# Corporations and Partnerships in Serbia

# Corporations and Partnerships in Serbia

**Mirko Vasiljević**
**Tatjana Jevremović Petrović**

This book was originally published as a monograph in the International Encyclopaedia of Laws/Corporations and Partnerships.

Founding Editor: Roger Blanpain
General Editor: Frank Hendrickx
Volume Editors: Koen Geens

Wolters Kluwer

*Published by:*
Kluwer Law International B.V.
PO Box 316
2400 AH Alphen aan den Rijn
The Netherlands
E-mail: lrs-sales@wolterskluwer.com
Website: www.wolterskluwer.com/en/solutions/kluwerlawinternational

*Sold and distributed by:*
Wolters Kluwer Legal & Regulatory U.S.
7201 McKinney Circle
Frederick, MD 21704
United States of America
E-mail: customer.service@wolterskluwer.com



ISBN 978-94-035-0686-9

e-Book: ISBN 978-94-035-0796-5
web-PDF: ISBN 978-94-035-0806-1

# The Authors

Mirko Vasiljević (born 1949, Pravoševo, Serbia) graduated from the University of Belgrade, Faculty of Law in 1973. He obtained a Master's Degree in 1976 at the University of Belgrade, Faculty of Law with a Master thesis *Altered Circumstances and Construction Contract* and a PhD Degree in 1980 with a thesis *Executive Management – Legal Aspects*. He started his academic career at the University of Belgrade, Faculty of Law in 1975 as Teaching Assistant, and then in 1980 as Assistant Professor and finally Full Professor in 1990. He was elected the Dean of the Faculty of Law, University of Belgrade for the 2004 to 2006 academic years, re-elected for the 2006 and 2009 and 2009 to 2012 academic years. He retired in 2020. He is the founder and was for more than two decades the President of the *Association of Business Lawyers of Serbia*, Founder and Honoured Editor-in-Chief of the legal periodical *Law and Economy (Pravo i privreda)*. He is a member of the *Academy of Sciences of Republika Srpska* from 2008, member of the *International Academy of Comparative Law* from June 2007. He was a President of the Foreign Trade Court of Arbitration of the Chamber of Commerce and Industry of Yugoslavia (1995–2001), and today he is a President of this Arbitration of the Chamber of Commerce and Industry of Serbia, and arbitrator in many institutional arbitrations abroad. He was a leading expert and head of expert teams for the preparation of numerous draft proposals of Commercial and Company Laws. He is the author of many published articles, monographs, textbooks and other legal writings in Serbian, English and French.

## The Authors

Tatjana Jevremović Petrović (born 1974, Belgrade, Serbia) graduated from the University of Belgrade, Faculty of Law in 1997. She obtained a Master's Degree in 2001 at the University of Belgrade, Faculty of Law with a Master thesis *Cross-Border Transfer of a Company's Seat in the Law of the European Union* and a PhD Degree in 2008 with a thesis *Cross-Border Merger in the Comparative Law and EU Law.* She was a research assistant (1998–2003) and research associate (2003–2009) at the Institute of International Politics and Economics in Belgrade. From 2009, she is Assistant Professor, from 2015 Associate Professor and from 2020 Full Professor at the Faculty of Law, University of Belgrade. During her studies, she was awarded a number of scholarships, including *Van Calker* Scholarship for the research at the Institute of Comparative Law, Lausanne (Switzerland) and Scholarship from the Swiss Commission for scholarships for foreign students at the Faculty of Law and the Institute of Comparative Law in Lausanne, Switzerland for the 2001–2002 academic year. She is a member of the Management Board of the *Association of Business Lawyers of Serbia* and the Editor-in-Chief of the *Law and Economy* since 2020. She is the Arbitrator in the Court of Honour (Serbian Chamber of Commerce) since 2018 and Member of the Extended Board of the Permanent Arbitration of the Chamber of Commerce and Industry of Serbia since 2021. She is the author of many articles and several books in the area of Company Law.

Professor Mirko Vasiljević wrote General Introduction (first and second title in Chapter 1, Chapter 2, titles on cooperatives and insurance companies in Chapter 3, Chapter 4) and Part II: Partnerships.

Professor Tatjana Jevremović Petrović wrote General Introduction (remaining titles in Chapter 1, Chapters 3 (excluding cooperatives and insurance companies), 5 and 6) and Part I: Companies.

# Table of Contents

**Table of Contents**

# List of Abbreviations

| | |
|---|---|
| Central depository | Central securities depository and clearing house |
| CGC | Corporate Governance Code |
| LCC | Law on Commercial Companies |
| Law on Conflict of Laws | Law on resolving conflict of laws with regulations of other countries |
| Law on Registration | Law on Registration procedure into the Business Agency Register |
| MTF | Multilateral Trading Facility |
| RS | The Republic of Serbia |
| RSD | Serbian dinar, the currency of the Republic of Serbia |

**List of Abbreviations**

# General Introduction

## §1. General Background of the Country

### I. Geography

*1.* Serbia (officially the Republic of Serbia – Republika Srbija) is a country covering the southern part of the Pannonian Plain and the central Balkans.[1] It borders Hungary to the North, Romania to the north-east, Bulgaria to the east, Macedonia and Albania to the south, Montenegro to south-west and Bosnia-Herzegovina and Croatia to the west. Its borders are 2,361.7 km long (out of which 1,567 km land border, 751.1 km river border and 43.3 km lake border).[2] Serbia (without Kosovo and Metohija) has a population of 7,186,862 (Census 2011), estimated 6,871,547 (out of which 51.3% female and 48.7% male) as of 31.12.2021 with a negative population growth rate of –6.7‰.[3]

The territory of Serbia occupies an area of 88,499 km$^2$. While Northern Serbia (Vojvodina and Mačva) is mainly flat, central and southern areas consist of highlands and mountains. The highest point is in the Prokletije Mountain (Đeravica at 2,656 metres), while the lowest point of 17 m is in Prahovo near Danube River. Apart from Danube, the longest river which flows for 588 km of its 2,857 km course through Serbia, the other most important and navigable rivers are Sava and Tisa. Serbia does not have a coastline, but is linked to Adriatic Sea via the Belgrade-Bar railway.

In terms of administrative and territorial division, the Republic of Serbia is divided into provinces, regions, administrative areas, the City of Belgrade, cities and municipalities. Serbia is divided into five regions (Belgrade Region, Vojvodina Region, Šumadija and Serbia West Region, Serbia South and East Region and Kosovo-Metohija Region), and it is organized into special territorial unit – the City of Belgrade and twenty-nine administrative districts. Serbia's capital and largest city is Belgrade, located at the confluence of Sava and Danube rivers.

1. Official general data available at: www.srbija.gov.rs (accessed 23 Mar. 2022).
2. Official statistical data on geographical review and climate are given according to *Statistical Annual of the Republic of Serbia for 2021 (Statistički godišnjak Republike Srbije 2021 – Geografski pokazatelji i klima)*, https://www.stat.gov.rs (accessed 23 Mar. 2022), 14.
3. Official statistical data (excluding Kosovo) are available from Statistical Office of the Republic of Serbia at: www.stat.gov.rs (accessed 23 Mar. 2022).

## II. Cultural Composition

2. Serbia is a multi-ethnical country. Although a majority of its population are Serbs (83.3%), there are many other ethnical groups, among which the most numerous are Hungarians (mostly in the Region of Vojvodina), Roma people (mostly in the Region of South and East Serbia), and Bosniaks (mostly in the Region of Šumadija and West Serbia).[4] Still, there are more than thirty different ethnicities living in Serbia. According to Serbian Constitution, all ethnicities have full equality and there is a guarantee of special protection to national minorities in order to exercise full equality and preserve their identity.[5]

Mostly inhabitants of Serbia are Orthodox (84.6% of the total population). There are other religious communities in Serbia, among which most numerous are Catholic (5%) and Islam religion (3%), but there are also Protestant, Jewish and other religions among its population.

The official language of the Republic of Serbia is Serbian language and Cyrillic script. In the areas inhabited by ethnic minorities, there is official use of languages and scripts of minorities. According to official statistics, most of its inhabitants (88.1%) consider the Serbian language as their mother tongue. The second language is Hungarian (3.4%), Bosniak (1.9%) and the Roma language (1.4%).

Numerous medieval monasteries and churches are the most valuable remnants of the Serbian cultural heritage. Some of them are enlisted in UNESCO World Heritage List, such as group of medieval monuments in Stari Ras and Sopoćani, Studenica Monastery, Medieval Monuments in Kosovo, as well as Gamzigrad – Romuliana, Palace of Galerius as late Roman fortification from the third and early fourth centuries.

Serbian culture especially flourished during its ages of national prosperity, such as in the medieval late twelfth to mid-fourteenth century, and from the nineteenth century. Since then, through ages to contemporary days, it produced many notable literary authors, including Ivo Andrić, Nobel Prize Winner for Literature in 1961, painters, composers and theatre and cinema artists. Serbia's renowned scientists, such as Nikola Tesla, Mihajlo Pupin, Mihajlo Petrović Alas, Milutin Milanković and many others gained world fame with their scientific contributions and inventions.

---

4. Official statistical data on ethnics, religion and language are given according to *Statistical Annual of the Republic of Serbia for 2021* (*Statistički godišnjak Republike Srbije 2021 – Stanovništvo*), www.stat.gov.rs (accessed 23 Mar. 2022), 41.
5. *See* General constitutional principles, Art. 14, as well as Ch. II on Human and Minority Rights and Freedom of the Constitution of the Republic of Serbia (Ustav Republike Srbije), *Official Gazette of Republic of Serbia (Službeni glasnik Republike Srbije)*, 98/2006 available in English at: https://www.srbija.gov.rs/tekst/en/130144/constitution-of-serbia.php (accessed 23 Mar. 2022).

## III. Political System

*3.* The Republic of Serbia is a country based on the rule of law and social justice, principles of civil democracy, human and minority rights and freedoms, and commitment to European principles and values.[6] Its fundamental principle is defined through rule of law.

Rule of law is confirmed and exercised by general principles of free and direct elections. Realization of that fundamental principle is also provided through protection of human and minority rights. Based on the premise that all are equal before the Constitution and the law, human and minority rights, guaranteed by Constitution and generally accepted in international law, ratified international treaties and laws can be applied directly.

Adopted principle of separation of power and independent judiciary, as well as principles of constitutionality and legality, constitute core principles whereby rule of law is exercised. Serbian Government system is based on the principle of division of power. It is divided into legislative, executive and judiciary power. Relationship between these powers guarantees balance and mutual control.

The supreme representative body and holder of constitutional and legislative power in the Republic of Serbia is the National Assembly. Its composition of 250 deputies is decided by general, direct and secret ballot elections, and it provides equality of genders and national minorities representation. The National Assembly has its elected president and one or more Vice-Presidents. Decisions adopted by National Assembly require a majority vote of deputies at the session at which majority of deputies are present, unless special majority of all deputies is required in most important decisions or on enactment of certain laws. The National Assembly has at least two regular sessions during a year, but other extraordinary sessions can be convoked upon the request of at least one-third of deputies or upon the request of the Government.

*4.* The Republic of Serbia has the President of the Republic. Candidate for the President is elected for the period of five years on direct elections, by secret ballot. Among the most important competences of the President of the Republic of Serbia are representation in the country and abroad, promulgation of laws, proposition for a candidate for the Prime Minister and other holders of positions determined by Constitution and laws, appointment and dismissal of ambassadors of the Republic of Serbia, and reception of letters of credit of foreign diplomatic representatives, grant of amnesties and commandment of the Army of Serbia.

In the Republic of Serbia, holder of executive power is the Government, accountable to the National Assembly for the policy of the Republic of Serbia, for enforcement of laws and other general acts of the National Assembly, as well as for the work of the public administration bodies. The Government has a Prime Minister, one or more Vice-Presidents and ministers.

---

6. For further general principles of political system, organization of government and basic principles of constitutionality and legality *see* Constitution of the Republic of Serbia, in particularly part I, V and VIII.

Management and direction of the Government and its representation are the main responsibility of the Prime Minister. He is also responsible for the activities of the Government and coordination of work of members of the Government. A candidate for the Prime Minister is proposed by the President of the Republic to the National Assembly. This candidate is presenting to the National Assembly the Government's Programme and its constitution. The National Assembly will make simultaneous decision on the election of the Prime Minister, Governments' Programme and members of the Government with the majority of the total number of deputies' votes. The term of office of the Government expires with the termination of office of National Assembly which elected the Government. Ministers are accountable for their work and affairs within the competence of their ministries to the Prime Minister, Government and National Assembly.

The organization of the Public Administration affairs is defined through Constitution and other laws. It is stipulated to be independent and bound to Constitution and the law, although accountable for its work to the Government. Public Administration affairs shall be performed by ministries and other public administration bodies. It is possible that particular affairs within the competences of the Republic of Serbia are delegated to autonomous provinces, local self-government units, enterprises, institutions, organizations and individuals, as well as to specific bodies in the performance of public functions.

The Civic Defender, elected by and accountable to the National Assembly, is an independent state body whose main competence is to protect citizens' rights and monitor the work of public administration bodies, body in charge of legal protection of proprietary rights and interests of the Republic of Serbia, as well as other bodies and organizations, companies and institutions to which public powers have been delegated.

Organization of judicial power is unique for the whole territory of the Republic of Serbia. The basic constitutional principles of separation and independent work of Courts are adopted, as well as the principle of performance of their duties in accordance with the Constitution, law and other general acts, as well as generally accepted rules of international law and ratified international contracts.

5. Judicial power in the Republic of Serbia is organized through courts of general and special jurisdiction. The Supreme Court in the Republic of Serbia is the Supreme Court of Cassation, whose President is elected for a period of five years by the National Assembly. Judges who are elected first time hold their position for three years, after which they can be elected permanently. Election of judges is done by the National Assembly and the High Judicial Council. Independent position of the judge is provided by fundamental principles of making decisions according to the Constitution and the law, while all other influences are prohibited. Judges enjoy immunity and the right of non-transferability. They are not permitted to perform any political or other activity which could be incompatible with their judicial function.

The High Judicial Council is an independent and autonomous body which shall provide for and guarantee independence and autonomy of courts and judges. It has eleven members, out of which three of them have their positions ex officio – President of the Supreme Court of Cassation, the Minister responsible for justice and the President of the authorized committee of the National Assembly, while other eight are elected for five years by the National Assembly. The most important competence of the High Judicial Council is the appointment and relief as well as proposal, of judges and Presidents of the courts of different levels and jurisdictions.

The Serbian judicial system provides for the Public Prosecutor's Office as an independent state body which shall prosecute the perpetrators of criminal offences and other punishable actions, and take measures in order to protect constitutionality and legality. The supreme Public Prosecutor's Office in the Republic of Serbia is the Republic Public Prosecutor's Office, elected for the period of six years by the National Assembly.

The supreme body which is protecting constitutionality and legality is the Constitutional Court. Constitutional Court is an autonomous and independent state body, and its main responsibility is protection of constitutionality and legality, as well as human and minority rights and freedoms. Decisions of the Constitutional Court are final, enforceable and generally binding. It has fifteen judges, elected and appointed for a period of nine years. Five of the judges are appointed by the National Assembly from among ten candidates proposed by the President of the Republic, the President of the Republic appoints five judges of the Constitutional Court from among ten candidates proposed by the National Assembly, and the general session of the Supreme Court of Cassation appoints five judges from among ten candidates proposed at a general session by the High Judicial Court and the State Prosecutor Council. Decisions of the Constitutional Court are made by the majority of votes cast by all judges of the Constitutional Court.

Serbian legal system is unique. Its supreme legal act is the Constitution. All other laws and general acts have to be in compliance with the Constitution. International treaties, ratified by the National Assembly and in compliance with the Constitution of the Republic of Serbia, as well as the generally accepted rules of the international law are part of the Serbian legal system. Laws and other general acts enacted in the Republic of Serbia must be in compliance with the ratified international treaties and generally accepted rules of international law.

Serbian territory is inseparable and indivisible, and it is a constitutional right of citizens to provincial autonomy and local self-government, subjected only to supervision of constitutionality and legality.

In Serbia, expression of political will of citizens is confirmed through organization of political parties, which are considered to represent important part of democratic life in Serbia. Political parties can be organized freely.

## IV. Population and Employment Statistics

*6.* According to the results of the Census done in 2011, the Republic of Serbia had a total population of 7,186,862 persons, among which 3,499,176 were male and 3,687,686 females.[7] It is estimated that population of the Republic of Serbia as of

7. All statistical data from Census 2011, as well as other official statistical data (excluding Kosovo), are available from Statistical Office of the Republic of Serbia at: www.stat.gov.rs (accessed 23 Mar. 2022).

1 January 2021 was 6,899,126. The average age among the population is 42.2 years. While men prevail in younger population, women prevail in middle-aged and aged population.

Among Serbian population aged 10 and over, only 1.96% are illiterate, usually in the older age groups. According to the official Census 2011 on educational attainment in population aged 15 and over, almost half of the total (6,161,584) has gained secondary education (3,015,092), while their number is lower in high education (348,335) and is reaching 652,234 in higher education. Proportion of male and female in educational attainment is relatively equivalent: out of 3,015,092 persons with secondary education, 1,613,356 are male and 1,401,736 are female; out of 348,335 persons in high education, there are 173,132 male and 175,203 female; and out of a total of 652,234 persons with higher education, there are 308,824 male and 343,410 female.[8]

Population in Serbia shows a decrease with average annual growth rate of -5.0 per 1,000 inhabitants and ageing of population. Birth rate is decreasing and was estimated to be 9.2‰, while mortality rate was 14.0 deaths per 1,000 inhabitants. Life expectancy is extended for men to 72.5 years and for women to 77.7 years.

There were 2,487,886 households, according to Census, whereby average household size is 2.88 with a decreasing trend of average household size. There was a total number of 2,125,772 families and 3,231,931 dwellings. The average population density in the Republic of Serbia is 92.6 inhabitants per 1 $km^2$. Distribution of inhabitants is unequal, with the highest density in Belgrade region of 515 inhabitants per $km^2$, compared to five times smaller density in other areas. Population density is the smallest in the South and East Serbia regions of only 60 inhabitants per $km^2$. Over half of all Serbian population (55.0%) lives in the same place from birth, with the highest rate in the Region of Šumadija and West Serbia.

Among Serbian population, 41.3% are economically active, out of which male (57.2%) prevail over female (42.8%). Employment rate of the population aged 15 and over is 37.4%.

Average net salaries and wages during December 2021 amounted to Serbian Dinars (RSD) 74 629 (equals approx. EUR 633).[9] The unemployment rate of unemployed persons in the active population (age 15 and over) for the second trimester of 2021 was 11.1%. Salaries showed a real increase compared to the previous year of 5.6%. In the first half of 2022, total consumer prices saw an average year-on-year growth of 8.0 % inflation rate (in comparison, in 2021 rate was in Q1 1.4%; Q2 3.2%; Q3 4.4%; Q4 7.3% while in 2022 Q1 8.5%).[10]

8. Official statistical data on educational attainment and sex are given according to *Statistical Annual of the Republic of Serbia for 2021 (Statistički godišnjak Republike Srbije 2021 – Stanovništvo)*, www.stat.gov.rs (accessed 23 Mar. 2022), 42.
9. All official statistical data on labour market are available from Statistical Office of the Republic of Serbia at: www.stat.gov.rs (accessed 23 Mar. 2022).
10. Statistical Office of the Republic of Serbia, Trends Q4, Quarter IV, 2021, Belgrade 2021, available at: https://www.stat.gov.rs/en-us/oblasti/deskriptivni-indikatori-i-ekonometrijske-analize (accessed 23 Mar. 2022).

## V. Enterprise, Corporations, and Partnerships Statistics

*7.* In the Republic of Serbia, official data from the Statistical Office of the Republic of Serbia on the enterprises and business structures are coordinated with the data from the Serbian Business Registers Agency.

According to the official data from the Business Registers Agency, on 4 January 2022, there were 414,705 active legal entities and natural persons registered to perform economic activity on the territory of the Republic of Serbia (with an annual increase of 14,059 persons compared to 2021 and 1,542 persons more compared to 2020). Out of the total of 414,705 active persons, there are 124,260 legal persons and 290,445 entrepreneurs – sole proprietors.[11] The most recent information on business activities of 106,111 enterprises can be found as aggregate data n the financial standing and business performance of legal entities and entrepreneurs in the Republic of Serbia in the past two years by the Official Annual Bulletin provided by the Serbian Business Registers Agency for statistical and other purposes.[12]

There was a total of 88,224 active incorporated enterprises in Serbia in 2019 which involved 1,207,098 persons employed. The total value of generated turnover out of all enterprises in 2018 was 10,379,074 (million RSD, approx. EUR 88,424), with the gross income from operating activities (value added at factor costs) of million RSD 2,368,001 (approx. EUR 22,474) in 2019.[13]

According to its size out of a total number of 87,407 enterprises in 2018, 73,663 are considered to be micro-size (with 0–9 employees), 10,778 small enterprises (with 10–49 employees), 2,430 medium-size enterprises (with 50–249 employees) and 536 large enterprises (with 250 or more employees). Out of all persons employed (1,161,577), less than half were employed in large enterprises (475,625), 252,191 in medium-size, 216,456 in small-size and 217,305 in micro-size enterprises.

## VI. Social and Cultural Values

*8.* The Republic of Serbia is a country that promotes traditional social and cultural values, common for European democratic societies. These traditional values are promoted in the Constitution of the Republic of Serbia, which is underlying their direct applicability.[14] Guarantees for inalienable human and minority rights in the

---

11. Official data from publication „Infografika – Osnivanje i zatvaranje privrednih subjekata (2017-2021)", 31.1.2022, available at: https://www.apr.gov.rs/infografike.4320.html?infoId=111# (accessed 23 Mar. 2022).
12. The most recent Official Bulletin for 2020: Republika Srbija Agencija za privredne registre, *Financial statements Annual Bulletin*, Belgrade april 2021, available at: https://www.apr.gov.rs/registri/finansijski-izvestaji/publikacije/godisnji--bilten-finansijskih-izvestaja.2127.html (accessed 23 Mar. 2022).
13. Official statistical data on business activities and units are cited according to *Statistical Yearbook 2021*, available at: www.stat.gov.rs (accessed 23 Mar. 2022), 187.
14. *See* in particular part II Human and minority rights and freedoms of the Constitution of the Republic of Serbia.

Constitution have the purpose of preserving human dignity and exercising full freedom and equality of each individual in a just, open, and democratic society based on the principle of the rule of law.[15] The fundamental principle of rule of law is provided through equality before the Constitution and the law, as well as the right of judicial protection.

Serbian social and cultural values are based on certain fundamental rights and freedoms. Human life is inviolable, and therefore death penalty is prohibited. Everyone has a right to dignity and free development of personality. Physical and mental integrity of every individual is inviolable. Torture or other degrading or inhuman treatment or punishment is prohibited, and medical or other experiment is forbidden without free consent.

It is the fundamental right of everybody to have personal freedom and security. Slavery, servitude and all forms of human trafficking, sexual and other financial exploitation, as well as forced labour are prohibited. All deprivation of liberty needs to be grounded in the procedure regulated by law, proclaimed by the court and based on its decision without delay, and with guarantees of information. During deprivation of liberty, all persons need to be treated with respect for their dignity and humanity.

Everyone has a right to fair trial without delay, in a public hearing in front of independent and impartial tribunal established by law with a right to free assistance of interpreter. All persons charged with criminal offence have right to defend themselves and provide evidence personally or through legal counsel, with right to free counsel if they are without sufficient means to pay for the legal counsel; right to be present during trial and with right to a hearing and defence before sentenced. According to fundamental principle, everyone shall be presumed innocent for a criminal offence until convicted by a final judgment of the court, and nobody can be found guilty for the act which did not constitute a criminal offence at the time committed, nor punished by the penalty not prescribed for this act. Criminal prosecution or execution of punishment for the war crime, genocide or crime against humanity is not subjected to time limitation. In the case of deprivation of liberty, detention or conviction without ground or unlawfully, any person is entitled to the right to rehabilitation and compensation of damage by the Republic of Serbia. Right of compensation is also available for everyone in the case of damage caused by the unlawful or irregular work of a state body and other entities or bodies exercising public powers.

Everyone is entitled to have legal capacity and to have the right to equal protection of rights and legal remedies. Every citizen of the Republic of Serbia has a right to citizenship, and every child born in the Republic of Serbia has the right to its citizenship, unless conditions are met to acquire citizenship from other countries. Everyone's right is to move freely and reside in the Republic of Serbia, including the right to leave and return, and restriction can be introduced only if necessary to conduct criminal proceedings, protection of public order, prevention of spreading contagious diseases or defence of the Republic of Serbia. Every person's home is inviolable, and entering without approval is permitted only with a court order and

15. Article 19 of the Constitution of the Republic of Serbia.

if necessary, in the situations prescribed by law. Right of confidentiality of letters and other means of communication and protection of personal data is guaranteed.

Everyone has a freedom of thought and expression, conscience, beliefs and religion. It is everybody's right to express national affiliation and understanding, recognition and respect of diversity of citizens are promoted. Therefore, all racial, ethnic, religious or other inequality or hatred is expressly prohibited and punishable.

Serbia is promoting freedom of the media and public information, forbidding censorship as unacceptable in a modern democratic society. Only exceptions allowed are connected to the protection of the constitutional system, peace and racial, ethnic or religious tolerance. Media are obliged to respect everyone's right to accurate, full and timely information.

Electoral right is given to every citizen of age (18 years) and working ability and is universal and equal for all. Free and direct elections are guaranteed, and they are carried in a secret voting ballot. Citizens are entitled to take part in the management of public affairs and to assume public services. They have the right to free assembly, restricted only by the law and only if necessary to protect public health, morals, rights of others or security. Every form of association, including political, union and others is guaranteed. It is the general principle that all associations are allowed to be formed freely and without prior approval.

Everyone is entitled to put forward petitions and other proposals to state and other public bodies without any detrimental consequences. Fundamental property rights include peaceful tenure of property and other acquired rights, including right to inheritance, and restrictions of property rights or seizure of property need to be in accordance with the law.

Right to work is guaranteed, and it includes right of free choice of occupation and under equal conditions. Everyone has a right to be respected at work, to work under safe and healthy conditions. General rights of limited working hours, daily and weekly rest intervals, as well as paid annual holiday are guaranteed, and they also include fair remuneration for work done and legal protection in the case of termination of work, with special protection and working conditions of certain categories, such as women, young and disabled persons. Employees have a constitutional guarantee to strike in accordance with the law.

The Republic of Serbia is protecting right to enter on a free consent or dissolve a marriage, and is providing equality of spouses. It is providing everyone a right to procreate or not and is putting special attention to protect children and their rights. Children enjoy human rights including right to personal name, entry into registry of births, right to information and identity and are protected from all forms of exploitation and abuse. Parents of children are provided with rights and duties, with the emphasis on the special protection of the families, mothers, single parents and children. It is expressly forbidden that children under 15 years of age are employed, or to be employed by the age of 18 years at jobs detrimental to their health.

Everyone is protected with the right of professional legal assistance, mental and physical health and promotion of social protection and pension insurance. Special protection of health of children, pregnant women or mothers on maternity leave, as well as other categories of persons, including single parent with children under 7 and elderly persons, is guaranteed. Social protection and insurance are guaranteed to employees and their families, as well to other citizens and families in social and existential difficulties. Special protection is provided for disabled persons, war veterans and victims of war.

Right of education is provided for all citizens. Primary education is compulsory and together with the secondary education is free of charge in public schools. While primary education lasts for eight years, secondary education can last three or four years, leading to vocational, specialization or general secondary school education. All citizens are provided with equal conditions for higher education, which is free to a certain number of students. There are several university centres in Serbia, including the University of Belgrade, Novi Sad, Niš and Kragujevac. Universities are provided with autonomy and freedom of their organization and work.

Fundamental rights and freedoms include special individual and collective rights belonging to national minorities. Bearing in mind national diversity and multiethnicity of its population, Serbia is not only providing full equality but also promoting preservation of specificity, including right to expression, preservation, fostering, developing and public expression of national, ethnic, cultural, religious specificity; use of their symbols, language and script in public places and in public bodies and institutions, as well as many other important rights conferred to these groups of Serbian citizens.

## VII. Privatization Efforts and Golden Shares

### *A. Privatization Efforts in Serbia*

*9.* Ownership regime in Serbia, at that time part of Socialist Federative Republic of Yugoslavia, as in many markets planned economies of Eastern Europe in the late 1980s and early 1990s with prevailing social ownership, faced major changes which led to the introduction of market economy and equality of all property regimes (including private property, state-owned, social ownership, as well as other forms of property regime, including cooperative and other).

First steps towards transformation of socially owned enterprises by privatization started during 1990s, through the adoption of the Law on socially-owned capital and Law on transformation of social property into other forms of ownership that adopted insider privatization models.[16] A major influence on establishment of market economy and change in ownership regime were privatizations undertaken according to the 1997 Law on social ownership transformation, which, again, followed an insider privatization scheme, whereby companies were privatized to current and former employees by free distribution of shares.[17] Privatization according to the

16. Law on Socially-owned Capital (Zakon o društvenom kapitalu), *Official Gazette of SFRY (Službeni list SRFJ)*, 84/1989 and Law on transformation of social property into other forms of ownership (Zakon o uslovima i postupku pretvaranja društvene svojine u druge oblike svojine), *Official Gazette of Republic of Serbia (Službeni glasnik Republike Srbije)*, 48/1991, later amended.
17. *See* in detail Law on social ownership transformation (Zakon o svojinskoj transformaciji), *Official Gazette of Republic of Serbia (Službeni glasnik Republike Srbije)*, 32/1997, later amended.

1997 Law was voluntary and decentralized.[18] However, seventy large firms and all state/public enterprises were excluded from this general approach and became subject to 'special privatization programmes' to be carried out by the government.

Privatization undertaken after major political changes initiated economic and social reforms, and according to the 2001 Law on Privatisation, was carried out by selling companies through tenders and auctions and has led to a second stage or 'wave' of privatization.[19] While tenders were intended to include medium- and large-scale enterprises, auctions were specifically aimed at small-size enterprises. Whole privatization, based on the market-oriented privatization methods, aimed at attracting major investors, including foreign ones into Serbian economy.[20] Therefore basic model of privatization was the share deal, although there were possibilities of free distribution of shares, either to employees or to citizens.[21] Privatization was forced and centralized through the Privatization Agency.[22]

In parallel to new methods of privatization, already privatized companies were intended to finish privatization through Share Fund, by deposition of remaining shares and minority blocks.[23] According to official data, only in the period between 2002 and 2004 privatization was completed through Share Fund and Belgrade Stock Exchange for 236 enterprises.[24]

According to other official data, as of 31 December 2004, nearly 2,000 enterprises have been privatized, 775 according to 1997 Law and 1,169 according to 2001 Law.[25] Analysis of companies privatized during the second stage shows general improvement of their performance, which was also the case for companies privatized according to 1997 Law, afterwards sold to major shareholders as strategic partners.[26] However, in those cases where companies were privatized to employees and still belong to them, statistics showed stagnation without improvement in performance.

---

18. *See* Nebojša Jovanović, 'Povlašćenost države kao akcionara u delimično privatizovanim privrednim društvima' (Privileges of a state as a shareholder in partially privatized companies), *Pravo i privreda (Law and Economy)* 5-8/2007, 148.
19. Law on Privatisation (Zakon o privatizaciji), *Official Gazette of Republic of Serbia (Službeni glasnik Republike Srbije),* 38/2001, later amended.
20. *See* for further details on privatization process during last decade in: Privatization Agency, Republic of Serbia, 'Impact Assessment of Privatisation in Serbia', Belgrade, 27 Oct. 2005, http://www.priv.rs/upload/document/Impact_Assessment_of_Privatisation_Final.pdf (accessed 23 Mar. 2022), 12–14.
21. *See*. Art. 9 of the 2001 Law on Privatisation.
22. Nebojša Jovanović, 'Povlašćenost države kao akcionara u delimično privatizovanim privrednim društvima' (Privileges of a state as a shareholder in partially privatized companies), *Pravo i privreda (Law and Economy)* 5-8/2007, 149.
23. *See* Law on Share Fund (Zakon o akcijskom fondu), *Official Gazette of Republic of Serbia (Službeni glasnik Republike Srbije),* 38/2001, later amended.
24. Privatization Agency, Republic of Serbia, 'Impact Assessment of Privatisation in Serbia', Belgrade, 27 Oct. 2005, http://www.priv.rs/upload/document/Impact_Assessment_of_Privatisation_Final.pdf (accessed 23 Mar. 2022), 14.
25. Privatization Agency, Republic of Serbia, 'Impact Assessment of Privatisation in Serbia', Belgrade, 27 Oct. 2005, http://www.priv.rs/upload/document/Impact_Assessment_of_Privatisation_Final.pdf (accessed 23 Mar. 2022), 8.
26. Privatization Agency, Republic of Serbia, 'Impact Assessment of Privatisation in Serbia', Belgrade, 27 Oct. 2005, http://www.priv.rs/upload/document/Impact_Assessment_of_Privatisation_Final.pdf (accessed 23 Mar. 2022), 8.

Privatization analysis showed that during 2006–2010 another 851 enterprises were privatized and that on 1 Sep 2011 there were still 537 non-privatized companies.[27] Most important data show that privatized companies increased profitability by 69% and profit of EUR 200 million was made by the end of 2010, while all non-privatized companies show negative business results for every business year. In both privatized and non-privatized companies, employment showed job reductions and negative impact. Investments in Serbia, including foreign direct investments, were significantly increased by the beginning of 2000s and privatization process. During the last decade, privatization showed immediate impact on the national budget, with slow increase in taxes and other social payments, usually within a period of two to three years after companies were turned around.[28] Serbian exports after privatization showed significant increase, but the data was inconclusive on the impact of privatization on that trend.

During 2014, a new Law on Privatisation was adopted in order to finish privatization with a time limit to the end of 2015, excluding strategic business entities and those with seat or principal place of activities or with their property in the territory of Kosovo and Metohija.[29] Tender and auctions remained the basic methods of privatization in this law, with the enhanced market orientation and several models of privatization, including share and asset deals, strategic partnerships or inside privatizations to employees.

### *B. Golden Shares and Public Enterprises*

#### 1. State as a Shareholder

*10.* While still remaining in the sphere of economy, the State became compelled, due to budget deficits and public sector inefficiency, to abandon the position of an exclusive owner in that sector, at both the national and local level. This was a ground for creating different forms of companies (joint-stock and limited liability companies). Creation of different forms of companies with state ownership was particularly high in Serbia during the privatization process. State ownership was created through a transfer of all non-privatized shares from the enterprises which started privatization under the provisions of the 1997 Law on Privatisation to the Share Fund. Non-privatized shares, unpaid shares from the privatization, as well as shares remaining after the share purchase, or after the nullity of the share purchase, were also transferred to the Share Fund, in order to be sold through the Privatisation Agency.[30] The Share Fund was later replaced with a Shareholders Fund, which

27. Agencija za privatizaciju, Republika Srbija, *Analiza efekata privatizacije u Srbiji (Analysis of effects of privatisation in the Republic of Serbia)*, http://www.priv.rs/upload/document/analizaprivatizacijewide.pdf (accessed 23 Mar. 2022), 15.
28. Privatization Agency, Republic of Serbia, 'Impact Assessment of Privatisation in Serbia', Belgrade, 27 Oct. 2005, http://www.priv.rs/upload/document/Impact_Assessment_of_Privatisation_Final.pdf (accessed 23 Mar. 2022), 168.
29. Law on Privatisation (Zakon o privatizaciji), *Official Gazette of Republic of Serbia (Službeni glasnik Republike Srbije)*, 83/2014, later amended. *See* in particular Art. 6 Law on Privatisation.
30. *See* in particular Art. 8 Law on Share Fund.

acquired shares of non-privatized companies or remaining shares and was in charge of privatization and particularly shares distribution free of charge to citizens and employees.[31] Its affairs were managed through the Privatization Agency, disbanded after the adoption of the Law on Privatisation, and substituted with the Agency for settlement of disputes related to privatisation.[32]

In certain circumstances, such as unattractive privatization, difficulties in finding a strategic partner, national interest, ensuring competitiveness and demonopolization before privatization, the State must remain a single owner of certain public sector enterprises. Therefore, in certain cases, state or other territorial units remained the single shareholder of public enterprises, with the possibility of creation of a new public enterprise in public utilities sector.[33] In the course of privatization of the public sector (along with restructuring), the new legislative trend in this field was the creation of legislative possibilities for demonopolization, by providing the possibility of entrusting certain public utilities to commercial companies, with or without state ownership.[34]

Although public enterprises are equivalent in many characteristics of organization and functioning with other market participants, their particularities cannot be underestimated. Therefore, the management of these public enterprises is under various instruments of state supervision. Preliminary supervision includes granting consent by competent authorities to specified documents, decisions, and especially management election (in particular CEO); supervision through a specially appointed supervisory board, as well as instruments of subsequent supervision by the government, specialized commissions and regulatory bodies.

## 2. Golden Shares

*11.* In the case where state is the shareholder, its position is the same as other shareholders, including right to participate in the company's profit and management in proportion to capital. However, if public interest, as specified by the law, requires it, the State or a territorial unit may acquire special rights in companies conducting a particular activity; this may occur even with minority interest or no interest in the capital at all. Special rights may be acquired by a state or territorial unit also in the privatization process applied to public sector enterprises, transformed into companies, through a special type of shares – 'golden shares'.

According to the position of the State as a shareholder through the Share Fund in the privatization process, it can be concluded that state had a special right in certain

31. *See* Law on the share distribution free of charge and other payments to citizens according to privatization process (Zakon o pravu na besplatne akcije i novčanu naknadu koju gra ani ostvaruju u postupku privatizacije), *Official Gazette of Republic of Serbia (Službeni glasnik Republike Srbije)*, 123/2007, last amended in 2014.
32. *See* additional Art. 31 introduced by the Amendments to the Law on Privatisation, *Official Gazette of Republic of Serbia (Službeni glasnik Republike Srbije)*, 112/2015.
33. Law on Public enterprises (Zakon o javnim preduzećima), *Official Gazette of Republic of Serbia (Službeni glasnik Republike Srbije)*, 15/2016, later amended.
34. Art. 3 Law on Public enterprises.

matters, including vetoing most important decisions, such as reorganization of capital (increase or reduction), structural changes, decisions concerning loans, sales or other changes to property and immovable and long-term loans, as well as management rights in the case of the nullity of share purchase agreement.[35] Since the Share Fund was later replaced with the Shareholders Fund and was acting through the Privatization Agency, its privileged position remained similar in the exercise of voting in the name and on behalf of the Shareholders Fund.[36] The same was the case in certain privatized companies, where in the articles of incorporation, the State was granted specific rights – veto or approval on most important decisions, as long as it holds a certain minority threshold.[37]

## §2. The Historical Background of Corporations and Partnerships

### I. Tradition

*12.* A period of economic liberalism and codifications of nineteenth-century company laws of many developed European countries influenced Serbia at that time. Serbia followed leading western countries in enacting its prestigious legislation at the time. The Kingdom of Serbia enacted a Civil Code as early as 1844, which contained a total of 950 paragraphs.[38] It did not include provisions regarding trade (commercial) companies, except those dealing with civil partnership in paragraphs 723–758.

In 1860, Serbia enacted the Commercial Code, under the strong influence of the French *Code de commerce* which was applicable until the end of the Second World War.[39] The Code included a chapter on 'commercial companies and relevant rules' (paragraphs 24-49), and provisions covering three types of commercial partnership:

35. *See* Art. 8a Law on Share Fund. Further on this issue: Nebojša Jovanović 'Država kao akcionar (State as a shareholder)', in: Mirko Vasiljević, Vuk Radović (eds), *Korporativno upravljanje (Corporate Governance),* Pravni fakultet Univerziteta u Beogradu, Beograd, 2008, 137; Nebojša Jovanović, 'Povlašćenost države kao akcionara u delimično privatizovanim privrednim društvima' (Privileges of a state as a shareholder in partially privatized companies), *Pravo i privreda (Law and Economy)* 5-8/2007, 153ff.

36. *See* in particular Art. 11b Law on Privatisation Agency (Zakon o Agenciji za privatizaciju), *Official Gazette of Republic of Serbia (Službeni glasnik Republike Srbije),* 38/2001, later amended.

37. *See* in detail for privatized company Naftna industrija Srbije – NIS. ad: Jelena Lepetić, 'Zlatne akcije u kompanijskom pravu Srbije (Golden shares in Serbian company law)', *Pravo i privreda (Law and Economy)* 4-6/2012, 172-173. On golden shares in Serbian law *see also*: Tatjana Jovanić, 'Zlatne akcije i neki oblici državne kontrole nad poslovanjem privatizovanih preduzeća koja obavljaju delatnost od opšteg interesa' (Golden shares and state control on the business of privatized companies in public sector), *Pravo i privreda (Law and Economy)* 5-8/2004, 246ff.

38. Serbian Civil Code (Gra anski zakonik za Kraljevinu Srbiju) published in: Gra anski zakonik za Kraljevinu Srbiju, ninth edition, Belgrade 1907 (printed and edited by the Royal Serbian Government Printing Office). Also available (in Serbian) at http://sr.wikisource.org/sr-el (accessed 23 Mar. 2022).

39. *See* in detail: Vladimir Jovanović, *Privredno pravo: privredne organizacije* (Commercial Law), Zavod za izdavanje udžbenika Narodne Republike Srbije, Beograd, 1961, 58.

public (under the same title), mixed (of the limited partnership nature) and anonymous – joint-stock companies.[40] In the autonomous province of Vojvodina, the 1875 Croatian-Hungarian Commercial Law was in force, and it included provisions on merchants and general partnerships, limited partnerships, joint-stock companies and cooperative societies – altogether 566 paragraphs.[41]

The first Law on Joint-Stock Companies of Serbia was enacted in 1896 and it contained 106 articles.[42]After the Kingdom of Serbs, Croats and Slovenes was founded; the Law on Extending the Validity of the Law on Joint-Stock Companies for the Kingdom of Serbia in the territory of Montenegro (1922)[43] was enacted, and slightly amended in 1930.[44] The Kingdom of Serbia also enacted its first Law on Shops in 1910, which was replaced by the new Law on Shops in the Kingdom of Yugoslavia in 1931.[45] In order to unify commercial law, the Kingdom of Yugoslavia adopted a Commercial Code in 1937 which never came to force. Written under the influence of German Commercial Code, it contained 513 paragraphs, including provisions on merchants and all forms of commercial, i.e., trading companies, but none relating to commercial transactions.[46]

## II. Period of Second Yugoslavia

*13.* The development of company and commercial law after the Second World War can be seen as several stages of legislative activity, although they can be generally considered very specific compared to their usual development in market-oriented economies. The first stage is marked by the adoption of the 1946 Law on State Economic Enterprises; the second one by the Law on Managing the State Economic Enterprises and Higher Economic Associations by Working Collectives (the so-called 1950 Self-management Law); the third stage is characterized by the enactment of the 1965 Principal Law on Enterprises; the fourth stage related to the Law on Associated Labour in 1976; and the fifth stage by the introduction of the market economy and enactment of the Law on Enterprises in 1988.

The first stage of development of post Second World War company law in Yugoslavia is characterized by the creation of state-owned economic (commercial) enterprises. These enterprises were organized on the federal level, the level of republics

40. Serbian Commercial Code (Trgovački zakonik), published in: G. Niketić (ed.), *Trgovački zakonik i stečišni postupak Kraljevine Srbije* (Commercial Code and the Insolvency Proceeding in the Kingdom of Serbia), Geca Kon, Belgrade, 1923.
41. *See*: N. Ignjatović (ed.), *Trgovinski zakon (1875 i 1908) – sa odnosnom sudskom praksom* (Commercial Code 1875 and 1908 with case law), Novi Sad (no indication of the year and publisher).
42. Law on Joint-stock Companies of Kingdom of Serbia (Zakon o akcionarskim društvima Kraljevine Srbije) (1896), available in Serbian at: http://projuris.org/RETROLEX/Zakon%20o%20akcionarskim%20drustvima%20Srbije%20%281896%29.pdf (accessed 23 Mar. 2022).
43. Published in the official gazette of the time: *Službene novine*, 105/1922.
44. Law amending the Law on Joint-stock Companies (Zakon o izmenama Zakona o akcionarskim društvima od 1896. godine), *Official gazette (Službene novine)*, 29/1930.
45. *See*: G. Niketić (ed.) *Zakon o radnjama (Law on shops)*, Geca Kon, Belgrade 1922; and later amended with Law on shops (Zakon o radnjama), *Official gazette (Službene novine)*, 262/1931.
46. *See*: M. Stražnjicki, *Tumač trgovačkog zakona od 1937. godine* (Commercial Code 1937 with commentary), Zagreb, 1930.

and on the local government level. They enjoyed legal personality, but they were managed by the government and with the state ownership. The main principles of management included formally prescribed economy planning and existence of bidirectional plans (determining both the manufacturer and the consumer and/or seller and buyer), as well as unidirectional ones, determining only the manufacturer and/or seller, while the sale was effected more or less autonomously.

The second stage of development was especially characterized by the introduction of the labour management (so-called self-management). Therefore, workers' councils as managing bodies were introduced with its executive body – director. This period led to the abolishment of administrative-operational management, abolishment of planning as the main source of private law and affirmation of commercial contracts. The main principle of distribution of income to salaries and funds led to gradual abolishment of state ownership.

The third stage indicates further development of autonomy of enterprises, begun in the second stage. This period is characterised by internal organization of enterprises through the establishment of different separate units with or without legal personality. The same period enhanced involvement and direct management by workers within separate units of the enterprise. Finally, this phase introduced the concept of social ownership.[47]

The fourth stage was characterized by the enactment of the Law on Associated Labour in 1976, although significant steps were made already in 1971 and 1972 Constitutional Amendments and 1974 SFRY Constitution and with the 1973 Law on Setting Up and Filing of Organisations of Associated Labour in the Court Register. This phase began by abandoning the concept of 'enterprise' and the development of the concept of the so-called organization of associated labour. The basic and inalienable right of workers in the basic organization of associated labour was the right to work using the socially owned property.[48] Organizations of associated labour had legal personality with property rights and were considered to be able to independently establish other forms of organization – so-called working organizations.[49] Affirmation of the concept of 'associated labour' was essentially negation of the classic 'capital (or market) relationship'. This concept involved workers in direct management through their personal votes either on referendum or workers' meeting or in indirect management through the workers' council. Organizations of associated labour were free to form so-called working communities as another statutory form of organization for workers performing various supporting services (administrative, professional and other), also available for 'working organization', or 'compound organization of associated labour'.[50] This stage of development

47. *See*: I. Maksimović, *Teorijske osnove društvene svojine* (Theory of social ownership), Belgrade 1975; A. Frimerman, *Društvena svojina i samoupravljanje u udruženom radu* (Social ownership and self-management in associated labour organizations), Belgrade, 1979; Group of authors, *Društvena svojina u Jugoslaviji* (Social ownership in Yugoslavia), Belgrade, 1976.
48. *See*: D. Radonjić, *Pravo rada društvenim sredstvima* (The right to work using socially-owned property), Titograd, 1985.
49. *See* particularly: A. Gams, *Svojina* (The property), Belgrade, 1987.
50. *See* more in: N. Balog, *Razvoj privrednog prava* (Development of Commercial Law), *Arhiv za pravne i društvene nauke*, 1-2/1986, pp. 273-284.

unfortunately lasted for much too long and left disastrous consequences on the economic, social, and political situation in Yugoslavia. Therefore, another phase which introduced market economy began in the late 1980s by the enactment of the Law on Enterprises.

## III. Introduction of Market Economy

*14.* The first law to eliminate the legal monopoly of social ownership was the 1988 Law on Enterprises.[51] This law introduced the principle of equality of all property law regimes: social ownership, private, state, i.e., government, cooperative and other forms of collective ownership, as well as the equality of domestic and foreign persons. Still, the provisions of this first law which returned to classic conception of the company were undeveloped and not numerous. Mostly they left rights and duties of members and shareholders to be dealt through articles of incorporation, which was also the case with the capital increase or reduction. The lack of provisions dealing with scrutiny by experts of contributions in kind and merger procedure, procedure with own shares and redemption of shares was also non-existent. Finally, the 1988 Law made the first steps towards corporate governance which was very rudimentary and still under the influence of the old socialist regime.

In order to remove all obstacles to the adoption of the first Law on Enterprises since the introduction of the market economy, the Federal Republic of Yugoslavia enacted in 1996 a new Law on Enterprises.[52] Its main task was to introduce more detailed provisions on new business forms and to establish legal certainty into the newly established market economy. The 1996 Law was dealing with not only all forms of business enterprises, including partnerships and corporations, but also state and public enterprises. It contained provisions to include workers' participation in corporate governance, with strong influences from the past. Although the 1996 Law was at the time an important improvement to the current company law regime, its classical approach and undeveloped registration and transparency regime, together with a difficult political situation and an unsuccessful privatization, led to major changes in this field at the beginning of the twenty-first century.

## IV. Modernization of Serbian Company Law

*15.* After the enactment of the Constitutional Charter for the State Union of Serbia and Montenegro in 2003,[53] and after the State was renamed Serbia and Montenegro, Montenegro enacted its own Law on Commercial Companies in 2002,[54] and Serbia followed with its own law in 2004.[55] After the independence referendum

51. *Official Gazette of the SFRY* (Službeni list SFRJ), No. 77/1988.
52. *Official Gazette of the FRY* (Službeni list SRJ), No. 29/1996.
53. *Official Gazette of the SCG* (Službeni list SCG), 1/2003.
54. Law on Commercial Companies (Zakon o privrednim društvima), *Official Gazette of Republic of Montenegro (Službeni glasnik Republike Crne Gore)*, 6/2002 later amended.
55. Law on Commercial Companies (Zakon o privrednim društvima), *Official Gazette of Republic of Serbia (Službeni glasnik Republike Srbije)*, 125/2004. Further in footnotes referred as LCC 2004.

held in Montenegro in May 2006, Serbia also declared its independence in June 2006, after which Law on Commercial Companies remained the major source of law.

The first law to introduce a modern company law regime in Serbia was enacted in 2004. Unlike previous laws focusing on enterprises, the new 2004 Law was dealing with Commercial Companies. Consequently, the status of basic commercial entities, in terms of legal regime of their governance, since 2004 is divided into three parts: one (and most important part) includes commercial companies subject to the Law on Commercial Companies. A smaller part of these commercial entities is socially owned including enterprises with a majority non-privatized capital subject to the Law on Enterprises from 1996, while the final, third part consists of public enterprises (at republic and municipal levels) subject to relevant public enterprise laws. Public enterprises were to be transformed into corporations (becoming companies of capital with the capital participation of the State or territorial units), independently of subsequent privatization, after which they would be the subject of the Law on Commercial Companies.

The 2004 Law on Commercial Companies was replaced in 2011 by the new Law on Commercial Companies aimed at improving certain inconsistent and unpractical solutions.[56] Still, the basic concept, and most important characteristics, including modernization, remained the same. Current Serbian company law has many provisions for efficient and competitive business environment regime. It is marked with modern corporate governance and is coordinated with other laws influencing company law regime. Therefore, introduction of the latest Law on Commercial Companies was followed by the simultaneous introduction of the Law on Capital Markets (2011) as well as the Law on Registration procedure into the Business Agency Register (2011). Finally, additional improvement of the current corporate law regime was done through the introduction of the new Corporate Governance Code.[57]

### A. *Position of Interested Parties*

*16.* Law on Commercial Companies from 2004, as well from 2011, holds the view that commercial companies belong, in terms of interest, to both owners and creditors, as well as to the employees. Consequently, there is a growing tendency for the structure of a company to include not only the natural and logical rights of the majority owners but also the rights of minority owners, creditors and employees. The tripartite nature of interest position, however, does not imply equality.

56. Law on Commercial Companies (Zakon o privrednim društvima), *Official Gazette of Republic of Serbia (Službeni glasnik Republike Srbije)*, 36/2011 with further amendments last amended 109/2021, available in English at: https://www.paragraf.rs/propisi/companies-act-of-serbia.html (accessed 23 Mar. 2022). Further in footnotes referred as LCC 2011.

57. Last Corporate Governance Code (Kodeks korporativnog upravljanja) – CGC 2012, *Official Gazette of Republic of Serbia (Službeni glasnik Republike Srbije)*, 99/2012, drafted by the Serbian Chamber of Commerce and Industry.

Specifically, the Law on Commercial Companies is conceived from the position of different stakeholders. Nevertheless, having in mind the fact that overemphasizing the concept of labour in corporate management through the self-management model produced a negative effect in Serbia during previous decades, the Law on Commercial Companies was chosen to leave the position of labour to its fundamental piece of legislation – the Labour Law. Therefore, at present, employee representation in corporate bodies is not provided for in the current company law regime.

### *B. Harmonization with EU Law*

*17.* The Law on Commercial Companies entirely integrates the corresponding EU directives relating to its key segments. However, many company law issues are yet to be harmonized even in the European Union. In regulating these matters, the Law on Commercial Companies applied considerable freedom of choice between continental law solutions (with conspicuous distinctions visible in the countries of developed legal tradition such as Germany or France) or, as the case may be, the ones in Anglo-Saxon law, having in mind the apparently irreversible trend of expansion of Anglo-Saxon company law institutes into the European continental law.

Therefore, modern regulatory trends in EU company law, as well as national company laws of most developed countries, had a strong impact on Serbian law. Besides, the influence of national company laws of those EU members who have common legal tradition and economic background during the existence of Yugoslavia such as Croatia and Slovenia is also evident.

### *C. Complete Regulation for all Commercial Forms*

*18.* In deciding whether to regulate all organizational forms of commercial entities within a single legal instrument (as is the practice in France, Italy, Switzerland, Hungary, Slovenia, Croatia, Macedonia, Bulgaria, Poland, the Czech Republic) or to regulate separately forms such as partnerships, from those of companies (as in Germany, USA, Austria, England), the Law on Commercial Companies had opted for the predominant solution. Therefore, in line with legal tradition in this region, the Law on Commercial Companies has provisions for all commercial forms, including partnerships. This concept was dictated by reasons of rationality, and the need to facilitate the position of those subjected to the law, as well as by codification needs.

### *D. Traditional Legal Forms of Commercial Entities*

*19.* The need to communicate in a unified business language with other countries, especially those from the region, has imposed standardized criteria of classification of commercial entities. Therefore, the Law on Commercial Companies stipulates only four ‘classical’ forms – types of commercial entities, together with provisions on sole proprietor – entrepreneur.

In addition to these four, in some countries, other types of companies are present as well, such as limited partnership by shares, unlimited liability company, company with liability covered by a guarantee, limited liability partnership, as well as other simplified or specific forms. They are not recognized in the 2004 Law, and the position of the 2011 Law on Commercial Companies is equivalent.

The reasoning behind this approach was not only that those company forms are not universally accepted but also that they are rarely established, even in the countries familiar with them. Moreover, mostly they were just the reaction of the business community to strict tax regulations. It seemed inappropriate for Serbia as a transition country to experiment with such solutions until the business practice suggested the necessity of their acceptance. Accordingly, the (2004 and) 2011 Law offers a choice of well-known forms of business organization that have been universally accepted and are legally well founded.

### *E. Flexibility and Possibility of Choice*

*20.* Reacting to justified and constant criticism of business practice according to which commercial legislation is too abstract and hard to implement, the Law on Commercial Companies, through its flexible solutions, offered a large number of choices to future founders of commercial entities when they are deciding on their entity form. The principle of *party autonomy* is the key element for all forms of closed commercial entities (partnerships, limited partnerships and limited liability companies), as well as for all the entrepreneurs. Only in matters concerning protection of third-party interests (such as liability issues, minimum legal capital requirement, effects on third parties of disclosed and published information in the business registers, etc.), imperative provisions prevail.

Therefore, Serbian company law is dominated by dispositive provisions which are, after all, essential characteristics of all forms of commercial companies except, to a degree, of (public) joint-stock companies. The intent of the law was to specify its inherently abstract nature in order to meet the needs of businesses, which seek possibilities of all commercial entities to be able to adapt to the market needs. The result is a simplified concept of legal capital in limited liability companies and its formation and flexibility of company bodies with the possibility of choice for the founders between a one-tier and a two-tier board structure.

### *F. Advanced Corporate Governance*

*21.* Corporate governance is a constant theme in reform of company laws and legislation not only in developed legal regimes but also for those in transition. Essential issues are flexible managerial structure in small and medium enterprises and mechanism of shareholders' protection, including permanent and effective shareholders' control over the company managing body (in the case of large companies where management is separate from ownership).

The Law on Commercial Companies provides advanced legal solutions for the above. Therefore, the main feature of corporate governance in small and medium-size enterprises is the possibility for establishing the managerial structure in accordance with their needs, either through simplified owners' management or, if required, a more developed management structure. An essential feature of the 2011 Law on Commercial Companies is party autonomy with regard to a one-tier board or a two-tier board structure in limited liability as well as joint-stock companies.

Large companies, especially joint-stock companies, including public companies, have to respect mandatory provisions on corporate governance. Therefore, the basic feature of this regime includes strengthening the role of shareholders and their rights, especially for minority shareholders; introduction and important role of non-executive and supervisory directors; strengthening duties of the board of directors and controlling shareholders. The interest of investors is specially emphasized through a developed system of transparency of information relating to companies, especially those trading on the regulated market, including provisions on market manipulation and inside dealing according to EU Directives. Provisions on external audit and financial reporting are also strongly influenced by EU regulation, and IFRS standards are an integral part of relevant accounting laws.

### *G. Advancing the Rights of Minority Shareholders*

*22.* Modernization of company law included advancement of the rights of minority shareholders, many of which were already introduced into Serbian company law in 2004. They were also confirmed in the 2011 Law on Commercial Companies.

These include advanced disclosure, such as information on the company's capital, financial results, management reports and information on related party transactions, as well as control structure, especially emphasized in public companies. Shareholders have rights with respect to information: pre-meeting and during the meeting especially through right to ask questions; with the appropriate use of modern electronic communication. General rights of shareholders include cumulative voting for the board of directors (when prescribed by the statute for public joint-stock company), qualified majority for certain decisions, including modification of capital, statutory changes, liquidation, etc., and appraisal rights. Minority shareholders have special rights connected to shareholders meetings' convocation, proposing agenda items, filing derivative suits and enjoying sell-out right, as well as limited investigation rights and minority oppression remedies, including right to initiate liquidation.

Unfortunately, modern company law regime for minority shareholders protection does not coincide with corresponding business culture and advanced share dealings. Undeveloped market regulation and inadequate and incompetent courts failed to protect these interests leaving many shareholders, especially minority shareholders of privatized companies unprotected in many cases.

## §3. Definitions and Structure of Corporations and Partnerships

*23.* Business or commercial entities are regulated in Serbian law with a single act, which defines these entities as those performing activities in order to gain profit.[58] All business entities under a general term *commercial companies* are considered legal persons with legal personality, and the law recognizes four basic commercial forms: partnership, limited partnership, limited liability company and joint-stock company. General provisions on business entities include provisions on sole proprietor, while other acts deal with other non-profit civil organizations, cooperatives, foundations, as well as commercial entities performing specific activities, such as those of insurance, banking and financial services (banks, insurance companies, regulated market, providers of investment services, etc.).

According to the prevailing theoretical concept, all commercial forms are independent holders of rights and duties, separate from their owners, and act in their own interest.[59] Therefore, *theory of reality and institutional character* of the company defines its basic features. Accordingly, commercial companies are not only 'companies-contracts' although created on the contractual basis but are also 'companies-institutions'. As a general consequence of this concept, companies are managed and represented through bodies and a legal representative – director, even in relation between the company and its members. In spite of this prevailing concept, commercial companies always remain linked to their contractual basis, not only through contractual nature of the foundation but also in relation to management and other issues in some forms, especially partnership, and also in other forms of closed companies. Non-contractual character is most evident in public company, regardless of the contractual nature of their foundation.

Commercial company acquires its *status of a legally independent person* for the purpose of performing a profit-making activity by registration, which is regulated by the Law on Registration into the Business Agency Register.[60] Therefore, all commercial companies have legal personality and are registered in the Business Register. Commercial companies are legal persons until dissolution which is effective upon deletion from the Business Register.

All companies have an independent *trade (business) name and seat*. Company's seat is defined as a place where company is managed from on a daily basis, and is determined in the articles of incorporation, statute, general meeting decision, or decision of all partners in general and limited partnership, after which registration is necessary.[61] Companies can have an additional address for business correspondence (including electronic address) which must be registered in addition to the company's seat in the Business Register.

---

58. Article 2 LCC 2011.
59. *See* further for theoretical affirmation of this concept: Mirko Vasiljević, *Company Law (Law of commercial companies of Serbia and the EU)*, Pravni fakultet Univerziteta u Beogradu, Beograd, 2006, 69-72 (in English).
60. *See* Arts 3 and 5 LCC 2011 and Law on Registration procedure into the Business Agency Register (Zakon o postupku registracije u Agenciji za privredne registre), *Official Gazette of Republic of Serbia (Službeni glasnik Republike Srbije)*, 99/2011, 83/2014, 31/2019 and 105/2021.
61. Article 19 LCC 2011.

Commercial companies can have either natural or legal persons for *founders and members*. Companies are free to choose and perform their *business activities* (although certain activities require special authority approval). Company is obliged to file prevailing activity in the Business Register, but can perform other activities as well, without obligatory denomination of these in its internal acts.

All forms of commercial companies are founded on the basis of the *articles of incorporation* (or unilateral decision by the only founder in limited liability or joint-stock company), which can be altered depending on the business form. Unlike all other forms, only joint-stock company has another obligatory document – *statute* – for the purpose of determining internal organization and other most important issues. While articles of incorporation serve as a general document necessary only for the establishment of a joint-stock company, and therefore being of a general nature and not amendable, statute is the main document to define internal organization and other issues and can be amended by a general meeting resolution. Articles of incorporation and statute for the joint-stock company are registered and disclosed in the Business Register. Other company forms can have additional internal acts on a voluntary basis, but they have internal nature without obligatory registration or disclosure.[62]

Being legally independent persons, all forms of commercial companies have their own *assets and liabilities*, separate from their owners gained during business activities through their bodies (organs). Company's assets are used to meet its liabilities to company's creditors, although in certain company forms, members have *unlimited liability* for the debts of their company. In those company forms where members are protected with a limited liability, there is a possibility of their unlimited liability in the case of piercing of the corporate veil. This responsibility, based on the concept of abuse of law towards creditors of the company, entitles creditors to prove misuse of the limited liability provisions in order to establish direct liability of those members.[63]

Company's assets are created by *contributions of its members*. Contributions of members can be in cash or in kind, unless otherwise provided for specific company form, and they need to be denominated in RSD. Contributions in kind include different assets (including contribution to perform work or supply services in partnership and limited partnership) which can be assessed either by members themselves or through the assessment of an independent expert, whose evaluation is obligatory in public companies. There is a general duty to contribute, once agreed by members, while provisions on contributions include time limits (of a maximum of five

62. *See* in detail Arts 11–15 LCC 2011 and Law on Registration.
63. Art. 18 LCC 2011. *See* Mirko Vasiljević, *Probijanje pravne ličnosti u kompanijskom pravu (član kompanije vs. poverilac kompanije) (Piercing the corporate veil in company law (company member vs. company creditor))*, Intermex, Beograd, 2020; Dragan Vujisić, 'Probijanje pravne ličnosti' ('Piercing the Corporate Veil'), in: Miodrag Mićović (ed.), *Uskla ivanje pravnog sistema Srbije sa standardima Evropske unije (Harmonization of the legal system of Serbia with the standards of the European Union)*, Pravni fakultet Univerziteta u Kragujevcu, Kragujevac, 2019, 405ff.

years) and equal treatment of members. Renunciation of contributions is forbidden unless capital is reduced, including general meeting approval and creditors protection.[64]

## I. Different Forms of Corporations and Partnerships

*24.* Serbian company law recognizes *four general forms* of business organization without further sub-classification. These are partnership, limited partnership, limited liability company and joint-stock company. There is also a separate chapter on the European Company, even though application of these provisions is postponed by the 1st of January 2025.[65] This time frame could be further postponed and is, in fact, related to the potential membership of the Republic of Serbia to the EU.[66]

In legal literature, it is common to divide these forms into two groups: companies of capital (limited liability company and joint-stock company) and companies of persons (partnership and limited partnership). A major trait of *companies of persons* is the integration of members in the formal structure and direct management of the company, usually through their unlimited liability. Because these companies are characterized by personal attributes, acquaintance and confidence between company members, and unlimited liability for company's commitments, transfer of stakes within these company forms is usually under various restrictions. Other personal circumstances of members (including death) can have important consequences for the company itself, such as dissolution of the company. *Capital companies* are characterized by the predominance of the interest of capital and not of persons. Therefore, they are less influenced by personal characteristics of its members, especially in the case of joint-stock company. Stakes (and particularly shares) are relatively easy to transfer. The company does not cease to exist due to matters involving individual issues of members or shareholders; there is no general unlimited liability of members. Capital companies are managed by company bodies and have an internal organization which can be quite diversified.

This classification is still present in legal writing. Still, it is evident that even the simplest criticism would require the introduction of the inter-category of *companies of persons and capital,* that would include limited liability company and limited partnership, because these two categories, more than other ones, possess the elements of both the first and the second category. However, even with this intermediate category, the above classification is losing its significance, especially bearing in mind that it is not included in the present Law on Commercial Companies.

Instead, the current legal regime is focusing on the difference between joint-stock companies, or sometimes only public companies, on the one hand, and all other –

64. *See* further on general rules applicable to all company forms on contributions in Arts 45–60 LCC 2011.
65. *See* Arts 577a–577š LCC 2011.
66. *See* Tatjana Jevremović Petrović, 'Osvrt na prekogranični element kao uslov osnivanja evropskog akcionarskog društva u srpskom pravu' ('The Cross-border Requirement for Creation of a European Company in Serbian Law'), *Pravo i privreda (Law and Economy)* 4–6/2019, 167ff.

closed companies on the other hand. Still, definition and other issues concerning public companies are dealt through Law on Capital Markets and will be discussed later.[67]

Other classifications can be of importance, such as those based on the criteria of the company's establishment (normative and establishment conditioned by the competent authority approval). While normative system prevails, certain company forms still require approval (which is the case for banks, financial institutions, investment funds, etc.). Classification can also be made according to general or special nature of the company's activities (financial or other special activities). In several cases, some specific companies (such as the Central Depository Agency) are formed directly by law. It is also worth noting the difference between commercial companies on the one hand and public and state-owned enterprises on the other hand, especially because of special legislation, which was already discussed in Chapter 1 section 7. Finally, criteria which focus on the time of incorporation distinguish companies founded for a definite or an indefinite period of time, and this classification is included in the current legal regime.[68]

Finally, the Law on Commercial Companies has additional provisions on business (non-profit) associations. Also, there is a separate chapter on the European Economic Interest Grouping, even though application of these provisions is postponed by the 1st of January 2025.[69] This time frame could be further postponed and is, in fact, related to the potential membership of the Republic of Serbia to the EU.

### *A. Joint-Stock Company*

*25.* Joint-stock company is a commercial company whose capital is divided into shares. It can have one or more natural or legal persons as its shareholders. Shareholders are protected with limited liability provisions, and they can be responsible for the company's debts only in the case of lifting of the corporate veil and other cases prescribed by law. Joint-stock company is a legal person. It has its own assets and liabilities with which it can be responsible for the debts incurred during business operations.

---

67. Law on Capital Markets (Zakon o tržištu kapitala), *Official Gazette of Republic of Serbia (Službeni glasnik Republike Srbije),* 31/2011, with last amendments by 153/2020, available in English at https://www.sec.gov.rs/index.php/en/regulations/legislation/laws/6458-law-on-the-capital-market (accessed 23 Mar. 2022), further cited as Law on Capital Markets 2011. The Republic of Serbia adopted new Law on Capital Markets (Zakon o tržištu kapitala), *Official Gazette of Republic of Serbia (Službeni glasnik Republike Srbije),* 129/2021 (further cited as Law on Capital Markets 2021) which came into force on 5 Jan. 2022, but with a postponement of the application of its provisions to one year – 5 Jan. 2023. Some provisions will be applicable upon the joining of the Republic of Serbia to the EU, while few provisions in regard to vesting authority to pass regulations, general and other enactments aligning the operations and work of specific entities with the provisions of this and other laws are already applicable. *See* Art 421 Law on Capital Markets 2021. For the purpose of this work, only provisions which are currently in force and applicable will be discussed in detail.
68. *See* Art. 10 LCC 2011.
69. *See* Arts 580a–580č LCC 2011.

*B. Limited Liability Company*

*26.* Limited liability company is a commercial company with one or more natural or legal persons as its members. Members are protected with limited liability, and they can be responsible for the company's debts only in the case of lifting of the corporate veil and other cases prescribed by law. Limited liability company is a legal person. It has its own assets and liabilities with which it can be responsible for the debts incurred during business operations. Its capital is divided between members, who have stakes in the company's capital.

*C. Partnership*

*27.* Partnership is a commercial company and is a legally independent person. It has its own assets and liabilities with which it can be responsible for the debts incurred during business operations. Partnership has at least two partners who are jointly and severally liable for company's debts. Their responsibility is of imperative nature, and partners cannot agree otherwise.

*D. Limited Partnership*

*28.* Limited partnership is a commercial company and is a legally independent person. It has its own assets and liabilities with which it can be responsible for the debts incurred during business operations. Limited partnership has at least two partners. At least one of them (partner) has joint and several liability for company's debts, and is, therefore, in the same position as partner in general partnership. Limited partnership has at least one member (partner with limited liability) whose responsibility is limited to the amount of unpaid but subscribed contribution.

## II. Distinction Between Structures and Consequences

*29.* Serbian company law distinguishes only four basic company forms. Their distinction, therefore, can be found in the basic features of the most important characteristics of the company. These include, among others, limited liability, as well as other issues inherent to classical distinction between companies of persons and companies of capital. These distinctions are usually essential in making a choice between company forms, although there are some activities which require specific forms.

First and by far the most important distinction between company forms is based on the associated risk. While companies of persons include personal unlimited liability of members for the companies' debts, companies in the form of limited liability company and joint-stock company include privilege of limited liability and therefore prevail in the business practice. From statistical data, it is evident that companies usually perform their business in the forms including limited liability of members (more than 110,000 companies compared to approximately 2500 partnerships and limited partnerships altogether).[70]

While all company forms have members with appropriate stakes depending on their contributions and company form, only joint-stock companies have capital divided into certain amounts of shares which are distributed to their shareholders. Contributions can be in cash or in kind in all company forms, although contributions to perform work or supply services are also possible, as an exception, in partnerships or limited partnerships. While contributions in kind can be assessed by owners, assessment of an independent expert is obligatory in public companies.

Distinction can also be made in relation to a minimum number of members – while a single member company can be formed only as limited liability or joint-stock company, partnerships (general or limited) must have at least two members.

It was already suggested that all forms of commercial companies are founded on the basis of the *articles of incorporation* (or unilateral decision by the only founder in limited liability or joint-stock company). This document can be amended in all forms except joint-stock company, which has other obligatory document – *statute* – which can be amended.

*30.* Second important distinction concerns company's structure. Company's structure is far less complicated in case of partnerships (or limited partnerships), whereby owners usually are in full charge of managing companies' affairs and representation. Limited liability companies and especially joint-stock companies have differentiated structure, involving different bodies with rights and liabilities. Although a limited liability company can be managed by the owners, it can, according to individual needs, be organized in a more complicated structure, including separate management and even supervisory boards.

If company's structure should be further compared between a limited liability company on the one hand and joint-stock company on the other, then it is evident that the same possibilities exist between the choice of a one-tier or a two-tier board structure. Although similarly organized, these forms usually differentiate between owners' management (and supervision) and indirect management in close connection between members and directors in limited liability companies to professional management and independent supervision in joint-stock, and especially public companies.

Nevertheless, it is the difference between imperative and dispositive rules on this structure which makes the distinction more prominent. While a joint-stock company is generally strictly organized according to prescribed structure, a limited liability company has, as the most important feature, party autonomy in relation to a majority of internal issues between company and members, as well as among members themselves. This far-reaching party autonomy, which can modify many

---

70. For more statistical data and sources *see* Ch. V in s. 1. *See* in particular: Mirko Vasiljević, 'Law on enterprises and the choice of legal form' (Zakon o preduzećima i izbor pravne forme preduzeća), *Collected regulations (Zbirka propisa)*, Belgrade, 1998, 1-3.

dispositive provisions, includes even powers of the general meeting and makes possible formation and functioning of this company form according to individual needs. This approach has been influenced by the need for simplification of this form.[71]

A limited liability company differs from a joint-stock company on other issues as well, including minimum capital requirement (which has a symbolic nature with equivalence of approximately EUR 1) and other simplified provisions on evaluation of contributions of members.

Distinction between company forms is also evident on the issue of limited transferability of stakes or partnership interest in all company forms except joint-stock company, which is also the case for the more prominent protection of members in closed companies through pre-emption and other priority rights or restrictions introduced to protect members.

*31.* Finally, only joint-stock company can issue its shares to public, respecting various public issue requirements, and with further constant supervision and periodical and *ad hoc* disclosure requirements. Therefore, certain characteristics are made according to distinction between closed and public companies, including stricter provisions on duty to contribute, assessment and failure to contribute, transfer of shares and their limits, purchase of own shares, capital increase and pre-emption rights, issues concerning corporate governance including convening of shareholders' meetings, proxy voting and voting, board structure, remuneration and directors' meetings, committees and internal audit.[72]

Although the choice of company form is made according to their prevailing characteristics, in some cases this choice is limited due to companies' activities. Therefore, certain activities have designated structure or company form.

This is especially the case in various financial activities. Examples for them include banks in the form of joint-stock company, insurance companies in the form of joint-stock (and limited liability company for certain additional insurance activities) or a special form of mutual insurance company. Various investment companies can have limited choice between only joint-stock, limited liability company and sometimes different contractual forms of organization, while stock exchange and providers of investment services and other investment activities take the form of joint-stock companies.

Certain independent professions are due to be organized in specific company or other business forms. Such as the case of auditors, who (if registered in the Republic of Serbia) are due to be organized either as a company (in all four existing forms

71. This 'oversimplification' was, nevertheless, criticized by some authors, especially on the issue of the possible negative effects on the company interest and members themselves, and also affecting other interested persons. *See*, for example: Mirko Vasiljević, 'Critical approach to the Law on Commercial Companies of Serbia 2011' (Kritički pogled na Zakon o privrednim društvima Srbije (2011)), in: Vuk Radović (ed.), *Harmonisation of Serbian business law with EU law (2012) (Uskla ivanje poslovnog prava Srbije sa pravom Evropske unije (2012)),* Pravni fakultet Univerziteta u Beogradu, Beograd, 2012, 14 (in Serbian).

72. *See*, in particular, Arts 261, 282, 290, 295, 306, 311, 331, 335, 375, 344, 354, 356, 368, 369, 453, 383, 387, 392, 400, 417, 437, 384, 393, 401-402, 409, 410, 451 LCC 2011.

according to LCC) or to be registered as sole proprietor – entrepreneur.[73] Certain activities – such as the law practice – can be organized, if not performing their activities independently on the individual basis or with other practising lawyers in the joint office, also through formation of partnerships of lawyers (law firms).[74]

As a general consequence of a free choice of company form as a rule (and with few exceptions), members can choose forms to protect their interests and business needs the best. Apart from that, all company forms have possibility of conversion to other company form without liquidation. This makes it easier for members to choose those forms which are suitable for business start-up (which is especially the case for limited liability company, bearing in mind simplified condition for its formation and operation) and with possibilities of further changes, according to market conditions.

## III. Commercial and Civil Corporations and Partnerships

*32.* Serbian law makes distinction between commercial entities (performing activities in order to gain profit) and other forms of civil associations, in various forms, which do not have prevailing commercial but social, political or other similar goals. As a basic characteristic, members of commercial companies are entitled to profit gained through their activities.

Commercial entities can be organized either in individual form as an individual entrepreneur or commercial companies in four basic forms (and several forms for certain specific activities). All other non-commercial organizations can have different forms and with possibility of having separate legal personality (including special forms of civil association – professional, citizens, sports, etc.: endowment, foundation, non-governmental organization, private and public institutions, etc.). Usual distinction between commercial and non-commercial entities is made according to activities performed. Therefore, commercial companies perform business activities in order to gain profit. Prevailing goal of civil associations and other organizations may be public or general interest, providing certain services or activities for beneficiaries, founders or members, etc. Still, certain civil organizations can, similarly to commercial companies, also perform business activities with the intention to make profit, but these goals are usually not prevailing. Nevertheless, although civil organizations, such as, for example, associations, can perform certain commercial activities, they are not entitled to profit distributions to founders, members, employees, directors and members of bodies, including connected persons.[75]

---

73. Article 4 Law on auditing (Zakon o reviziji), *Official Gazette of Republic of Serbia (Službeni glasnik Republike Srbije)*, 73/2019.
74. Articles 44, 45 and 47 Law on the legal practice (legal profession) (Zakon o advokaturi), *Official Gazette of Republic of Serbia (Službeni glasnik Republike Srbije)*, 31/2011, further amended.
75. *See*, for example, Art. 37 Law on associations (Zakon o udruženjima), *Official Gazette of Republic of Serbia (Službeni glasnik Republike Srbije)*, 51/2009 and later amended. It entitles these organizations to perform business activities in order to gain profit under certain conditions but limits profit distribution. On the difference between civil and commercial organizations *see* in detail: Mirko Vasiljević, *Company Law (Law of commercial companies of Serbia and the EU)*, Pravni fakultet Univerziteta u Beogradu, Beograd, 2006, 45-49; Vladimir Vodinelić, *Gra ansko pravo: Uvod u gra*

Finally, according to the constitutional right of association, there is a choice between not only regulated forms of different civil organizations but also other non-regulated forms, which is not the case for commercial companies. Prescribed forms of commercial companies which pursue business activities with the intention of distribution of profit to members are of limitative nature and are under imperative requirements of the Law on Commercial Companies. Still, freedom of choice exists between these forms, with exceptions in certain specific activities, as mentioned before.

General (civil) partnership, unlike partnership as a commercial form under the Law of Commercial Companies, is not specifically regulated in Serbian civil law. Its basis, as a partnership contract without separate legal personality, failed to regulate Law on Obligations.[76] This legal vacuum is especially problematic bearing in mind that Law on Associations defines and underlies all associations without legal personality to provisions on civil partnership. Bearing in mind that in Serbian law a clear distinction exists between general and partnership as a form of commercial company, these problems relate to general Civil and Obligations law and will not, therefore, be analysed further.

## IV. Non-profit Associations and Other Corporate Legal Persons

*33.* Organizations of different kinds are regulated in many different sources of law. The most important forms of private organizations include associations, foundations, endowments, cooperatives, etc.

### *A. Associations*

*34.* Serbian Law on Associations defines this organization as a voluntary, non-governmental and non-profit organization founded by association of several natural or legal persons, in order to fulfil common or general goals and interests, not excluded by Constitution and law.[77]

Associations can be registered in the Business Agency Register on voluntary basis, after which it gains legal personality. Associations can be founded by three or more natural or legal persons on the constitutional assembly signing of the articles of incorporation and statute. It has its own name and seat, as well as other individual designations. Associations have members who can be directly involved in

*ansko pravo i Opšti deo gra anskog prava*, Pravni fakultet Univerziteta Union, Službeni glasnik, Beograd, 2012, 392-393.

76. Law on Obligations (Zakon o obligacionim odnosima), *Official Gazette of SFRY (Službeni list SFRJ)*, 29/1978 and later amended, including *Official Gazette of FRY (Službeni list SRJ)* 31/1993 and *Official Gazette of Republic of Serbia (Službeni glasnik Republike Srbije)*, 18/2020 available in English at: https://www.mpravde.gov.rs/files/The%20Law%20of%20Contract%20and%20Torts_180411.pdf (accessed 23 Mar. 2022).

77. *See* in particular Arts 2ff. Law on Associations.

management of the association or through designation of representatives in the association's bodies. It has an assembly as the supreme body, but can also organize other bodies.

Associations are entitled to have rights and own property. They have obligations of their own, and are liable to third persons with their property. Members and directors can be jointly and severally liable in the case of abuse of the association and its property. Associations can perform different activities, including commercial ones, but they are not entitled to distribute profit to its members, founders, directors, employees and other connected persons. Loss of legal personality after liquidation or insolvency proceedings is registered and becomes effective after the entry into Business Register.

The Law on Commercial Companies has additional provisions on business (non-profit) associations.[78] The business associations have legal personality and are formed jointly by two or more commercial companies or sole proprietors in order to achieve various non-profit goals and interests. Business associations are registered in the register of the Business Registers Agency and have status (including general provisions applicable to them) of associations.

### *B. Foundations and Endowments*

*35.* Endowment is a legal person, characterized by the absence of members, but with own property, which is established in order to achieve charitable goals in the public or private interest. Foundations are legal persons characterized by the absence of members and property and established in order to achieve charitable goals in the public interest. Both organizational forms are non-profitable and non-governmental organizations. Their goals must be in accordance with the Constitution and other laws.[79] If assets of foundations and endowments are contributed without reimbursement, a special tax regime is applicable.

Foundations and endowments can be founded by one or more natural or legal persons by signing of the articles of incorporation, or, in the case of endowment, by a legacy. They have their own name and seat, as well as other individual designations. Foundations and endowments are registered in the Business Agency Register after which they gain legal personality.

Foundations and endowments have a management board and a director, but can also have other bodies if provided for in statutes. Similar to associations, foundations and endowments can perform different activities in order to achieve their goals, and these include business activities. Still, assets can be used only in order to perform goals and tasks provided by the statutes of these organizations and all distributions to founders, management, employees and other connected persons are forbidden. Foundations and endowments are responsible for all debts with their assets. Unless there is a ground for piercing of the corporate veil, founders and management are not responsible for the debts of these organizations.

---

78. *See* Arts 578ff LCC 2011.
79. *See* Law on Endowments and Foundations (Zakon o zadužbinama i fondacijama), *Official Gazette of RS (Službeni glasnik RS)* 88/2010, further amended.

Similar to associations, loss of legal personality after liquidation or insolvency proceedings is registered and becomes effective after its entry into the Business Register.

### *C. Cooperatives*

*36.* Cooperatives are a specific form of organization of natural persons in order to pursue specific economic, social and cultural interests. They are organized according to principles of solidarity and voluntary organization, democracy and equal rights of management, independence and the possibility of being connected into specific cooperative unions.[80]

Depending on their activity, the cooperatives may be classified as: farming cooperatives – general and specialized – housing cooperatives, consumer cooperatives, handicraft cooperatives, healthcare ones, youth and pupils' cooperatives, as well as other types of cooperatives engaged in manufacturing, trade of goods and rendering services. Among other things, different classes of cooperatives have specific rules, including the number of founders, in each category prescribed by law.

The principles of cooperative organization and operations include the principle of formation and maintenance of capital and permanently open door to accept new members in a non-discriminate manner (*the cooperative's openness and non-discrimination principle and the principle of formation and maintenance of capital*). Second, membership status in a cooperative entitles the members to a dual position: a cooperative member and a client (consumer and credit cooperatives), employee (manufacturing and handicraft cooperatives) or supplier and service provider (sales and service cooperatives). That principle binds a cooperative to work only for the cooperative members – *the exclusivity principle*. Still, there are possible exceptions to this principle. Thirdly, preserving the principle of cooperative members' equality and voting 'by heads', however, this principle is relative for specified cooperatives either by assigning votes according to the size of contribution to the capital or according to the scope of business done with the cooperative. Prevailing principle of *the altruism* whereby interest rate is fixed on the share and not the dividend is sometimes altered by the distribution of net profit to cooperative members according to the work performed or pursuant to the value of doing business with the cooperative. Finally, cooperatives are characterized by *the principle of voluntary status of cooperative members* (entering and leaving the cooperative).

Cooperatives are granted with legal personality which they gain after the registration in the Business Register. They have their own rights and obligations, and their own property. Members of a cooperative have limited liability in proportion to

80. *See* Law on cooperatives (Zakon o zadrugama), *Official Gazette of RS* 112/2015. *See* in particular: Dobrosav Milovanović, Vlado Kovačević, 'Pretpostavke i značaj razvoja zadružnog sektora u Republici Srbiji' ('Preconditions and Importance of Development of Cooperative Sector in the Republic of Serbia'), in: Vuk Radović (ed.), *Uskla ivanje poslovnog prava Srbije sa pravom Evropske unije (2017) (Harmonisation of Serbian Business Law with EU Law (2017)),* Pravni fakultet Univerziteta u Beogradu, Beograd, 2017, 30ff; Vuk Radović, 'New trends in Serbian cooperative law', in: Bojan Milisavljević, Tatjana Jevremović Petrović, Miloš Živković (eds.), *Law and Transition: Collection of Papers*, University of Belgrade Faculty of Law, Belgrade, 2017, 147ff.

their contributions for the obligations of the cooperative. Obligatory documents include memorandum of association and cooperative rules (statutes), adopted at the constitutive general meeting by majority vote. They can be amended or supplemented at the general meeting of members by absolute majority of votes. The general meeting elects initial cooperative bodies, which include management and a supervisory board and a director.

Similar to other organizations, loss of legal personality after liquidation or insolvency proceedings is registered and becomes effective after the entry into Business Register, while it is also possible for cooperative to be dissolved after statutory changes, not including those with commercial companies.

### *D. Specialized Commercial Companies*

#### 1. Banks

*37.* Setting up and business operation of commercial banks and other financial organizations are regulated by a special law.[81] Although a bank is established as a joint-stock company, and autonomously performs its activity in order to earn profit based on the principles of liquidity, profitability and security, its foundation, management and activities are under significant National Bank of Serbia supervisory powers. A bank is established in order to perform various banking activities, including deposit, credit, payments, foreign currency exchange, issuance of guarantees and various other activities in financial markets.

Bank is established as a joint-stock company by natural or legal domestic or foreign persons with initial capital of at least EUR 10.000.000 equivalent in RSD. The most important provisions on the organization and functioning of the bank are included in its obligatory documents – articles of incorporation and statute. A bank is constituted at a *constitutive meeting of shareholders* that must not be held prior to the receipt of a preliminary approval from the National Bank of Serbia, although it gains legal personality by registration in the Business Register.

Banks are subject to strict provisions on a minimum capital requirement, adequacy of capital, its modifications, acquisition of own shares, obligatory reserves and liquidity requirements, which are under the supervision of the National Bank of Serbia. There are other strict requirements for banks on risk management, including liquidity risk, credit risk, interest and foreign exchange risk and other market risks, risks of bank's exposure to specific person or group of related persons, investment risk and operational risk.

A bank is expected to respect various provisions in order to protect its clients and their interests, especially including secrecy in relation to their clients. Special provisions on disclosure of information, as well as direct information of the National Bank of Serbia, are introduced for a bank and their connected persons (subsidiary and other members of the group) regarding most important information on the bank

81. Law on banks (Zakon o bankama), *Official Gazette of RS* (*Službeni glasnik RS)* 107/2005, 91/2010, 14/2015 available in English at: https://nbs.rs/en/drugi-nivo-navigacije/propisi/zakoni/ (accessed 24 Mar. 2022).

management, functioning of its organizational parts, business activities, liquidity, solvency and profitability, including consolidated reporting. External control, including auditing and consolidated auditing, is also under the supervision of the National Bank of Serbia.

Banks have an obligatory internal organization, including general meeting of shareholders, management and board of executive directors. Each bank has an obligation to establish at least several committees, including an audit committee with internal audit function, a credit committee and an assets and liability committee, but is free to establish other committees as well.

Supervision of the National Bank of Serbia, apart from mentioned, includes also consent for the acquisition of certain amount of ownership which establishes direct and indirect voting rights and control on other legal persons; supervision over solvency and legal compliance of bank operations and consolidated supervision of a banking group; consent to bank statutory changes and establishment of the bank representation offices and subsidiaries abroad. Finally, an important influence of the National Bank of Serbia is evident in the possibility of bank restructuring in the case of inability to operate because of various reasons, and is based on the principle of creditors' protection and shareholders' risk. Special insolvency proceedings for banks and insurance organizations are introduced through Law on insolvency and liquidation of banks and insurance organizations.[82]

## 2. Insurance Organizations

*38.* Insurance organizations are regulated by a special Insurance Law.[83] These companies are subject to provisions of the Law on Commercial Companies as well, unless otherwise regulated in certain matters by special laws.

Insurance activities can be performed through insurance companies, under condition of approval of the National Bank of Serbia either as a joint-stock company or mutual insurance company or as a branch of a foreign insurance company. Other insurance activities, including agency and representation in insurance, can be performed through joint-stock company or limited liability company forms or a natural person after approval of the National Bank of Serbia.

Joint-stock insurance company can be founded by two or more natural or legal, domestic or foreign persons. Their activities include one or several insurance activities within the same group of insurance activities, or re-insurance activities, including other connected insurance activities. Minimum capital requirement depends on the insurance activities, starting from EUR 3.200.000 in equivalent sum in RSD for life insurance, EUR 2.200.000 for certain activities in regard to non-life insurance, and EUR 3.200.000 for re-insurance.

---

82. *See* Law on insolvency and liquidation of banks and insurance organizations (Zakon o stečaju i likvidaciji banaka i društava za osiguranje), *Official Gazette of RS* (*Službeni glasnik RS)* 14/2015 further amended, available in English at: https://nbs.rs/en/drugi-nivo-navigacije/propisi/zakoni/ (accessed 24 Mar. 2022).

83. Law on insurance (Zakon o osiguranju), *Official Gazette of RS* (*Službeni glasnik RS)* 139/2014, further amended, available in English at: https://nbs.rs/en/drugi-nivo-navigacije/propisi/zakoni/ (accessed 24 Mar. 2022).

A joint-stock insurance company is established after registration in the Business Register conditioned on the approval of the National Bank of Serbia under certain requirements, such as the submission of the articles of incorporation, statutes, evidence of minimum capital requirement payments, business policy and plan proposal, possible shareholders and percentage of their holdings, persons to be nominated as director, as well as other data and documents. Insurance company has an obligatory two-tier internal structure, with obligatory general meeting, executive board of directors and supervisory board. Consent to the election of board of directors and supervisory board members is granted by the National Bank of Serbia.

A mutual insurance company is an organization with legal personality performing insurance activities for its members – insured beneficiaries and is based on the principle of mutuality and solidarity. It can perform all insurance activities without the possibility of performing re-insurance activities. There are two different forms of this organization, either with unlimited or limited contributions of members, depending on the limits of contribution. Other provisions on the minimum capital requirements, articles of incorporation, statute, as well as internal organization are applied by analogy to the joint-stock insurance company.

Insurance companies are under specific provisions on capital formation and maintenance, including insurance premiums, obligatory, specifically technical, mathematical, warranty and other reserves, liquidity requirements, investment limitations and minimum solvency requirements. Insurance companies have risk management obligations, limits in assets and obligation fulfilment, as well as various limits in distributions.

An insurance company has to organize internal auditing, that is autonomous and independent, and accountable directly to the company's supervisory board. Its control is continuous and comprehensive, and includes all company activities. These companies are also subject to mandatory auditing and disclosure of their financial reports.

Supervision of insurance company activity is exercised by the National Bank of Serbia primarily in order to protect the interests of the insured and other insurance beneficiaries. To reach that objective, the bank issues an operating licence to the company, grants consent to specified company documents and actions, adopts rules and decisions as specified by law, processes statistical and other data, maintains prescribed registers and examines complaints by the insured, insurance beneficiaries and third parties that suffered damage from company operations and the activity of other persons engaged in insurance business.

In exercising supervision over company activity, the National Bank of Serbia may order measures to remedy non-compliance and irregularities, those caused by failing to comply with the risk management rules, order that the insurance portfolio be transferred to another insurance company, take control over company operations and appoint a receiver, revoke the licence to carry out one or several insurance activities, impose injunctions and propose specific steps against members of company bodies. Specific provisions on insolvency and liquidation are applicable, same as for banks.

3. Investment Funds

*39.* Serbian law regulated investment funds as a form for collective investments for the first time with a special Law on Investment Funds in 2006.[84] It provided provisions for open-end funds with units, closed-end funds with share capital and private funds. Further regulation in this area introduced specific provisions for open-ended investment funds subject to public offering (UCITS funds).[85] Separate law addressed other alternative investment funds.[86]

An open-ended investment fund subject to public offering (undertaking for the collective investment in transferable securities – UCITS, also referred to as UCITS fund) is organized and managed by a management company of an open-ended investment fund subject to public offering. This type of management company may also manage other collective investment undertakings. Organization and foundation of open-end and closed-end and management of all alternative funds are performed through an investment fund management company. Registration of all open-end and closed-end funds is conditional upon approval of the Republic of Serbia Securities Commission.

There are special conditions on the investment policy and diversification of risk according to investment structure and limitations, while risk management is performed through open-ended or alternative investment fund management company.

*An open-ended investment fund subject to public offering (undertaking for the collective investment in transferable securities – UCITS fund)* is defined as an open-ended investment fund, the sole object of which is the collective investment of capital. Its capital is raised by public offering of the fund's investment units, in transferable securities or in other liquid financial assets. UCITS fund operates in compliance with the principle of investment risk spreading, and the investment units of which, at the request of unit holders, are redeemed, directly or indirectly, out of the assets of the open-ended investment fund.

UCITS fund is without legal personality. It is organized by an open-ended investment fund subject to public offering management company. The assets of UCITS fund are managed by the management company in its own name, and on behalf of fund members.

Its minimum capital requirement is the RSD amount equivalent of EUR 200.000. The assets of a UCITS fund must be managed according to diversification of investment risk and upon investment policy and investment objectives of the UCITS fund stated in the prospectus. Various restrictions on the investment and use of UCITS fund assets are applicable. A proportionate share of the UCITS fund net assets is

---

84. Law on investment funds (Zakon o investicionim fondovima), *Official Gazette of RS* (*Službeni glasnik RS)* 46/2006, further amended.

85. Law on open-ended investment funds subject to public offering (Zakon o otvorenim investicioni fondovima sa javnom ponudom), *Official Gazette of RS* (*Službeni glasnik RS)* 73/2019, available in English at: https://www.sec.gov.rs/index.php/en/regulations/legislation/laws/7181-law-%D0%BEn-open-ended-investment-funds-subject-to-public-offering (accessed 24 Mar. 2022).

86. Law on Alternative Investment funds (Zakon o alternativnim investicionim fondovima), *Official Gazette of RS* (*Službeni glasnik RS)* 73/2019, available in English at: https://www.sec.gov.rs/index.php/en/regulations/legislation/laws/7177-law-on-alternative-investment-funds (accessed 24 Mar. 2022).

calculated in investment units, conferring the same rights to fund members, including right of disposal and redemption of investment units.

*An open-end alternative investment fund* is not a legal entity, but a purely contractual form, organized through an alternative investment fund management company and managed on behalf of the fund members. Here also fund assets belong to fund members, and not the fund itself. Various limits prescribed to investment and diversifications are fully applicable to this alternative fund type.

Units of alternative investment funds without legal personality shall be dematerialized transferable financial instruments. Members of the open-end alternative investment funds are entitled to be redeemed at their own request, and at any time, either directly or indirectly from assets of this fund.

*A closed-end alternative investment fund* can be either a closed-end AIF without legal personality or a closed-end AIF with legal personality. While a closed-end AIF without legal personality is of contractual nature and organized by an alternative investment fund management company, a closed-end AIF with legal personality can be in the form of joint-stock or limited liability company.

*A closed-end AIF without legal personality* has a separate set of assets, managed by AIF management company on its own behalf and for the joint account of members of the AIF. Its investment units may not be redeemed from assets of the AIF by its members.

*A closed-end AIF with legal personality* is established and managed by an AIF management company on its own behalf and for its (and not its members) account. Its members and also not allowed to request redeem of their shares or parts in the funds capital. When a closed-end AIF is organized as a joint-stock company or a limited liability company, its minimum share capital must be equivalent to EUR 200.000 and must have a two-tier governance structure.

Finally, there is a possibility to establish *a closed-end AIF with internal management*. This fund has legal personality. It manages its assets internally, acting at the same time as an alternative investment fund management company.

Investments in assets of alternative investment funds are subject to various limits. Alternative investment funds can be subject to public offering or private placements. Its shares are allowed to be marketed to not only professional but also semi-professional investors.

## 4. Investment Fund Management Company

*40.* The Law on open-ended investment funds subject to public offering and the Law on alternative investment funds regulate the open-ended or alternative investment fund management companies. Their main activities include organization and foundation of open-ended funds subject to public offering as well as alternative open-ended and closed-ended funds, their management, rights and various obligations.

A management company of an open-ended investment fund subject to public offering must be organized as a legal person in a form of joint-stock closed company. Its internal organization must be regulated as two-tier management and control system. This type of management company may also manage other collective investment undertakings. The minimum capital requirement for a management company of UCITS fund must be RSD equivalent of EUR 125.000.

All management companies of alternative investment funds can be organized as legal personalities, in the form of limited liability company or closed joint-stock company. Management companies of alternative investment funds may be large and small, depending on their total assets of alternative investment funds under management and the categories of investors (professional/semi-professional) that alternative investment funds are offered to. Large management company of alternative investment fund must be internally organized as a two-tier management and control system. Registration of these companies' forms is under the approval of the Republic of Serbia Securities Commission. Among other legal requirements, it is worth mentioning that necessary approval is conditional upon ownership structure (and further modifications of qualified participation in ownership), suitability and reliability of shareholders and connected persons, including sources of their capital.

The minimum capital requirement for a large management company of alternative investment fund is set to EUR 125.000 (or EUR 300.000 for internally managed closed-ended AIFs with legal personality) while it is EUR 70.000 (or EUR 150.000 for internally managed closed-ended AIFs with legal personality) in the case of small management company of alternative investment fund.

Apart from other capital requirement provisions, there are specific provisions on other organizational and technical requirements. All investment fund management companies have special provisions of disclosure of certain information to the public and Securities Commission, such as financial information, assets and obligations, portfolio structure, investment units and all their changes.

Management in these companies is regulated according to general provisions of the Law on Commercial Companies with additional requirements for directors, including special experience, qualifications and other conditions in the Law on open-ended investment funds subject to public offering and the Law on alternative investment funds, respectively. Nomination of a director needs to be approved by the Securities Commission.

## 5. Investment Services Companies

*41.* Basic provisions on financial markets, participants on financial markets, including Securities Commission and Central securities depository and clearing house, are contained in the Law on Capital Markets. The most important specialized form to provide investment services is the investment company, exclusively authorized to trade on regulated markets under the approval of the Securities Commission. Investment companies have to be organized either as broker-dealer companies or authorized banks – a special organization unit of a credit institution.

The minimum capital requirement for an investment company depends on the investment activities, starting from EUR 125.000 equivalent to RSD, paid in cash. These companies are also required to fulfil other technical, equipment, professional and organizational conditions in order to gain approval of the Securities Commission to perform particular investment activity (or activities).

*Broker-dealer companies* are organized according to general provisions of the Law on Commercial Companies, with further conditions introduced with regard to directors and board members and under the preliminary approval of the Securities Commission.

It has articles of incorporation and statute, common for all joint-stock companies, and obligatory procedures and rules, including tariff rules. It operates under the principles of safety, fairness and professionalism, in the interest of its clients. Special provisions apply on the minimum capital requirement, risk evaluation and management, as well as financial reporting and disclosure under the supervision of the Securities Commission.

Broker-dealer companies can be authorized to keep separate money accounts in a credit institution for its clients and are able to keep separate securities accounts at the central depository and clearing house, including professional recording and information obligations.

*Authorized banks* for broker-dealer and other investment services on financial markets are separate organizational units of credit institutions, authorized by Securities Commission under certain conditions. These include separate organizational structure and bookkeeping, as well as other necessary conditions same as for investment (broker-dealer) companies, except capital adequacy and risk evaluation and management provisions.

## §4. Sources and Hierarchy of the Law on Corporations and Partnerships

*42.* Corporations and partnerships are regulated with general sources, typical to civil law, such as the Constitution, laws, by-laws enacted by public authorities, as well as customs, general legal principles and other private sources of law, including general terms of business, corporate governance codes, etc. Finally, case law, legal tradition and theory can have an important impact on the law on corporations and partnerships.

### I. International Sources

*43.* Serbian Constitution adopts a principle of direct application of generally accepted rules of international law and ratified international treaties. They are considered to be an integral part of the legal system in the Republic of Serbia.[87] Nevertheless, ratified international treaties must be in accordance with the Serbian Constitution, which is a consequence of the hierarchy of sources, whereby the Constitution is considered to be the highest formal source of law. The majority of international sources are of the general nature and usually have an indirect impact on the content of the law regulating corporations and partnerships.

87. *See* Art. 16 of the Constitution of the Republic of Serbia.

*44.* On the other hand, the Stabilisation and Association Agreement between the European Communities and the Republic of Serbia, signed on April 29th 2008, is of direct relevance to Serbian Company Law, influencing structure, definitions, principles and many important particular provisions related to corporations and partnerships.[88] According to provisions of the Stabilisation and Association Agreement, the Republic of Serbia agreed to ensure that its existing laws and future legislation will gradually be made compatible with the EU acquis and that such laws will be properly implemented and enforced.[89] The same obligation the Republic of Serbia expressed within the Resolution on the accession to the EU, adopted by the National Assembly on October 13th 2004.[90] After the signing of the Stabilisation and Association Agreement, the Republic of Serbia started to harmonize its laws with the EU, including issues related to Company law. The process is still ongoing, even though Serbia already harmonized its provisions with EU Law in most relevant issues (*see also* §2.IV.B).

## II. National Sources

### A. *Legislation*

*45.* The term *law* is understood to mean, first of all, a legislative instrument in the formal sense, enacted by the legislature, i.e., parliament. In that sense, the term also designates normative instruments of the executive and the administrative branches of power (decrees, orders, conclusions, decisions). The need for these legislative instruments in company law, in contrast to civil law, is particularly emphasized. The reason is in the dynamics and complexity of company law legal relations whereby the law regulates only the key principles, giving it a less active role than is the case with civil law.

Company law provisions follow the needs of practice. However, in Serbian law, they have a noticeable tendency to changing often. This is understandable bearing in mind major reasons for these changes. First, many provisions and norms typical for a market economy were introduced after almost fifty years of their exclusion from Serbian law. It is understandable that many of them are still new and that business practice, theory and case law still try to accommodate certain company law instruments and fit them into the legal system. Second, developments in this area were remarkable in company laws in many countries and within EU, and were sometimes too eagerly followed in Serbian company law by way of harmonization and legal transplantation. These developments particularly include modernization

88. *See* the full text in English at: https://www.mei.gov.rs/upload/documents/sporazumi_sa_eu/saa_textual_part_en.pdf (accessed 18 May 2022).
89. *See* Art. 72 of the Stabilisation and Association Agreement.
90. Full text of the Resolution in Serbian can be found at: https://www.mei.gov.rs/upload/documents/nacionalna_dokumenta/rezolucija_narodne_skupstine_o_pridruzivanju_eu.pdf (accessed 18 May 2022).

and introduction of new technologies, electronic registration and other communication developments; development of financial markets and the process of dematerialization of securities, including online trading, business activities to include online trade, wide use of electronic signature and the like. They also include modernization efforts in corporate governance, including board structures, increased transparency and further simplification of capital requirements for closed companies.

A basic law to deal with corporations and partnerships is the Law on Commercial Companies.[91] It governs general statutory issues for commercial companies, especially foundation, governance, statutory changes, change of legal form, dissolution and other issues.[92] It is also a general source of law to govern legal status of entrepreneurs – sole proprietors. This law is of general nature, and is applicable to general but also specific forms of companies, even though specific laws can by governing their formation and activities provide for different solutions.

Among these specific laws, the most important include Law on Capital Markets, particularly important for the legal status and functioning of public companies and other participants on capital markets; Law on financial leasing, Law on Public Enterprises, Law on Banks, Law on insolvency and liquidation of banks and insurance organizations, Law on Insurance, Law on open-ended investment funds subject to public offering and Law on Alternative Investment funds, etc.[93] Finally, for commercial companies, many other laws have a high level of importance, including Law on the registration procedure into the Business Agency Register, Law on Takeovers of Joint-stock companies, Law on Insolvency, Law on Auditing, Law on Accounting, Law on Investments, Law on Public-Private Partnerships and Concessions, Law on Privatization, etc.[94]

Normative instruments of the executive and the administrative branches of power play an important role in this field of law. They include numerous by-laws passed by the Government authorities in particular in the sphere of privatization and taxes,

---

91. Already cited as LCC 2011.
92. *See* Art. 1 and further in LCC 2011.
93. All other laws already cited except Law on financial leasing (Zakon o finansijskom lizingu), *Official Gazette of RS* (*Službeni glasnik RS)* 55/2003, further amended and available in English at: https://nbs.rs/en/drugi-nivo-navigacije/propisi/zakoni/index.html (accessed 24 Mar. 2022). As already mentioned above, The Republic of Serbia adopted new Law on Capital Markets (Zakon o tržištu kapitala), *Official Gazette of Republic of Serbia (Službeni glasnik Republike Srbije),* 129/2021 (further cited as Law on Capital Markets 2021) which came into force on 5 Jan. 2022, but with a postponement of the application of its provisions to one year – 5 Jan. 2023. Some provisions will be applicable upon the joining of the Republic of Serbia to the EU, while few provisions in regard to vesting authority to pass regulations, general and other enactments aligning the operations and work of specific entities with the provisions of this and other laws are already applicable. *See* Art 421 Law on Capital Markets 2021. For the purpose of this work, only provisions which are currently in force and applicable will be discussed in detail.
94. Law on Takeovers of Joint-stock companies (Zakon o preuzimanju akcionarskih društava), *Official Gazette of RS* (*Službeni glasnik RS)* 46/2006, further amended; Law on insolvency (Zakon o stečaju), *Official Gazette of RS* (*Službeni glasnik RS)* 104/2009, further amended, available in English at: https://alsu.gov.rs/en/dokumenta/zakoni/ (accessed 24 Mar. 2022); Law on accounting (Zakon o računovodstvu), *Official Gazette of RS* (*Službeni glasnik RS)* 73/2019, further amended; Law on Investments (Zakon o ulaganjima), *Official Gazette of RS* (*Službeni glasnik RS)* 89/2015, further amended; Law on Public-Private Partnerships and concessions (Zakon o javno-privatnom partnerstvu i koncesijama), *Official Gazette of RS* (*Službeni glasnik RS)* 88/2011, further amended. Law on Registration, Auditing and Privatization already cited.

as well as the National Bank in matters of monetary market supervision and Securities Commission in relation to financial markets supervision.

### *B. By-Laws or Articles*

*46.* Company law has other sources of law which can be important in the governance of business organizations. Among these, special attention is given to general principles of law, case law and other provisions.

#### 1. General Principles of Law

*47.* Since it is also impossible in company law to regulate all legal matters with written sources of law (laws passed in the parliament, through normative instruments of the executive and the administrative branches as well as other sources) – of particular significance in this branch are *the general principles of law*. In Company law, this is particularly the case with the principle of good faith, principle of good business practice and duty of care, principle of the interest of the company and duty of loyalty to the company, and the like. All of these principles are incorporated in the Law on Commercial Companies by reference. General principles of law, especially those existing in the General part of civil law (or rather Law on Obligations), are also applicable in Company Law. Those general principles include party autonomy, contractual freedom, principles of equality, good faith, *pacta sunt servanda*, prohibition of abuse of law, etc. Finally, most of the general principles of law, even those not formally included in written laws, including principle of fairness, legal certainty, solidarity, etc., are applied in the courts.[95]

#### 2. Case Law

*48.* In continental legal tradition, including Serbian law, *case law* is not a formal source of law. This means that lower instance courts are not obliged by decisions of higher courts (and the higher court is not obliged to pass the same judgment in a subsequent similar case). Still, in reality lower instance courts nevertheless conform to legal opinions expressed in judgments passed by the higher courts. Reasons for such vertical influencing are numerous. First of all, the practice established in such a way is highly authoritative, which is genuine and not formal, and is based on the worthiness of the reasoning expressed in the judgment of the superior court. This is even more the case for the so-called legal positions and opinions taken at the judge meetings of the superior courts (in Serbia for commercial matters it is the Commercial appellation court). Finally, *general legal positions* are pronounced by the general meeting of the Supreme Cassation Court with regard to the interpretation of

---

95. *See* in particular Vladimir Vodinelić, *Gra ansko pravo: Uvod u gra ansko pravo i Opšti deo gra anskog prava (Civil law: Introduction to civil law and General part of Civil law)*, Pravni fakultet Univerziteta Union u Beogradu, Javno preduzeće 'Službeni glasnik', Beograd, 2012, 75.

specific legal norms and are obligatory for all chambers of this court until changed by a different general legal position taken at the general meeting of the Supreme Cassation Court.[96] Another motivation for influence of case law is psychological: people stick to positions already taken by a superior court – and thus become inert. Finally, there is also the line of least resistance; the judge believes that his/her decision will be modified if it deviates from current practice (shifting the responsibility to higher courts). Nevertheless, it can be said that case law of courts and arbitrations in Serbia is still undeveloped in the matters dealing with commercial companies. However, case law plays in this, as well as in many other relatively new and undeveloped branches of law, an exceptionally important role in eliminating contradictions in relevant legislation, interpretation and understanding of new legal instruments, and creation of those provisions in issues not being regulated. For this important task, there is a general need for further professionalism and specialization, but especially for independence of judges.

## 3. Customs

*49.* Customs (usage) do not have the same role in company law as they do in civil law or the trade – commercial law. There are many reasons for this, one of them being the fact that a certain amount of time is necessary to establish a custom. Company law has been developing in Serbia for just over three decades, with a constant change of primary sources to deal with commercial companies, which is a rather short period for an initial practice to become customary. However, the nature of that source, as an unwritten rule of conduct, is in itself not favourable for raising the level of legal certainty among participants in the market, particularly not for investors and other participants on capital markets.

## 4. Code of Conduct (Corporate Governance Code)

*50.* Corporate Governance Code is an important source of law, developed in contemporary company law. Serbia followed this modern approach by enactment of Corporate Governance Code first in 2006 and more recently in 2012 through the Serbian Chamber of Commerce and Industry.[97] It is intended for all companies of capital – companies with limited liability of its members on a voluntary basis.[98]

96. For general legal positions of the Supreme Cassation Court and legal positions of the Commercial appellation court *see* Arts 26 and 31 Law on the organization of the courts (Zakon o ure enju sudova), *Official Gazette of RS* (*Službeni glasnik RS)* 116/2008, further amended; available in English at: https://www.mpravde.gov.rs/en/tekst/1700/judicial-package.php (accessed 24 Mar. 2022 ).
97. Data on the Corporate Governance Code (CGC 2012) already cited.
98. *See* Introduction remarks in the CGC 2012.

Still, the Law on Commercial Companies promotes the introduction and application of Corporate Governance Codes on the 'comply or explain' basis especially for public companies.[99]

It is true that these Codes play an increasingly important role in regulating the conduct of businesses, even though sanctions for their breach are not of the imperative, but rather moral nature. Still, Serbian business culture needs to be developed further in order to promote a wider application of these principles of good business practice.

## 5. Autonomous Instruments (Articles of Incorporation and Statute)

*51.* It was already mentioned that all forms of commercial companies are founded on the basis of the *articles of incorporation* (or unilateral decision by the only founder in limited liability or joint-stock company), which can be altered depending on the business form. Only the joint-stock company has a further obligatory document – *statute*, for the purpose of determining internal organization and other most important issues. While articles of incorporation serve as a general document necessary only for the establishment of the joint-stock company, and therefore being of a general nature and not amendable, statute is the main document to define internal organization and other issues and can be amended by the general meeting resolution.

Therefore, Law on Commercial Companies gives the founders an opportunity to autonomously regulate numerous matters of their organization, management, relations between the owner and his/her company, creating in such a way a source of law applicable to specific and not general matters. This is especially so for the closed commercial companies, while public companies are under a stricter regime of legislative control through imperative solutions and the resulting supervision by public law bodies. In any case, these instruments – articles of incorporation, statutes, as well as all other internal acts, including shareholders', members' or partners' agreements have an important role in the implementation and application of the corresponding laws. They must be in accordance with imperative requirements, as well as public policy and good faith. While articles of incorporation of all forms of closed companies allow for greater party autonomy, it is much more limited in the statutes of joint-stock companies, due to numerous imperative legal requirements regulating this company's form.

Since these instruments are also grounds for certain court decisions, the interpretation of the pertinent piece of legislation through these instruments is exceptionally important for both the quality of a piece of legislation and its application, and in turn the quality of law in general and legal certainty.

---

99. *See* in particularly Arts 368 and 452 LCC 2011. On the rather 'controversial nature' of these sources of law in Serbian law *see* Zoran Arsić, 'Kodeks ponašanja – Kodeks korporativnog upravljanja (Code of conduct – Corporate Governance Code)', *Pravo i privreda (Law and Economy)* 5-8/2005, 73-82.

*C. Relationship Between By-Laws or Articles and Legislation*

*52.* Provisions contained in the articles of incorporation, statutes and other internal acts are appropriately positioned in the hierarchy of their sources. Namely, after the application of legislative acts, including laws and other normative instruments of the executive and the administrative branches of power (decrees, orders, conclusions, decisions), there is a possibility to introduce and apply these sources once there is either an express authorization or, otherwise, where this is implied in the optional nature of the provisions contained in the legislation. These provisions are considered to be of a permissive nature, leaving the possibility to regulate certain issues according to business needs.

Modern company law is characterized by a considerable number of laws that include constraints or rules of the imperative nature – the so-called *renaissance of formalism*. This is also the case in Serbian company law. Although there are many imperative requirements, they are usually only applied to specific forms of companies – usually joint-stock companies and particularly public companies. However, there is a strong trend of introducing provisions with permissive nature, available to introduce party autonomy for all other company forms, being of the closed nature. For them, there is an important number of provisions being optional or leaving a choice in order to provide flexibility. This choice is therefore particularly exercised through articles of incorporation, statute (where allowed), as well as other internal acts of the company.

## III. Hierarchy of the Law on Corporations and Legislation

*53.* Serbian law defines the Constitution as a supreme legal act of the Republic of Serbia.[100] Ratified international treaties and generally accepted rules of the international law are considered to form an integral part of the Serbian legal system, but they need to be in compliance with the Constitution.

All laws and other general acts enacted, therefore, must be in compliance with the Constitution, as well as ratified international treaties and generally accepted rules of International Law. All by-laws of the Republic of Serbia, general acts of organizations with delegated public powers, political parties, trade unions and civic associations, as well as collective agreements must be in compliance with the law.

If autonomous provinces and local self-government units are allowed to enact statutes, decisions and other general acts must be in compliance with the law. All their general acts must be in compliance with their statutes, and all individual acts and actions of state bodies, organizations with delegated public powers, bodies of autonomous provinces and local self-government units must be based on the law.

Bearing in mind the most important sources of corporations and partnerships law, the basic hierarchy shall be as follows: Law on Commercial Companies must be in compliance with the Constitution and with the ratified international treaties and generally accepted rules of International Law. Other laws, particularly those regulating

100. For general principles of hierarchy of legal acts *see* Arts 194–198 of the Constitution of the Republic of Serbia.

specific company forms, have *lex specialis* character and are applied in regulating specific issues covered by their provisions, while all other (general) provisions of the Law on Commercial Companies, in accordance with specific provisions, will be applicable.

By-laws have an important role in company law and are to be in accordance with legislative sources. For those legal provisions with permissive nature, there is a place for party autonomy and possibility of choice. Therefore, articles of incorporation and statute, as well as other internal acts, are available to regulate certain issues within party autonomy principle, which is especially so in the case of closed commercial companies.

## §5. International Private Law (Conflict of Law Rules)

*54.* The Law on resolving conflict of laws provides basic provisions to determine company's nationality as well as the *lex societatis* for companies.[101] This provision implies the application of the theory of incorporation, modified with the real seat concept.

Namely, nationality of the legal person (including commercial companies) shall be determined according to the law of the country where it has been incorporated.[102] Nevertheless, if a legal person has its seat in a country other than a country of incorporation and that country considers the legal person to have its own nationality, this criterion shall prevail.[103] Therefore, there is a possibility to apply national law of the company's seat only in the case whereby that country considers company to have its own nationality only on the seat criteria. There are still no provisions on the change of the applicable law, including company's nationality, even though it is to be expected that Serbian law will be harmonized in due time with the recent EU provisions on cross-border conversions.[104]

Nevertheless, definition of the seat in Serbian law is made according to the real seat criteria, whereby it is considered to be the place from where the company's affairs have been conducted. It should coincide with the statutory seat of the company and must be registered –these additional criteria introduce the method of a company's seat determination and disclosure to third parties. Therefore, there is a legal presumption of identity of the place of real, statutory and registered seat. Nevertheless, the real seat may be different from the registered seat. However, due to

101. Law on resolving conflict of laws with regulations of other countries (Zakon o rešavanju sukoba zakona sa propisima drugih zemalja), *Official Gazette of SFRY* (*Službeni list SFRJ)* 43/1982, further amended 72/1982, 46/1996 and *Official Gazette of RS* (*Službeni glasnik RS)* 46/2006, available in English at: https://www.mpravde.gov.rs/en/tekst/1699/civil-matter.php (accessed 24 Mar. 2022). *See*: Tatjana Jevremović Petrović, 'Državna pripadnost, *Lex Societatis* i sedište privrednog društva' ('Nationality, Lex Societatis and the Company Seat'), *Pravni život (Legal Life)* 11/2010, 155ff; Tatjana Jevremović Petrović, 'Right of Establishment: Serbian Company Law', in: *SEE*, EU Cluster of Excellence in European and International Law (Ed.), *South East Europe and the European Union – Legal Aspects*, Verlag Alma Mater, Saarbrücken 2015, 77ff.
102. Article 17 para. 1 of the Law on conflict of laws.
103. Article 17 para. 2 of the Law on conflict of laws.
104. *See* in particular Directive (EU) 2019/2121 of 27 Nov. 2019 amending Directive (EU) 2017/1132 as regards cross-border conversions, mergers and divisions.

the importance of registration of companies' data in the Business Register, the significance of the real seat concept is diminished in practice.[105]

## §6. The Labour Law Connection: Co-determination and Corporate Structure

*55.* The Law on Commercial Companies has no particular solutions regarding employees' participation in the company's management and control. Namely, it is conceived from the position of capital and not of labour. The controversial nature of labour position was viewed from the perspective of labour involvement in company's affairs in the past decades of socialist Yugoslavia. After the period of overemphasizing the concept of labour in corporate management through the self-management model, which produced a negative effect in the sphere of working discipline and economic effectiveness, new commercial legislation in Serbia has chosen to leave the position of labour to the Labour Law and limit employees' rights to information and consultation.[106]

Under the Law on labour provisions, employees are granted certain rights, including right to associate with labour unions (syndicates) emphasizing their right to be informed.[107] There are several other possibilities of employees' involvement in the companies' affairs, including their involvement in the adoption and application of collective agreements. Law on labour specially introduces protection of employees in the case of statutory changes, and adopts the concept of acquired rights and continuation of contracts.[108]

Finally, the most important provisions for involvement of employees in the management of a company are provided by the possibility for employees to be organized as a separate body – employees' council when a company has more than fifty employees. Where this body is organized, its main use is to promote consultation rights and to be involved in decision-making in the case of decisions affecting employees' rights.[109] Nevertheless, it must be emphasized that these provisions are of optional and not obligatory nature.

105. *See* in detail part dealing with identification of the company, particularly company's seat. Otherwise *see* Art. 19 LCC 2011.
106. Law on labour (Zakon o radu), *Official Gazette of RS* (*Službeni glasnik RS)* 24/2005, further amended.
107. General provisions on employees' rights are particularly regulated under the Art. 13 Law on labour. Further rights concerning labour unions and their information rights are stipulated in the Arts 206ff Law on labour.
108. *See* Arts 147–151 Law on labour.
109. *See* Art. 205 Law on labour.

# Part I. Companies

## Chapter 1. Joint-Stock Company

*56.* Joint-stock company (*akcionarsko društvo* – abbreviation a.d. or ad) is defined as a company whose capital is divided into shares and with one or more shareholders who are not responsible for company's debts, except in the case of lifting of the corporate veil or other cases prescribed by law.[110]

### §1. Characteristics

*57.* Joint-stock company has all typical characteristics of a capital company. Applicable provisions are usually of the *imperative nature* with important constraints on the organization and functioning of this company type. Because of all characteristics of this company form, a joint-stock company may pursue any kind of profitable activity that, as a rule, is not the case with other commercial companies.

It has *legal personality* upon registration and is responsible for all debts incurred during business operations. Members of the joint-stock company – shareholders have *limited liability*; meaning that they only bear the business operation risk up to the amount of their subscribed contributions, and are not responsible for the companies' debts, except in the case of lifting of the corporate veil. Other exceptional liability exists only for controlling shareholder in the case of compulsory liquidation.

A joint-stock company can have either one or more shareholders – natural or legal persons. An important implication of this is the possibility of this form to have only *one member* – natural or legal person (single member joint-stock company), while still applying provisions on limited liability.

Unlike other company forms, only joint-stock company has its *capital divided into shares*. The most important provisions on this company type include the principle of fixed legal capital and *minimum and capital protection requirements*. Shares issued by the joint-stock company must have nominal, or where there is no nominal – an accountable par value.

---

110. *See* Art. 245 LCC 2011, as well as Art. 548 for additional liability of controlling shareholder in the case of compulsory liquidation.

A joint-stock company can issue *fully transferable shares which may be listed for trading* on an organized securities exchange. It is the only company form which can issue its shares to public, respecting various public issue requirements.

Finally, organization of this company provides *separation of ownership from management*. It is organized through either a one-tier or two-tier board structure with important features of modern corporate governance.

## §2. Formation

### I. Formal Requirements and Minimum Contents of Articles

*58.* A joint-stock company is formed simultaneously in a formal procedure which implies obligatory registration.[111] It is founded on the basis of the articles of incorporation (or unilateral decision if there is only one founder), and adoption of another obligatory document – statute, for the purpose of determining initial internal organization and other most important issues.[112]

Articles of incorporation have to be in written form, signed by all founders, and their signature has to be certified.[113] Articles of incorporation can be drafted as an electronic document, when company members can apply their qualified electronic signature, when there is no need of additional certification of the document by the public notary, with the exception of the transfer of immovable property. If articles of incorporation are in electronic form or are digitalized by a person entitled to digitalize document with his qualified electronic signature, this document is registered in the Business Register in electronic form. All founders are also due to adopt and sign the statute of the company. Registration is obligatory for both documents.

*Articles of incorporation* have obligatory minimum content, including identification of the company (name and seat) and its founders (name, gender, identification number and domicile or seat of the natural or legal person), objects clause including principal activities, contributions in cash and in kind (including their value and content) and when these contributions are due.[114] Articles should also include data on the shares issued (including their number, class, nominal or accountable par value). Finally, articles need to include founders' expression of intent for company formation and that they are taking over responsibility to pay or perform their contributions upon share subscription.

Unlike articles of incorporation in other company forms, this document has its main purpose during incorporation of the joint-stock company, and is, therefore, not to be changed, once signed and registered.

111. On the foundation formalities *see* Arts 264–268 LCC 2011.
112. *See*: Tatjana Jevremović Petrović, *Modeli osnivačkih akata (Model Articles of Incorporation)*, Pravni fakultet Univerziteta u Beogradu, Beograd, 2019.
113. At the moment, Serbian legal regime prescribes certification of signatures by public notary, or solemnization in the case of transfer of immovable property. *See* Law on Public notaries (Zakon o javnom beležništvu), *Official Gazette of RS* (*Službeni glasnik RS*) 31/2011, further amended.
114. *See* Arts 9a, 11–14 and 264–265 LCC 2011.

Under limited circumstances, there is a possibility that articles of incorporation are pronounced null and void.[115] These conditions include that articles were made against obligatory formal requirements, that the objects of the company in the articles of incorporation are unlawful or contrary to public policy, when articles do not state the name of the company, the amount of individual subscriptions of capital, the total amount of capital subscribed or the objects of the company; or when there is incapacity of all founder members when articles were signed. Nullity must be pronounced only in front of the court, when there is no possibility to remedy conditions for nullity. When the company was registered, nullity pronounced by court shall entail the winding-up of the company. Nullity shall not affect the validity of any commitments entered into by or with the company to third parties acting in good faith. Members of the company with limited liability shall remain obliged to pay up the capital agreed, or make other contributions, to the extent necessary to fulfil commitments entered into with creditors.

A joint-stock company has an obligatory *statute*, and its main purpose is to determine initial internal organization and other issues.[116] Therefore, this document has minimum content, including name and seat of the company, principal activities, information on the capital (subscribed and paid), as well as the number and nominal value of shares issued. It should also include all information on the issued shares, including class, type and nominal or accountable par value, as well as all obligations, limits and privileges in each class of shares. Statute contains information on shares and other financial instruments authorized for issuance, including their type and class, special conditions of share transfer, if any. Finally, the statute must include information on the convening of the shareholders' meetings and how the company is to be organized, including designation of the bodies and their functions, number of members, further provisions on the appointment requirements and dismissal, as well as decision-making within company's bodies. Statute can also include other provisions important for the organization and functioning of the company.

Statute can be changed through approval of the general meeting with at least simple majority of the total voting rights of members or higher majority, if provided in the statute.[117] In the case of change of capital and shares, there is an obligatory change of statute at least once a year.

The companies' statute may stipulate the obligation for the company to pay *expenses of its formation*, or to provide payment to shareholders, including maximum payments possible.[118] Otherwise, it is the obligation of the founders to pay all expenses related to the formation of the company. Companies' statute will also include all special rights conferred to founders or advantages granted to third parties in relation to foundation of the company or acquisition of necessary approvals. The statute should also include their content, including duration and persons to

115. For nullity grounds and procedure *see* Arts 13–14 LCC 2011. *See also* Tatjana Jevremović Petrović, 'Ništavost osnivačkog akta u srpskom pravu' (Nullity of the Articles of Incorporation in Serbian Company Law), *Pravo i privreda (Law and Economy)* 4–6/2017, 71ff.

116. *See* Arts 246–247 LCC 2011.

117. Article 247 LCC 2011.

118. *See* Art. 267 LCC 2011.

whom they are conferred. Once approved, these rights or advantages might be revoked through changes in the company's statute.

Founders of the company are due to make contributions according to the articles of incorporation through a temporary account at a commercial bank in the Republic of Serbia.[119] After all formalities are met, company gains legal personality after *registration in the Business Register.*

## II. Notification, Registration, Incorporation and Publicity

*59.* Registration procedure is regulated by the Law on Registration procedure in the Business Agency Register.[120] Business register is a central electronic database for all data and documents relevant for registration. It operates under the principles of publicity, accuracy and protection of third parties.

Registration procedure is acted upon the administrative procedure rules. It can be initiated by the application for registration submitted by authorized person, or upon request of a competent authority. Applications can be made in person, in paper or electronic form, or by mail.[121] New amendments in regard to registration of the incorporation of all commercial companies, including joint-stock company, will make this procedure to be *in electronic form only*, and this provision will be applicable starting from May 2023. All new data or documents necessary for registration, including changes to the data or documents already registered, must be applied for registration within fifteen days (or within other prescribed time limit).

Registration procedure is performed by the *registrar – a person who performs registration* whose position and authority are prescribed by the provisions on the Registration Agency. He performs registration upon *registration application* under provision of certain conditions. First, there must be competence to act upon application, application must be submitted by a competent person(s), data or documents applied for registration must be within the scope of registration, submitted in prescribed time limits (if any) and in accordance with special laws and competent authority decisions. Data or documents must not already be registered. The data from the application form must be in accordance with documents submitted and already registered in the case of publicly available data or documents. Finally, in the case of incorporation of a new company, a legal person or sole proprietor cannot be registered under the same name (or applied for registration). The name of the company must be in accordance with legal provisions applicable and all relevant fees must be paid.[122]

The person performing the registration needs to *decide on the application* within a time limit of five working days, whereby this decision needs to be affirmative in the case where all conditions for application are met. Therefore, only formal

119. For further requirements on the payment and contributions and the minimum payments required *see* part V and VI of this chapter on the initial share capital and contributions.

120. Further referred as the Law on Registration, already cited.

121. *See*: Tatjana Jevremović Petrović, 'Elektronska registracija osnivanja privrednih društava u Republici Srbiji' (On-line Registration of Companies in the Republic of Serbia), *Pravo i privreda (Law and Economy)* 3/2021, 305ff.

122. *See* Art. 14 Law on Registration.

requirements, and not the authenticity and credibility of data or documents enclosed with the application form, are relevant for the positive registration decision. Should the person who performs registration fail to decide on the application within five working days from the day of its submission, it shall be considered that the request in the application is granted.

The person performing the registration can make a negative decision by *rejection of the application* only when conditions for registration are not fulfilled. If there is negative decision and conditions can be additionally fulfilled, applicant can reapply within thirty days, although only once, and keep the right of priority of the previously submitted application by payment of half of the prescribed fee.[123]

On decisions made by the person who performs registration, there is a *right of appeal* to the competent Minister through the Registration Agency within thirty days.[124] Registration Agency can reject the appeal on procedural grounds, accept appeal and make a positive decision on the application or forward appeal to the competent Minister. The Minister has to make a decision within thirty days, and he can reject the appeal on procedural grounds or refuse the appeal on material grounds; accept the appeal and make affirmative decision or forward the appeal to a registrar to reconsider application. This decision is final, and to object there is a possibility to bring a lawsuit in front of a competent court.[125]

The person performing the registration can act independently and delete documents and data already registered, but only in the case of a registration made contrary to registration conditions and within a short period of time of twelve months since the registration was performed. There is a possibility to ask for a court decision of the nullity of registration only in regard to registration of incorporation and on limited grounds, including short period of time: within thirty days of the knowledge of these conditions but no later than a year after the registration of incorporation took place.[126] Conditions for nullity of registration of incorporation include that registration application contained false data or registration was made upon false, illegal or untrue documents, as well as in other cases provided by law.

Decisions on the registration are publicly disclosed. *Publication* of the affirmative decision is made together with data and documents whose registration is obligatory. Other information on the company, including financial information and documents, can also be disclosed, while other information can be obtained upon request.

The *effects of the registration* take place one day after disclosure, and cannot have a retroactive effect.[127] Third parties may rely on all registered data, documents and particulars (*positive effect* of registration), and they cannot bear negative effects

123. *See* Art. 17 Law on Registration.
124. On the appeal procedure *see* Arts 25–32 Law on Registration.
125. Article 32 Law on Registration.
126. Article 33 Law on Registration. *See* Tatjana Jevremović Petrović, 'Nullity of companies' registration in Serbian law under the influence of European legal systems', in: Bojan Milisavljević, Tatjana Jevremović Petrović, Miloš Živković (eds.), *Law and Transition: Collection of Papers*, University of Belgrade Faculty of Law, Belgrade, 2017, 215ff.
127. Article 22 Law on Registration.

because registered information was incorrect.[128] Nevertheless, third parties can prove that it was impossible to have the information within fifteen days after disclosure of registered information. The company may also prove that third parties had knowledge of the information and documents before they were registered.

## III. Contracts Made on Behalf of a Company in Formation

*60.* Law on Commercial Companies 2004 had a provision on the issue of pre-incorporation contracts and other liabilities taken with respect to company's foundation before its registration.[129] It was prescribed that founders and other persons have joint and several unlimited liability with respect to obligations made in connection to the company's formation. It was possible to arrange this issue with contracting parties otherwise. Once registered, company was considered to have joint and several liability with founders and third parties for these obligations only if accepted by the company after registration procedure was completed.

Current Serbian Law on Commercial Companies does not have any specific provision on pre-incorporation contracts and other liabilities taken before registration. Therefore, general provisions of the Law of obligations (including assignment of contract and substitution of creditor or debtor, as well as agency and invalidity of contract) must be applied.[130]

## IV. Number of Subscribers

*61.* A joint-stock company is a commercial company whose capital is divided into shares to at least one or more shareholders. Shareholders can be natural or legal persons. Therefore, there is no limitation on the minimum number of subscribers. The current legal regime does not provide for a maximum number of shareholders in joint-stock companies.

---

128. For registration effects *see* Art. 6 LCC 2011. On this issue *see* further: Mirjana Marković, 'Pozitivan publicitet registra privrednih subjekata' ('Positive effects of registration of commercial companies'), *Pravo i privreda (Law and Economy)* 5-8/2008, 357ff.

129. Article 12 LCC 2004.

130. *See* in particular provision on the assignment of contract in Art. 145 and general provisions on the substitution of creditor or debtor in Arts 436–453 Law on obligations. *See also* Mirjana Radović, 'Pravna analiza ugovora u ime budućeg društva u nedostatku posebnih kompanijskopravnih pravila' ('Legal analysis of pre-incorporation contracts in lack of specific rules of company law'), in: Vuk Radović (ed.), *Uskla ivanje poslovnog prava Srbije sa pravom Evropske unije (2014) (Harmonisation of Serbian business law with EU law (2014)),* Pravni fakultet Univerziteta u Beogradu, Beograd, 2014, 75ff. On other obligations upon company formation *see also* Zoran Arsić, 'Troškovi osnivanja akcionarskog društva' (Expenses during foundation of the joint-stock company), *Pravo i privreda (Law and Economy)* 1-4/2002, 21-25.

## V. Initial Share Capital

*62.* Joint-stock company has a minimum capital requirement of RSD 3.000.000 (or other higher amount in the case of specialized companies, which is equivalent to EUR 25.559).[131] The initial capital amount and its modifications have to be registered and published.

The principle of fixed capital applied in the Law on Commercial Companies implies application of the principle of nominal equivalence between contributions and subscribed capital.[132] According to general provisions on the contributions, they can be either in cash or in kind, and their value must be expressed in RSD.

There is a general duty to contribute.[133] This means that all persons who agreed (or otherwise are obliged) to contribute are liable for the fulfilment of the obligation to contribute to the company. This obligation needs to be performed in time, prescribed in the articles of incorporation or general meeting decision and within time limits set by law. These limits include duty to perform contributions in cash right away in the case of a public company for the public issuance of its shares paid in cash. In other cases, the time limit for performance of an obligation to contribute in the public company is two years, or five years for the contributions in closed joint-stock company, except those made as a result of an initial public offering of shares, when contributions must be paid immediately.

Duty to contribute implies not only an obligation to contribute in the amount but also in the existence: renunciation of this obligation is not possible, and shareholders may not be released to pay up their contributions unless there has been a capital reduction beforehand. The only possible exception is through allowance of change of obligation. This change can be made only by the approval of the general meeting of shareholders by qualified majority of three-fourths of shareholders present at the meeting, or other higher majority prescribed in the statute. Change of contribution includes that contribution in cash is substituted by contribution in kind of equivalent value, or contribution in kind for contribution in cash or by substitution of one contribution in kind to other of equivalent value. Contributions in cash are not allowed to be substituted to contributions in kind in the case of a public company for the public issuance of its shares.

In the case of failure to fulfil an obligation to contribute, the company may offer additional time, which is at least thirty days, to shareholders to fulfil their obligations. Public company is obliged to offer this additional time to no less than ninety days from the due date to contribute (or other shorter period prescribed in the articles of incorporation or statute). After expiration of additional time for performance of the contribution obligation, joint-stock company may and public joint-stock company must decide on the exclusion of shareholder(s). Joint-stock company may also provide in the articles of association or its statutes for liquidated damages (stipulatio poenae) for non-performance or undue performance of contribution in kind.

---

131. Article 293 LCC 2011.
132. Article 44 LCC 2011.
133. Article 46 LCC 2011.

In the case of share transfer, there is a joint and several liability of previous shareholder as well as a person who acquired shares towards the company.[134] In this case, a lawsuit can be brought by either the company itself or its shareholders holding at least 5% of shareholdings. Nevertheless, there is a limited possibility of share transfer in the case of unpaid (in total or in part) contributions, but this provision is applicable only to public joint-stock companies.[135]

Finally, initial share capital is protected by the provision on prohibition of return of paid or performed contributions, including payment of penalties, as well as of prohibition of direct and indirect financial assistance (loans, guarantees, providing for securities) by the company for the acquisition of its shares by members, employees or third parties.[136]

## VI. Contributions in Kind

*63.* Provisions on contributions in kind, including their evaluation and exceptions, were made under considerable influence of the regime prescribed by the former Second Company Law Directive, now Directive (EU) 2017/1132 relating to certain aspects of company law.[137] It is prescribed that contributions may be formed only of assets suitable for economic assessment. Therefore, contributions in kind may consist of different tangible assets (immovable and movable) as well as intangible and financial assets (different kind of rights).[138] In a joint-stock company, contributions cannot consist of obligations to perform work or provide services.

Value of contributions in kind can be determined either by shareholders or by evaluation, whereby evaluation is obligatory for public companies.[139] Evaluation is done by an authorized independent expert or company. The designation of the expert is made by the members of the company in the case of foundation, or by director, board of directors, or supervisory board (in case of a two-tier system), unless otherwise provided by the statute. If evaluation in the joint-stock company is determined by shareholders, there is a possibility for creditors to address the court within five years of completion of contribution in kind to make such an evaluation in the case when the company is unable to fulfil its obligations in the regular course of business. If a lower value is determined by the court compared to the value agreed by shareholders, shareholder whose obligation was to furnish the contribution in kind will be asked to pay up additional value to the company up to the value determined by the court, and to meet jointly with the company all expenses regarding court proceedings. The burden of proof for the value of contribution in kind is with the member who was obliged to furnish it.

Evaluation made by an authorized independent expert or company must be made within one year of the provision of contribution in kind, and it has to be registered

134. Article 49 LCC 2011.
135. *See* Art. 252 LCC 2011.
136. *See* in particular Arts 60, 154, 279 LCC 2011.
137. Directive (EU) 2017/1132 of the European Parliament and of the Council of 14 Jun. 2017 relating to certain aspects of company law, *OJ L* 169, 30 Jun. 2017.
138. Article 45 LCC 2011.
139. For evaluation *see* in particular Arts 51–59 LCC 2011.

and disclosed. Evaluation of contributions in kind must include their description, methods of evaluation applied and opinion whether the value arrived at by the application corresponds to either nominal value or, where there is no nominal value, to the accountable par and, where appropriate, to the premium on the shares to be issued for them.

In the case of decrease in value of the contribution in kind from the date when evaluation is performed until the date of its provision, there is an obligation for the company to undertake a new evaluation of the contribution in kind. Any member due to provide contribution in kind, whose value decreased is due to make additional contribution in cash, if necessary, at the same time when providing the contribution in kind is due. If the company does not undertake revaluation, one or more shareholders, holding an aggregate percentage of at least 5% of the company's subscribed capital on the day the decision on the share issue is taken and still having their share interest on the day to address the company, can make a demand for an evaluation by an independent expert, or if nothing is done can address the court after the expiration of fifteen days in order to make an evaluation. Right to court appeal expires after ninety days of the provision of the contribution in kind to the company.

Board of directors, or, in case of a two-tier system, supervisory board, or other persons defined by the statute may decide not to make an evaluation of contributions in kind (other than transferable securities and money-market instruments) if these assets have a fair value which can be determined by previous evaluation in the financial reports of the member providing the contribution, in case these reports have already been subject to a fair value opinion by a recognized independent expert in the previous year. In the cases of new qualifying circumstances that significantly change the fair value of an asset at the effective date of its contribution, a revaluation needs to be carried out as in the case of decrease in value of the contribution in kind from the date when evaluation is performed until the date of its provision and with same rights granted to one or more shareholders holding an aggregate percentage of at least 5% of the company's subscribed capital on the day the decision on the share issue is taken.

In cases when contributions in kind consist of transferable securities and money-market instruments, they can be evaluated either by independent expert or by their value on regulated market or MTF (multilateral trading facility). If an evaluation is made by the value on regulated market or MTF, it needs to be made at least sixty days before the provision of the contribution to the company. The value is determined as the weighted average price at which they have been traded in a regulated market or MTF during the six months preceding the date of the evaluation if the market for such securities or instruments was liquid – at least 0.5% of the total amount of issued shares were traded within the period of six months. It is also necessary that trading reached at least one-third of the trading days on a monthly basis within the period of six months. If this was not the case or if the price in the period since the evaluation until the effective date of contribution has been affected by exceptional circumstances that would significantly change the value of the asset, the company has to re-evaluate that contribution in kind. If this is not the case, one or more shareholders holding an aggregate percentage of at least 5% of the company's subscribed capital have the right to address the court to make such an evaluation within ninety days of the provision of the contribution in kind to the company.

Where consideration other than in cash occurs without an experts' report in case when it has a fair value according to financial reports or it was determined during trade of securities or money-market instruments on regulated market or MTF, a President of the board of directors, or in case of a two-tier system, of the supervisory board has to make a declaration, which is registered and published, including a description of the consideration other than in cash at issue; its value, the source of that valuation and, where appropriate, the method of evaluation; a statement whether the value arrived at corresponds at least to the number, to the nominal value or, where there is no nominal value, the accountable par and, where appropriate, to the premium on the shares to be issued for such consideration; and a statement that no new qualifying circumstances with regard to significant change of the original evaluation have occurred.

Finally, if, before the expiry of two years from the date the company is registered, the public joint-stock company acquires any assets belonging to a shareholder who founded the company for a consideration of or higher than one-tenth of the subscribed capital, the value of these assets must be determined by provisions on the evaluation of contributions in kind. The contract with the shareholder must be in written form and approved by the general meeting of shareholders by a qualified majority of three-fourths of votes present at the voting, or higher majority, prescribed by the statute. The acquisition and the effects of the contract are conditional upon general meeting approval. These provisions are not to be applied to contracts made in the normal course of company's business, to acquisitions effected at the instance or under the supervision of an administrative or judicial authority, or to stock exchange acquisitions.[140]

## VII. Other Material Formation Requirements

*64.* Formation of a joint-stock company is usually followed by several technical and administrative requirements. They include opening of bank accounts and performance of other administrative requirements. The procedure of registration of formation of joint-stock company performed by the Business Agency Register is carried out through as *one-stop shop* procedure, and includes that company once registered simultaneously obtain company identification number, assigned by the Statistical Office of the Republic of Serbia; taxpayer identification number (*PIB – poreski identifikacioni broj*), which is assigned by the Tax Administration Office, VAT registration, as well as a certificate (*M-A form*) confirming submission of the application for the compulsory social security of the founder who is registered as the representative of the company.[141]

---

140. *See* Art. 268 LCC 2011 applicable only to public limited liability companies.

141. *See* official site of the Business Agency Register, including information of the one-stop shop procedure available in English at: https://www.apr.gov.rs/registers/companies/instructions/formation.4339.html (accessed 24 Mar. 2022).

Pursuing certain activities requires applying with competent inspection agencies or other authorities (market, sanitary, labour, building inspection authorities, etc.) in order to obtain necessary certificates and approvals on meeting necessary requirements for performing registered business. These approvals and certificates are dependent on the company's activities. Therefore, it is prescribed as a general provision in the Law on Commercial companies that registration or pursuit of certain activity may be, under specific laws, conditioned upon approval, permission or other authorization of the competent authority.[142] As already mentioned, among other requirements, they include formation of most important specialized commercial companies, such as banks, insurance organizations, investment funds and other participants in the financial markets.

## §3. Essential Elements of the Legal Person

*65.* It is common in Serbian legal literature to understand a company as a specific form of organization with several essential (constitutive) elements.[143] They include its contractual origin, leading to its legal personality (and to the institutional character of a company as was previously emphasized) and association of persons and their contributions in order to gain profit. Finally, a decisive constitutive element of every commercial company is the intention to establish a company, and the decision to cooperate within it with other company founders and members ('*affectio societatis*'), since not every contribution aimed at making profit is considered a commercial (trading) company. Such intention should always involve an active, enthusiastic approach, convergence of interests, and equality in the position of members. The intensity of this intention depends on the type of company – where partners' risk is higher (unlimited liability), the *affectio societatis* is more intensively expressed. Also, in smaller companies, ties between the members and founders within the company usually tend to be stronger, although not always equally manifested. Therefore, in joint-stock companies *affectio societatis* exists, but is not always strong, nor equal to all shareholders. As already emphasized, a joint-stock company gains its personality upon registering in the Business Register, which is also mentioned in literature as one of the essential elements for company's existence.[144]

Apart from these essential elements, it is usually considered that companies have certain distinctive features in order to make their individualization.[145] They include name, seat, objects clause and identification and other numbers.

---

142. *See* Art. 4 LCC 2011.

143. On these issues in Serbian literature *see* further: Mirko Vasiljević, *Company Law (Law of commercial companies of Serbia and the EU),* Pravni fakultet Univerziteta u Beogradu, Beograd, 2006, 61ff.

144. *See*: Nebojša Jovanović, Vuk Radović, Mirjana Radović, *Kompanijsko pravo: pravo privrednih subjekata* (*Company Law: Law of Commercial Subjects*), Pravni fakultet Univerziteta u Beogradu, Beograd, 2021, 109–119.

145. *See*: Mirko Vasiljević, *Company Law (Law of commercial companies of Serbia and the EU),* Pravni fakultet Univerziteta u Beogradu, Beograd, 2006, 86ff; Zoran Arsić, Vladimir Marjanski, *Pravo privrednih društava (Commercial companies law),* Pravni fakultet Univerziteta u Novom Sadu,

## I. Seat

### A. *Definition*

*66.* Serbian law determines the seat of a company as a place and address in the territory of the Republic of Serbia from where the company is being managed and which is determined in the articles of incorporation, statutes or by a general meeting decision or decision of partners.[146] If not otherwise provided in the articles of incorporation or statutes, change of seat will be made upon a general meeting's decision. New amendments to the Law on Commercial companies made further precision on the address of the company (city, municipality, place, street or square, house number, floor and flat number). A company's seat needs to be registered in the Business Register and is obligatory content of the articles of incorporation and statute.

Therefore, a company's seat is determined by the real seat criteria in combination with statutory seat criteria. Although determination of the company's seat has prevailing real seat character, parallel application of the statutory seat introduces presumption that these places coincide. Additionally, provisions regarding registration provide for obligation of the registrar to take into account whether information on the registration application is identical to that on the documents provided. It should, therefore, be presumed that statutory and registration seats coincide. In this situation, practical relevance of the real seat of the company becomes less important, bearing in mind general provisions on the effects of registration, including that third parties can rely on information contained in the register, irrespective of consideration of whether they are true.[147] Therefore, although Serbian law applies real seat parallel to statutory seat, in practice it is the statutory and registered seat that is relevant for third parties.

Original text of the Law on Commercial Companies contained a provision intended to protect third parties acting in good faith. It was possible if a company is permanently pursuing its activities in a place different from its seat, for third party to invoke this place for the purpose of determination of court jurisdiction. This provision had the obvious intention of third-party protection, especially in the case when the real seat and place of exploitation do not coincide with statutory and registered seat of the company. Nevertheless, this provision is in the last revision of the Law on Commercial Companies deleted, and replaced with a new one, based on negative effects of practice to register a seat without any substantive control, and with limited possibilities of protection of interested parties, once a data or document has been registered. Namely, according to new provisions, if a person with property rights did not agree on the use of place for a company's address as a place from where the company is being managed, interested party is entitled to initiate a court proceeding in order that registered address of the company's seat is deleted

---

Novi Sad, 2013, 19ff; Mirko Vasiljević, Tatjana Jevremović Petrović, Jelena Lepetić, *Kompanijsko pravo: pravo privrednih društava (Company Law: Law of Commercial Companies)*, Službeni glasnik, Beograd, 2020, 73ff; Nebojša Jovanović, Vuk Radović, Mirjana Radović, *Kompanijsko pravo: pravo privrednih subjekata* (*Company Law: Law of Commercial Subjects*), Pravni fakultet Univerziteta u Beogradu, Beograd, 2021, 139ff.

146. *See* Art. 19 LCC 2011 on the seat of the company.

147. *See* in particular Art. 3 para. 1 under (2) Law on Registration.

from Business Register. If successful, a court will accept the claim and instruct Business Register to delete registered address of the company's seat. In that case, a company has a possibility to register the new address of the seat during thirty days of final decision of the court. Otherwise, a procedure of compulsory liquidation must be initiated in front of the Business Register.

### *B. Change of Company's Seat*

*67.* Once determined, a company's seat can be changed by general meeting's decision or in other way provided in the articles of incorporation or statute. According to this provision, it is obvious that the prevailing concept of the seat is closer to its statutory, or even registered seat concept. On the effects of the seat concept on determination of the proper law of the company (*lex societatis*), *see* §5 in General Introduction.

There are no clear provisions on the effects of change of the real seat. Internal effects of the real seat change can be seen in relation to an obligation of the company to make the registration application after changes of certain information, whose registration is obligatory. This obligation is due fifteen days after the change occurred.[148] Although registration provisions should affect efficient and true information to interested parties, sanctions prescribed for their breach are not complete, since they provide only for criminal liability in the case of application of false (untrue) information or documents. Bearing in mind that the registrar can only make (positive) registration decision by considering only formal requirements, and not the authenticity and credibility of data or documents enclosed with the application form, it can happen that factual situation does not coincide with the registered one. Therefore, it must be understood that change of real seat should not affect third parties' rights, especially when acting in good faith.

### *C. Correspondence Address*

*68.* Apart from seat, companies can also register correspondence (mail delivery and receipt) address at the territory of the Republic of Serbia in the Business Register, which can be different from its (registered) seat, which is otherwise presumed to be the place for all business correspondence.[149]

In the case of unsuccessful mail delivery (if delivery is registered and includes a return receipt) to the registered seat or registered address (different from the company's seat if such address is registered), there is an obligation for a second attempt of registered mail delivery with at least fifteen days between first and second mail delivery attempt. If the second mail delivery to the registered seat or registered address (if there is any) is unsuccessful, it shall be presumed successful eight days after the second unsuccessful attempt for delivery to the registered seat or address

148. *See* Art. 10 Law on Registration.
149. Article 20 LCC 2011.

(if there is any). These provisions are relevant for all business correspondence, but special provisions deal with mail delivery in the court, administrative, tax or other procedures.

### *D. Electronic Address*

*69.* Since last amendments of the Law on Commercial Companies, companies must have an electronic address for business communication. This electronic address must also be registered in the Business Register. Before last amendments, electronic address was an optional (not obligatory) address of the company. New provisions on the obligatory registered electronic address will not be applicable until mid-2023. All communication with the company by using electronic address will be regulated by relevant provisions on the electronic documents, electronic identification and trusted services in electronic business, as well as according to provisions on e-Government.[150]

## II. Name

### *A. Definition*

*70.* Commercial companies must be identified in business transactions under a specific name, known as the business name (former term was 'firm'). Designation of business name is an obligatory element of the articles of incorporation and the statute of every commercial company, including joint-stock company, and it has to be registered in the Business Register. Decision on the business name is made by a general meeting of shareholders.

There are several principles related to the company's business name. They include *the principle of accuracy,* according to which business name content must correspond to actual state of affairs – to be authentic. Second, *the principle of publicity* not only in the Business Register but also including display of business name on business premises and its use in business correspondence. *The principle of protection of one single – unique name* means that every commercial company must have only one business name to be used while performing business activities (including branches and other parts of the company). Business name is also characterized by *the principle of exclusivity (distinctiveness)*, according to which a name that was used and registered previously is protected against the possibility of repeated use of the same or similar name by another commercial company (or entrepreneur). A business name is protected under the *principle of priority* and is to be

150. *See* in particular Law on electronic document electronic identification and trust services in electronic business (Zakon o elektronskom dokumentu, elektronskoj identifikaciji i uslugama od poverenja u elektronskom poslovanju), *Official Gazette of RS* (*Službeni glasnik RS*) 94/2017, 52/2021, available in English at: https://epotpis.mtt.gov.rs/download/law-on-electronic-document-electronic-identification-and-trust-services-in-electronic-business-official-gazette-rs-94-17/ (accessed 24 Mar. 2022); as well as Law on e-Government (Zakon o elektronskoj upravi), *Official Gazette of RS* (*Službeni glasnik RS*) 27/2018.

registered for the company who applied (or made reservation of the business name) first. The interest of business reputation requires that a business name remains as *permanent* as possible. Finally, a business name is generally *free to choose*, although there are certain conditions and limits.

### *B. Content*

*71.* Commercial companies are required to have *minimum obligatory content* of a business name. They should always include distinctive name (designation), legal form and the place of company's seat.[151]

*Distinctive name (designation)* is the most important part of a company's name whose main purpose is to achieve individualization of a company. Therefore, its main task is to provide a distinction from other companies by the choice of unique and distinctive name.

All joint-stock companies must have designation of their form in the business name in full or abbreviated. Therefore, joint-stock companies shall include *the form: akcionarsko društvo* (in Serbian) or abbreviation *a.d.* or *ad* within company's name. Finally, company's name shall include *the place of the company's seat.*

Company must include *additional obligatory content* in its name in special circumstances. These include denomination 'in liquidation' (u likvidaciji – in Serbian) or 'in compulsory liquidation' (u prinudnoj likvidaciji – in Serbian) after registration of the liquidation decision in the Business Register and related to liquidation procedure. Similarly, a company's name shall include an additional denomination 'in insolvency' (u stečaju – in Serbian) as a consequence of the opening of the insolvency proceedings and after publication of this act on the notice board of the competent court.[152] Other obligatory content may be introduced by law for certain specific contents.

Finally, a company's name may include other content (*voluntary additional content*) like description of the business activity.[153] Also, when using the company's name, it can be followed by a coat of arms, flag, emblem, designation or other symbols of the Republic of Serbia, foreign country or other territorial unit or autonomous province or international organization only with their explicit consent.

When a company's name is too long or difficult for everyday use, the company may choose to have an *abbreviated name.* This abbreviation must include the distinctive name (designation) and legal form. It is additional to company's business name, and it can be used under the same preconditions as full business name. Therefore, company must register abbreviated name, if there is any, together with its (full)

---

151. *See* Art. 22 LCC 2011.
152. *See* Arts 73 and 78 Law on insolvency.
153. Dragan Vujisić, 'Poslovno ime privrednog društva' ('Company's Trade Name'), in: Slavko Đor ević (ed.), *Uskla ivanje pravnog sistema Srbije sa standardima EU (Harmonization of the legal system of Serbia with EU standards),* Pravni fakultet Univerziteta u Kragujevcu, Kragujevac, 2017, 314.

business name. Business name or abbreviated name may be *translated* into a foreign language or national minority language excluding distinctive name – designation. For the reasons of legal certainty, this translation should be registered together with full and abbreviated names in the Business Register.

### C. *Positive and Negative Conditions*

*72.* Although there is a general freedom in choice of a name, there are certain restrictions.[154] They include certain conditions with regard to language and letter of the business name, as well as usage of certain terms or personal, national or official names and signs. Also, there are certain restrictions in choice of business name related to public policy issues or to legal certainty. The registrar who performs registration has an obligation to check whether all requirements including content of business name and positive and negative conditions are satisfied.

#### 1. Conditions Regarding Language and Letters

*73.* When it comes to conditions with regard to language, although company may be named after general freedom principle, it should be in Serbian language, either in Cyrillic or Latin letters. Still, business names can be in a foreign language or with foreign words or letters, Latin letters in English, as well as Arab or Roman numerals.

#### 2. Conditions Regarding Use of Personal Name(s)

*74.* A business name may contain a personal name of a natural or a legal person. When it contains the name of a natural person, there is an obligation to obtain consent to use the personal name either from the person himself/herself or from the legal successors of a deceased person.

Personal name of a shareholder may be used in the company's business name only while retaining this status. If the shareholder (natural or legal person) ceases to be in the position of a member of the company, continuing use of his personal name in the business name will be under general restrictions, including his/hers consent or consent from his/her legal successors. In the case when a personal name is included in the company's name, and irrespective of the consent, the company must respect his/her personality and reputation while doing business. Otherwise, a person whose name is contained in the business name or his/her legal successor(s) may demand in front of the competent authority (court proceedings) for his name to be deleted from the business name and include compensation of damage, if caused.

In the case of a breach of these provisions, general provisions on the protection of a business name will be applicable.

---

154. *See* in particular Arts 24, 26, 27, 29 and 30 LCC 2011.

3. Conditions Regarding Use of National or Official Designations and Terms

*75.* Use of domestic or foreign national designation has certain conditions related to the consent of the competent authority. When using designation of the Republic of Serbia, territorial unit or autonomous province, it is necessary to obtain consent from the competent domestic authority; use of a foreign state designation or designation of international organization requires consent of a competent authority of that state or organization. Exceptions are allowed if founders' business name already contains designation of a state, domestic territorial unit or autonomous province or international organization. Consent of the domestic or foreign competent authority is not unconditional and can be revoked. Therefore, the Business Registration Agency must delete designation from the business name upon request of the competent authority.

4. Negative Conditions

*76.* The most important condition regarding the distinctive nature of a business name is difference from other business names. First of all, it cannot be identical to other company's names. Business name also has to be distinctive enough from other company's name to avoid confusion regarding company's identity. Therefore, it is not only forbidden to have the same (identical) name as another company but also distinctive enough from other similar names. Legal theory underlines that confusion can happen not only if a name is identical or similar but also when a company is engaged in the same or similar line of business (activity).[155] There are several possibilities of legal protection in the case of a breach of these provisions (*see* later under section F).

Business name cannot be in contravention of public policy or lead to confusion regarding company's legal form or principal activities. Business Register has to refuse a registration in the case where business name falls under these restrictions. When a business name is in contravention of public policy, the State attorney may bring legal action in front of the competent court related to the change of a business name. Final and enforceable judgment ordering the change of a business name is registered in the Business Register and has for a result obligatory change of business name or compulsory liquidation.

155. *See* Mirko Vasiljević, *Company Law (Law of commercial companies of Serbia and the EU)*, Pravni fakultet Univerziteta u Beogradu, Beograd, 2006, 106.

*D. Use of Business Name*

*77.* Companies may use their full name, abbreviated name or their translation *in business correspondence*, including electronic communication.[156] Business correspondence should always include full or abbreviated name, company's seat and correspondence address (if there is any), identification number and tax identification number.

There is a possibility to *use a business seal* in business correspondence. Use of a business seal cannot be required, not even by special provisions. Finally, third parties acting in good faith cannot bear any negative effects regarding the form of business correspondence, regarding which company cannot imply any formal errors.

*E. Transferability of Business Name*

*78.* There is a general restriction on transfers of a business name to another company.[157] Therefore, a business name is not allowed to be the subject of legal transactions independently. There is only one exception when it is possible to transfer business name together with the business itself. Namely, the law prescribes that business name can be transferred in the case of statutory change whereby business name is transferred to the acquiring company from the company being acquired which ceases to exist. This provision should be applicable not only to the acquiring or recipient and company being acquired or divided (merger by acquisition or division by acquisition) but also to the companies involved in a merger or division by formation of a new company.

*F. Protection of Business Name*

*79.* Business name of a company needs to be distinctive in order to avoid confusion with other companies. There is a general provision prohibiting that one company has an identical name to another company or to make confusion regarding identity with other company. The business name of a commercial company enjoys manifold protection: by the operation of law (ex officio), based on justified business interest (action in front of the competent court), on the ground of unfair competition, and through criminal law protection.

Ex officio *protection* is performed by the Business Registration Agency. It is prescribed that the registrar performs registration upon registration application under certain conditions, including whether there is already registered legal person or sole proprietor or pending application under the same name or the name is already reserved.[158] The registrar is obliged to check all legal conditions and content of the

156. Article 25 LCC 2011.
157. Article 26 LCC 2011.
158. *See* Art. 14 para. 8 Law on Registration and Art. 28 LCC 2011. Protection ex officio was before limited to the territorial jurisdiction of the competent court, performing inscription into business register. After LCC 2004 and Law on registration of commercial companies (Zakon o registraciji

business name.[159] Registrar is obliged to reject the application and include reasons for his negative decision in the case if these conditions are not met or if there is an identical registered name, pending registration or reserved name.

*Legal action* in front of a competent court is an important mechanism of legal protection in the case of registration of the same or similar business name leading to confusion regarding company's identity. Interested persons are allowed to request judgment ordering the change of a business name and/or claim damages caused within three years after the registration of a business name. According to case law, such interest did exist whenever, due to registration of the same or similar name, confusion of business names might take place in the market, regardless of whether such confusion really has taken place.[160] As already mentioned, when a business name is in contravention of public policy, the State attorney is entitled to bring legal action in front of the competent court and require that a company changes its business name.

Final and enforceable judgment ordering the change of a business name is registered in the Business Register and has for a result obligatory change of business name or compulsory liquidation.

Important protection of a business name is contained in the unfair competition or intellectual property provisions, as well as criminal law.

### G. *Reservation of Business Name*

*80.* Person(s) intending to establish a commercial company or to start performing business activities as entrepreneurs are allowed to make a reservation of a business name.[161] Reservations are made in the Business Register within five working days of a registration application and if all prescribed fees are paid for.

Reservation of a business name is conditional under the same requirements as registration of business name, including that there is not already registered legal person or sole proprietor or pending application under same name, or name is already reserved, and under all conditions for legality of business name.

Reservation of a business name is made for the period of sixty days after registration publication, and can be extended for further sixty days upon payment of the prescribed fee. It is possible to make a transfer of the reserved name to other persons within the period of reservation.

---

privrednih subjekata), *Official Gazette of Republic of Serbia (Službeni glasnik Republike Srbije),* 55/2004 (with further amendments) were introduced, these limitations were removed, bearing in mind that Registration Agency has jurisdiction for registration on the whole territory of the Republic of Serbia. For case law with regard to business name protection, *see* in detail: Mirko Vasiljević, *Company Law (Law of commercial companies of Serbia and the EU),* Pravni fakultet Univerziteta u Beogradu, Beograd, 2006, 107-108.

159. *See also* Art. 27 para. 2 LCC 2011.

160. *See* Mirko Vasiljević, *Company Law (Law of commercial companies of Serbia and the EU),* Pravni fakultet Univerziteta u Beogradu, Beograd, 2006, 107.

161. *See* Arts 39–41 Law on Registration.

## III. Objects Clause

*81.* Serbian company law has a general provision that every company, including joint-stock company, has principal activity which is registered in the Business Register.[162] Activities, which can be registered, are defined by the Act on classification of activities, and include the name of the activity, numerical code and description.[163] Activities are defined and divided into sectors, areas (there are currently 99 different areas), sub-areas and groups.

*82.* Apart from principal activity, which has to be registered, companies can engage in all other (unregistered) activities, unless prohibited by law. It is not necessary that other activities are registered, and company does not need to specify them in the articles of incorporation or its statute. It is possible for a company to change its principal activity, which is decided by general meeting of shareholders and must be registered in the Business Register. Therefore, it can be concluded that there is a general legal capacity of a company in performing all activities allowed by law. This means that objectives of a company are unrestricted.

Although there is a general freedom of choice in performing business activities, it is possible that certain activities are under special regime, including provisions on obligatory registration or their performance and/or registration is conditional upon approval of competent authorities. Typical examples include not only activities in financial, banking and insurance sector (*see* above under General Introduction, chapter 3, title D) but also other activities, such as the production, trade, and storage of dangerous or harmful to human health substances, armament, etc.

*83.* During incorporation, founders of the company apply for registration with specifying *one principal activity*, which will be registered in the Business Registers Agency. Company can in further business operations perform not only principal but also any other activity. If a company wants to pursue an activity for which prior approval, consent or other act of competent authority is necessary, such approval, consent or other act is necessary for the registration of such an activity. Other restrictions in business operations of certain activities (including special premises or equipment, safety or other measures, etc.) do not impede registration of the activity. Therefore, if the company wants to conduct such an activity, it can register activities including special conditions and restrictions, after which it is the company itself obliged to respect that all conditions for their performance are met. Breach of these restrictions will result in various penal sanctions for the company and/or authorized person, but will have no impact on its registration.

*84.* Serbian law does not have particular provisions on foreign trade or trade services operation as a special business activity, which was the case during socialist regime and little afterwards. Since 2012 all companies are free to perform trade or trade in services at home as well as abroad, without the necessity to register that

162. *See* Art. 4 LCC 2011.
163. Act on classification of activities (Zakon o klasifikaciji delatnosti), *Official Gazette of Republic of Serbia (Službeni glasnik Republike Srbije)*, 54/2010.

activities will be performed abroad. In other words, foreign trade or trade in services is not conditioned anymore by registration into the register.[164]

## IV. Commercial Character of Activities

*85.* Commercial character of activities is one of the essential elements in defining a commercial company generally. It is also necessary in order to make a distinction from other forms of (non-commercial) associations. Still, as it was already mentioned in the General Introduction, all commercial companies are clearly distinct from other forms of civil associations and other organizations. Distinguishing features include not only formal ones – such as the fact that all general commercial forms are regulated in the Law on Commercial Companies – but also the fact that commercial companies perform business activities in order to gain profit, which can be distributed to its members.

Therefore, all joint-stock companies in Serbian law are of commercial character and perform different activities in order to gain profit. This is also the case for specialized commercial companies, including banks, insurance organizations, investment service companies and other specialized forms of joint-stock companies.

## V. Identification Number

*86.* Registration procedure implies ex officio grant of ID, tax ID number, as well as a registration number for the Health Insurance Agency. It is based on the unique registration application for commercial companies (in Serbian: Jedinstvena registraciona prijava privrednog subjekta – JRPPS).[165]

Identification number (in Serbian *matični broj*) is a unique number, different for each company and identical to registration number. It is conferred by the Statistical office ex officio after fulfilment of all conditions for registration in the Business Agency Register. It includes eight-digit numbers, which are used for company's identification in the Business Register, as well as with third parties. Once given, the identification number cannot be changed.[166]

Tax identification number (in Serbian *poreski identifikacioni broj – PIB*) has tax purposes and is obligatory for all commercial companies, individual entrepreneur,

164. *See* information on the registration of foreign trade or trade in services at the official site of the Business Registers Agency at: https://www.apr.gov.rs/registers/companies/instructions/general-instructions.4338.html#9 (accessed 18 May 2022).

165. *See* Art. 4 Decision on the content of the Business Register and documents necessary for registration (Pravilnik o sadržini Registra privrednih subjekata i dokumentaciji potrebnoj za registraciju), *Official Gazette of Republic of Serbia (Službeni glasnik Republike Srbije)* 42/2016.

166. *See* Zoran Arsić, Vladimir Marjanski, *Pravo privrednih društava (Commercial companies law)*, Pravni fakultet Univerziteta u Novom Sadu, Novi Sad, 2013, 28.

as well as permanent establishments of non-residual commercial companies (as well as to other legal persons). It is also given through a unique application procedure in the Business Agency Register.[167]

## §4. Capital and Shares

### I. Different Concepts of Capital

*87.* According to the accepted provisions on legal capital within European company laws and under considerable influence of the former Second Company Law Directive, now Directive (EU) 2017/1132 relating to certain aspects of company law, Serbian company law also pays special attention to legal capital, as one of the core areas of provisions regarding joint-stock companies. General definition of a joint-stock company underlines, therefore, as a particularity of this company form and unlike all other forms that it has *initial (nominal) capital divided into shares* to one or more shareholders.

Among principles related to the legal capital of a joint-stock company dominate those related to capital formation, in particular minimum capital requirement, limitations regarding contributions and obligatory evaluation on contributions (on contributions *see* this chapter §2. under V and VI). Apart from the principle of fixed legal capital, special attention is paid to the provisions on capital maintenance, especially distribution of profits (and other payments) and possible capital reorganizations, including capital increase or reduction. These mechanisms are intended to protect creditors and shareholders, at which the principle of equal treatment is predominantly aimed.

The basic concept on the company's capital is the initial–nominal (also referred to as registered) capital as the value of the capital subscribed. Therefore, legal capital is related to the concept of nominal, i.e., subscribed capital. As already stressed (in this chapter §2. under section V), there is a general duty to contribute, including that all persons who agreed to contribute are liable for the timely performance of the obligation. Nevertheless, there is a possibility that a certain amount of capital is paid or contributed within time limits set by law. Therefore, certain amount of company's capital must be paid up, while there is a provision for subscribed but unpaid capital.

Finally, because of the flexibility and economy of the financing of the company, there is an explicit authorization for the general meeting to approve certain amount of the authorized capital, if that option was provided for by its statutes. All mentioned concepts of capital will be discussed further below.

---

167. *See* Art. 26 Law on tax procedure and tax administration (Zakon o poreskom postupku i poreskoj administraciji), *Official Gazette of Republic of Serbia (Službeni glasnik Republike Srbije)* 80/2002 with further amendments. Also, *see* Decision on the conferment of the tax identification number to legal persons, individual entrepreneurs and other persons in the registration authority of the Business Register Agency (Pravilnik o dodeli poreskog identifikacionog broja pravnim licima, preduzetnicima i drugim subjektima za čiju je registraciju nadležna Agencija za privredne registre), *Official Gazette of Republic of Serbia (Službeni glasnik Republike Srbije)*, 32/2009 with further amendments.

*A. Nominal Capital*

*88.* Serbian law defines company's capital as a value of contributions subscribed by its members and divided into shares to one or more shareholders.[168] Although the terminology used refers to *basic capital* (*osnovni kapital*), it must be understood as nominal capital. This capital is also referred to as registered capital because of the obligation to register the amount of nominal–subscribed capital, including further changes.

The amount of nominal–subscribed capital is one of the essential contents in the articles of incorporation and the statute, and in the case when such information is not provided, there is a possibility for nullity of the articles of incorporation.[169]

Serbian company law adopts the principle of fixed capital, which is the basis of many other provisions. They include, among others, those on contributions, and duty to contribute, once shareholders agreed to subscribe a certain amount for shares at the time of the foundation of the joint-stock company, or later based on capital increase decision. This duty to contribute includes that shareholder may not be released to pay up their contributions unless there has been a capital reduction beforehand and that there is a prohibition of return of paid or performed contributions to shareholders.

Nominal capital is divided into shares to one or more shareholders. Position of shareholders, including their rights and duties, is determined according to the amount of the shares (within each class of shares) subscribed in proportion to the nominal capital of the company, if not otherwise prescribed or allowed.[170]

*B. Issued Capital*

*89.* Companies are allowed to issue certain amount of capital, determined on the basis of the articles of incorporation or further capital increase. Concept of the nominal (registered) capital defined as the value of the subscribed capital is at the same time defining the amount of issued capital. Nevertheless, companies are allowed to have a certain amount of capital authorized for issuance. This is discussed further below.

*C. Paid-Up Capital*

*90.* There is a general duty of all shareholders to contribute, once agreed or otherwise stipulated, to make their contribution. Therefore, shareholders are liable for the provision of their contribution – either in cash or in kind, depending on the obligation (*see* above under this chapter §2.V.). General duty to provide is essential for

168. Article 44 para. 3 and 245 LCC 2011.
169. *See* Art. 13 para. 1, under 3 LCC 2011.
170. Nevertheless, certain rights are conditional or restricted (including share transfer or right to vote) depending on the amount of shares subscribed, but unpaid for. For general provision on these restrictions in the case of non-fully paid-up shares, *see* Art. 252 LCC 2011.

the formation of the legal capital. Therefore, shareholders cannot be released to pay up their contributions unless there has been a capital reduction.

Although duty to contribute is unconditional, performance of this obligation is prescribed in the articles of incorporation or decision on the capital increase and within time limits set by law. These limits include the duty to provide contributions in cash right away in the case of public company for public issuance of its shares paid in cash. In other cases, time limit for performance of obligation to contribute in the public company is two years, or five years for the contributions in closed joint-stock company, except those made as a result of an initial public offering of shares, when contributions must be paid right away.[171] Liability for the performance is strengthened with the provision of joint and several liability of the previous shareholder as well as a person who acquired the shares in the company in the case of share transfer (*see* above under this chapter §2.V.).

From provisions dealing with time limits set for performance of the obligation to contribute, it is clear that a company can have capital, which is paid up at the time of subscription. Still, certain amount can be unpaid. Minimum payment or other performance of consideration before registration of the joint-stock company is prescribed to the amount of at least 25% of the subscribed capital, whereby cash consideration paid must be at least equivalent to the minimum capital requirement (RSD 3.000.000, equivalent to EUR 25.559).[172] If there is a capital increase, shares issued for consideration must be paid up according to the capital increase decision, but at least up to 25% of their nominal, or accountable par value, including issue premium, if any.[173] The rest of the amount subscribed for is to be paid or otherwise contributed within the time limits set by law for the duty to contribute (*see* above).

A company must include in the articles of incorporation and its statute provisions on the total amount of capital subscribed, as well as capital paid up. The amount of paid-up capital is particularly relevant for the issues on limits regarding distribution on profits and other payments as well as acquisition of shares by the company itself (*see* below under II and VII); condition for capital increase (*see* below under II) as well as certain shareholders' rights, including preferential right of subscription (*see* below under III).

### *D. Minimum Capital Requirements*

*91.* Joint-stock companies have a minimum capital requirement of RSD 3.000.000 (approx. EUR 25.559), unless a higher amount is prescribed by law.[174] In the case of specialized companies having the legal form of a joint-stock company (such is the case of banks, insurance companies, investment companies, etc.), there are special provisions on minimum capital requirement, usually significantly higher compared to the general amount of minimum capital prescribed by the Law on Commercial Companies.

---

171. Article 46, para. 2 LCC 2011.
172. *See* Art. 266 LCC 2011.
173. Article 298 LCC 2011.
174. Article 293 LCC 2011.

As already explained above, minimum payment or other performance of consideration before registration of the joint-stock company is prescribed to the amount of at least 25% of the subscribed capital, whereby cash consideration paid must be at least equivalent to the minimum capital requirement.

The main task in prescribing a minimum capital requirement is to protect creditors, as well as to bring about seriousness in investments. It is for this reason that companies need to have a minimum amount of capital not only at the time of company's formation, but also later on. Therefore, a company can reduce nominal capital using the procedure prescribed by law, but the capital reduction cannot result in subscribed capital amount going below the minimum capital amount requirement. In the case when minimum capital requirement is not satisfied, capital reduction decision, if not simultaneously followed by capital increase decision up to minimum requirement prescribed, is null and void and must not be registered.

Serbian law does not recognize company law provisions aimed at assessment of undercapitalized companies. This includes lack of general provisions dealing with capital adequacy (except minimum capital requirement) and related to activities performed or risk connected to those activities (excluding financial markets participants) at the time of company's formation or later on. Also, Serbian company law does not deal with the issue of financing the company from the perspective of the equity to debt ratio, or further structure of the capital subscribed.

Finally, there are very few provisions dealing with serious capital loss. The most important provision requires that a general meeting of shareholders must be called in cases when a company has a serious loss. They imply that net assets as set out in the company's accounts fall below 50% of the amount of the subscribed capital.[175] Nevertheless, it is only stressed out that general meeting of shareholders must be called, including specification in the convening of the general meeting of the reason for its convening, as well as decision proposal, either to liquidate or to adopt other adequate measures. By allowing the possibility to adopt 'other adequate measures' and not to pursue either liquidation or to prescribe obligatory capital increase, legal protection of companies' capital was left incomplete.

### *E. Authorized Capital*

*92.* Joint-stock company is allowed to have a certain number of shares authorized to be issued if provided by company's statutes. Their amount is set up to be less than half of the number of ordinary shares already issued.[176]

The purpose of authorized capital is capital increase by new subscriptions or conversion of the securities convertible into shares or with a right to subscribe for shares. Even thought it was allowed that general meeting can authorize the board of directors (or supervisory board in two-tier system) to issue shares during a time limit prescribed by the general meeting's decision, this possibility is no longer available. Newest amendments of the Law on Commercial Companies provide that authorized capital can be made by general meeting decision only. This decision

175. Article 371 para. 2 LCC 2011.
176. Article 313 LCC 2011.

must include details on authorized shares, including period for their issuance, which is set to a maximum of five years with the possibility of the extension of this period through change of statute or new general meeting's decision, for further five years in each extension. General meeting's decision on the authorization for share issues needs to be registered.

## II. Alteration of Capital Requirements

*93.* Maintenance of legal capital is a fundamental principle of Serbian law governing joint-stock companies, which is in line with the former Second Company Law Directive, now Directive (EU) 2017/1132 relating to certain aspects of company law. Many mechanisms serve this principle, although the most important include capital increase and capital reduction provisions.[177]

### *A. Capital Increase*

*94.* Legal capital of a joint-stock company can be increased by new subscriptions, conditionally – through conversion of securities convertible to shares or with right to subscribe for shares, or through a share issue to board members or employees; from the company's reserves or profits and, finally, as a result of statutory change (for this last case *see* below under this chapter §7.I.).

In every case, there is an obligatory general meeting decision on the capital increase. Even thought there was an exception in cases when the board of directors (or supervisory board in two-tier system) was authorized to issue shares (*see* above under section I.E.), new amendments of law deleted this possibility, leaving only general meeting to decide on the capital increase.[178] General meeting's decision must be registered within six months in which time no shares subscription can be made. If decision on the capital increase is not registered within the time limit, it is null and void.

Capital increase is conditional upon all issued (subscribed) shares being paid up or otherwise contributed. The reason behind this provision is to prevent further investment if previously subscribed shares are not fully paid up.[179] This is the reason for exceptions, including capital increase by subscription of contributions in kind or statutory change, which results in a capital increase.

---

177. In this section only capital increase and reduction will be analysed. Other issues, including contributions, evaluation, distribution, company's acquisition of its own shares, etc., are discussed in other sections of this chapter above and below.
178. On the capital increase *see* Arts 294ff LCC 2011.
179. Zoran Arsić, Vladimir Marjanski, *Pravo privrednih društava (Commercial Companies Law),* Pravni fakultet Univerziteta u Novom Sadu, Novi Sad, 2013, 285.

### 1. Capital Increase by New Subscriptions

*95.* Subscribed capital can be increased by new subscriptions. In the case of a closed joint-stock company (which is not allowed for a public company), there is a provision for conversion of a debt into shares.

Decision on the capital increase by new subscriptions must include certain information, especially those on the amount of capital increase, method(s) of increase, conditions for successful increase and deadlines; issue price or methods of determining the price and other information on shares; as well as financial institution where payment for shares has to be made. In the case of the increase by contributions in kind, further details on contributions and its evaluation are necessary.

For the purpose of capital increase subscription, the company must publish a subscription form including all elements in order to determine the time, date and the amount of increase in general, as well as general information of shares issued (class, number and other information, including issue price), information on the subscriber and contribution (description, time and date of performance of contribution), as well as number and class of shares subscribed. The time of subscription is determined as the moment of submission of the signed subscription form to the company or other authorized persons. Conditions for payment and/or provision of contribution have already been discussed above (under section I C).

For public issue requirements special provisions are applicable (*see* further under section V).

If there is successful share issue, company must request inscription of all shares issued and all shareholders subscribing shares into the Central securities depository and clearing house (later referred to as Central depository; in Serbian – *Centralni registar hartija od vrednosti*) within five working days since successful share issue procedure is completed. The company must also register capital increase within eight days after the share issue is recorded in the Central depository.

### 2. Conditional Capital Increase

*96.* Serbian law refers to 'conditional' capital increase in the case of a share issue in several situations: conversion of convertible debentures to shares or in order to exercise the rights from securities to subscribe for shares; for the share purchase of that company or other connected person to board members or employees, if provided in the statute. Capital increase cannot be made above 50% of the capital subscribed at the moment of the capital increase decision in all situations, except when shares are issued to board members or employees, when this limit is set to 3% of the capital subscribed.

The decision on capital increase must include certain information, especially those on the amount and purpose of capital increase, persons having rights to subscription and further conditions, time limit for the capital increase, issue price or the methods of determining the price and other information on shares.

In the case of capital increase for the purpose of conversion of securities convertible to shares, persons who enjoy right of conversion need to make a statement on conversion of their securities to shares in writing, which is considered to represent a share subscription. In other cases of conditional capital increase general provisions on the subscription (including form, content and procedure), registration in the Central depository and registration of the capital increase are applicable. In all cases, full payment for shares is necessary, even though in the case of capital increase upon conversion of convertible debentures company's reserves formed for that purpose can be used.

### 3. Capital Increase from Company's Reserves or Profits Made

*97.* Company can increase capital from the profits made or reserves accumulated and available for this purpose. It is necessary that financial results (annual accounts) show that the company did not incur a loss, or if losses were made, they can be covered and capital increased from the sums drawn from reserves and profits brought forward from previous years. Financial results, which serve as a basis for the capital increase, must be approved by the auditor for all public and other companies required to have their financial accounts audited, and the decision on the capital increase must be registered within six months of the approval of financial results at the general meeting.

The aim of such an increase may be in strengthening the capital position, adopting a new policy of dividend payment, intensifying trade in shares, etc.[180] The decision on the capital increase must include certain information, especially those on the amount of capital increase, amount and type of reserves used, or profits accumulated and used for the capital increase; specification of the share issue – change of nominal (or accountable par) value of the already issued shares or a new share issue, including information on newly issued shares (if that is the case).

All shareholders (including shares acquired by the company itself) on the date of the capital increase are entitled to shares issued in proportion to their paid-up (or in other way contributed) shares to the total amount of paid-up capital. If company issued securities convertible to shares, the number of shares (or their nominal or accountable value) entitled for conversion is increased proportionately.

In case of a capital increase from the profits made or reserves accumulated, shares issued entitle for the dividend payment for the whole business year period within which capital increase decision was made. Eventually, it can be decided that capital increase entitles shareholders to a dividend distribution for the period of the previous business year if capital increase decision was made before the previous year's dividend distribution to shareholders was made.

Capital increase must be applied for registration in the Central depository and registered and disclosed in the Registration Agency, and, for public companies, reported to the Securities Commission.

---

180. *See*: Zoran Arsić, 'Povećanje osnovnog kapitala akcionarskog društva iz neto imovine' ('Capital Increase out of Company's Net Asset'), *Zbornik radova Pravnog fakulteta u Novom Sadu (Collected Papers of the Faculty of Law in Novi Sad)* 4/2018, 1140.

### *B. Capital Reduction*

#### 1. Capital Reduction Procedure

*98.* A joint-stock company's legal capital may be reduced by a resolution of the general meeting via a three-fourths majority of votes of the shareholders present, and within each class of shareholders having vote on the issue. If the capital reduction is made by the cancellation of shares acquired by the company itself, the decision can be made by the board of directors (or supervisory board in two-tier system), if that is provided by the general meeting's decision (*see* below under VII).[181]

Decisions on capital reduction must specify aim, amount and the methods of capital reduction, especially indicating whether there is an exception for creditor's protection, or by publication and invitation to creditors to claim for securities (on the creditors' protection *see* below).

Capital reduction decision must be registered within three months of the adoption, or is otherwise null and void. Company has to apply for the registration of all changes made by the capital reduction in the Central depository by submitting application and all necessary documents. They include a written statement of the president of the board of directors and supervisory board that all legal conditions for the capital reduction were fulfilled, especially with regard to creditors' protection. Otherwise, if the statement was untrue in connection to creditors' protection, there is a joint and several liability of the board members to creditors for damage incurred as a result of the capital reduction.

After completion of the capital reduction procedure, registration is again obligatory in the Registration Agency.

#### 2. Withdrawal of Shares and the Principle of Equal Treatment

*99.* Subscribed capital can be reduced by the withdrawal of shares from shareholders and their cancellation, by the cancellation of shares acquired by the company itself, or by the reduction of the nominal or accountable par value of the already issued shares. For the withdrawal of shares from shareholders and their cancellation to be possible, this needs to be prescribed by the statute before subscription of the shares which are to be withdrawn is subscribed for; or if not prescribed by the statute before subscription only with the consent of every shareholder whose shares are withdrawn and cancelled or other interested person having certain rights on shares concerned. Withdrawal decision must comply with general provision on equal treatment of shareholders within each class. It is specifically achieved by the withdrawal and cancellation *pro rata* of the number of shares (or their nominal or accountable par value).

181. On the capital reduction *see* Arts 314ff LCC 2011.

3. Creditors' Protection

*100.* Capital reduction usually implies an obligation for creditors' protection. For that purpose, there is an obligation of registration and publication of the capital reduction decision for three months since registration. The company must inform in writing all creditors with claims above RSD 2.000.000 (approx. EUR 17.040) of the decision, at least thirty days after registration was made. All creditors whose claims antedate thirty days of the end of publication period of the capital reduction decision can claim in writing for securities by the end of time limit for the publication of the capital reduction decision.[182] If those creditors, who claimed for securities within prescribed time limit, are not adequately safeguarded or their claims were not fulfilled within two months of the publication period of the capital reduction decision, they may bring legal action in front of the competent court within a period of one month, requiring adequate safeguards, if their claims are at stake due to the reduction in the subscribed capital. Creditors are required to inform the company on the court proceedings. The court will especially take care whether safeguards are necessary with regard to the assets of the company. Creditors whose claims are secured or are privileged in the insolvency proceeding are not entitled to additional safeguards. Finally, no payment may be made for the benefit of shareholders within thirty days of registration of the capital reduction.

As an exception, provisions on creditors' protection are not applicable in the case of cancellation of shares acquired by the company itself, fully paid and made available to the company free of charge or using reserve sums available for this purpose (under general limitation of distribution of profits and other payments); in case of share reorganization without capital reduction. Also, certain cases of capital reduction without net asset changes (such as to offset losses incurred, or to include into reserves not more than 10% of the reduced subscribed capital) are also excluded from the creditors' protection provision application, unless no payments are made to shareholders.

## III. Preferential Right of Subscription

*101.* Shareholders on the date of capital increase by new subscription (except in cases of share issues effecting statutory changes) are entitled to preferential right of subscription in proportion to their paid-up shares (within the same class of shares to be issued) to the total amount of the shares of the same class and type.[183] The shareholder has the same preferential right in the case of issues of securities entitled for conversion of shares of the same class that the shareholder has.

It can be provided by company's statute that shareholders have preferential right of subscription of different class and type of share issued after preferential rights of the shareholders of that class and type are satisfied.

182. *See also*: Zoran Arsić, 'Smanjenje osnovnog kapitala akcionarskog društva i zaštita poverilaca' ('Reduction of Share Capital and Protection of Creditors'), *Zbornik radova Pravnog fakulteta u Novom Sadu (Collected Papers of the Faculty of Law in Novi Sad)* 3/2017, 631.
183. Article 277 LCC 2011.

Procedure for the exercise of the preferential right of subscription is to be prescribed by the statute, including obligatory notification of each shareholder having preferential right of subscription on the share issue or issue of other securities. The company must also provide an adequate period of time for the exercise of the preferential right of subscription, at least within thirty days of the notification of the decision on the share issue or issue of other securities.

Preferential right of subscription can be restricted or withdrawn only in the case of closed share issue (when public issue is not obligatory) on the written request of the board of directors (or supervisory board in the two-tier system) by decision of the general meeting taken by a three-fourths majority of the shareholders of the same class present.[184] The decision must state the reasons for the restrictions or withdrawal of preferential right of subscription, as well as a detailed explanation on the share issue price. Decision on the restrictions or withdrawal of preferential right of subscription needs to be registered.

On the infringement of this right Serbian case law still has no answer, but legal theory is inclined to recognize, in addition to the right to damages pertaining to shareholders whose pre-emptive right of acquisition is infringed upon, the possibility for avoidance of a contract of acquiring such shares, while the subscriber of such shares would be entitled to damages from the company involved.[185]

## IV. Issues of Shares at a Premium and at a Discount

*102.* General principle determines that shares are issued at the *issue price.*[186] This price is determined by a decision of the general meeting on share issue.

Issue price can be determined either as equivalent to nominal value or above nominal (or accounting par value). Therefore, it is possible to issue shares at a premium. Premium can be used for capital increase, formation of company's reserves formed for the capital increase, cover up of company's loss in subscribed capital, share purchase from dissenting shareholders or expenses during capital increase or reduction.

Another important limit in determination of the issue price is the requirement that the issue price cannot go below the market price, except in the case of initial public offering. While provisions on the issue price being equivalent or above market price have the purpose of protecting existing shareholders and preventing dilution of their shareholdings, provisions that the issue price cannot go below nominal (or accountable par value) have a purpose in capital formation and maintenance.

There are possibilities of a share issue at discount, although the issue price in this case cannot be below the nominal or accountable par value. Shares can be issued at a discount only in the case of a public offer when issuing to investment companies

184. On this formal requirement *see* critically in Vladimir Marjanski 'Formalno pravni uslovi isključenja prava prečeg upisa akcija' (Formal requirements for exclusion of the preferential right to shares), *Anali Pravnog fakulteta u Beogradu* (*Annals of the Faculty of Law in Belgrade*) 2/2014, 273ff.

185. Mirko Vasiljević, *Company Law (Law of commercial companies of Serbia and the EU),* Pravni fakultet Univerziteta u Beogradu, Beograd, 2006, 298-299.

186. Article 260 LCC 2011.

providing underwriting services on a firm commitment basis.[187] In the case when an issue of shares is closed (non-public) and if not otherwise provided in the statute of the company, it is possible to issue shares at a discount of up to 10% of the issue price to existing shareholders in realization of their preferential right of subscription.

## V. Public Issue Requirements

### A. *Public Company*

#### 1. Conditions

*103.* Although the Law on Commercial Companies prescribes only the form of joint-stock company, many provisions refer to public companies (which are predominantly in the form of a joint-stock company). They also include many important rights and obligations if a joint-stock company is also a public company, or otherwise are specific to public companies.[188] Still, all provisions on the public issue and the status of the public company, including initial public offer, obligations for public companies and termination of that status are prescribed by the Law on Capital Markets.

Public company is the issuer of securities provided that either securities were successfully issued in the public offer procedure on the basis of a prospectus, whose publication was approved by the Securities Commission (*see* below under section C); or whose securities are introduced to trading on the regulated market, or multilateral trading facility in the Republic of Serbia (*see* below under VI).[189]

#### 2. Obligations for Public Companies

*104.* Public companies have important privileges in collecting equity capital from the public. Therefore, it is their duty, once becoming public, to respect several obligations. The most important ones include financial and other non-financial reporting, special provision on the supervision and control of the Securities Commission and other obligations, including those related to capital and contributions,

187. On difference between investment company acting as an agent or underwriter *see* Art. 2 para. 1 under 14 and 15 Law on Capital Markets.
188. Such as the example of the provisions on contributions (including time limits, evaluation and consequences of non-performance), share market and issue price, shareholders' rights (including rights of the shares not fully contributed or paid, transfer of shares, in determining dividend day of record and shareholders (vote) record date, publications related to the general meeting, proxy voting and voting majority required), capital increase, acquisition of shares by company itself, general meeting, board structure and meetings, as well as board remuneration, different financial and other reporting obligations, application of the Corporate Governance Code and statutory change procedure. All mentioned provisions related to the public companies are included in the Law on Commercial Companies and will be mentioned where appropriate.
189. *See* Art. 2 para. 1 under 43 Law on Capital Markets.

obligations related to shareholders, general meeting and board of directors (or supervisory board in a two-tier system), as well as others, prescribed by law. Here we discuss only several reporting and disclosure requirements, while all other obligations are mentioned where appropriate.[190]

Public companies have a different set of obligations regarding financial reporting. Their financial results, including independent expert report, need to be disclosed *annually* for all public companies, *half-yearly* for all public companies whose securities are traded on the regulated market and *quarterly* for the companies whose securities are traded and quoted on the listing of the regulated market during the period of listing.

*Notification of acquisition or disposal of major holdings of shares* of an issuer whose shares are admitted to trading on a regulated market or MTF is an obligation for shareholders reaching, exceeding or falling below the 5%, 10%, 15%, 20%, 25%, 30%, 50% and 75% thresholds to which voting rights are attached. This obligation requires notification to the company, Securities Commission and regulated market or MTF where shares are admitted for trading. Should a person under obligation to submit the notification fails to do so, Securities Commission shall adopt a decision on temporary suspension of the voting rights for shares held by such a person, until fulfilment of the obligation. Following the notification of the shareholder, public company must disclose to the public this information, as well as the total number of voting rights and capital at the end of each calendar month during which an increase or decrease of such a total number has occurred. Public company whose shares are admitted to trading on a regulated market or MTF must also disclose all changes related to their shares or other securities issued, as well as to disclose a document including all information disclosed to public in the last twelve months at least once a year. Finally, public companies are also obliged to disclose acquisitions or sale of voting shares held by the company itself.

A public company that is the issuer of equity securities traded on the regulated market, or MTF have a general obligation on *equal treatment and information of its shareholders*, especially those related to the availability of all terms and information necessary for the shareholders to exercise their rights.

In the fulfilment of various public companies' obligations, *supervision* is *performed by the Securities Commission*. This supervision includes, as the most important, authorization of requests for various information, documents and statements, public disclosure of information, suspending trading or requests from the regulated market of MTF to suspend trading or their exclusion.

### 3. Termination of Public Company Status

*105.* Public companies may terminate their public company status after submitting relevant documents to the Securities Commission which will delete the public

190. On different special obligations for public companies *see* in particular Ch. V of Law on Capital Markets.

company from the public companies register.[191] There are several cases when a public company may submit an application for the termination of its public company status.

These include the application of the termination of the public company status if a company publicly issued debt securities owned by a limited number of persons (less than 100) at the end of any calendar year after the year when the public offer was successfully completed.

Public company can decide on the exclusion of issued shares admitted to trading on the regulated market or MTF from that market (*see* below under VI.B.) and submit an application for termination of the status if all dissenting shareholders were redeemed.

Finally, public company status will be terminated if, during one calendar year, all publicly issued shares were acquired on the basis of a takeover bid, sell-out or squeeze-out right, or cancelled after the merger or other statutory change procedures.

## *B. Public Offer*

*106.* Serbian law has detailed provisions on public share issues, mainly contained in the Law on Capital Markets. A general rule is that public offers can be made only in relation to shares or other securities, but it is forbidden for stakes in other company forms, including limited liability company.[192] Therefore, for the purpose of public funding, companies can only use the joint-stock company form to collect equity capital. Other legal persons can publicly issue other securities (excluding shares and other securities representing equity capital), including debentures.[193]

A public offer of securities is any information made, providing enough details on the public offer and securities to be issued to investors, who can, based on this information, make decisions on the purchase or subscription of securities.[194] A public offer can be made either by the company (legal person) directly or through financial intermediaries – agents or underwriters. While agents provide investment services regarding placing of financial instruments without a firm commitment basis, underwriters are under firm commitment basis in relation to the securities issued.

Several requirements need to be satisfied in order to make a public offer, including prospectus publication, upon approval of the Securities Commission (*see* below under section C). All other public offers of securities within the Republic of Serbia are to be considered null and void.

---

191. Article 70 Law on Capital Markets.
192. *See* Art. 2 para. 1 under 2 Law on Capital Markets and Art. 150 LCC 2011.
193. Law on Capital Markets is referring to these persons as issuers or public companies, without referral to company forms prescribed in the LCC 2011.
194. On the legal nature of public offer *see* Mirko Vasiljević, *Company Law (Law of commercial companies of Serbia and the EU),* Pravni fakultet Univerziteta u Beogradu, Beograd, 2006, 255; Ivica Jankovec 'O javnom pozivu za upis akcija' (Public issue of shares), *Pravo i privreda (Law and Economy)* 5-6/1994, 42-43.

Exceptions provided for when *publication of a prospectus is not necessary* include public offers in the case of professional or offers to other specific investors.[195] They include qualified investors (most important are participants on the financial markets, the Republic of Serbia, territorial and other administrative foreign and domestic units, Central bank and international financial organizations and other natural or legal persons who have the position of the qualified investors after Securities Commission admission), important investors (investing at least EUR 50.000 per investor) or securities with a nominal value of at least EUR 50.000 each in RSD equivalent; offer of securities with a total consideration of less than EUR 100.000 in RSD equivalent during a twelve-month period; or offers made to few investors (not exceeding 100). The same exceptions apply in the case of final placement through financial intermediaries.

Exceptions to publication of a prospectus also include issues of securities to existing shareholders, board members or employees; in exchange to shares already issued, or to be offered as compensation after a takeover bid or a merger. In case when publication of a prospectus is not necessary, the issuer or other person involved in share trade must inform investors on all information necessary for the public issue of securities.

Subscription of securities is made in the investment company, while payment has to be made in the credit institution, who is a member of the Central depository. Subscription and payment can also be made on the regulated market or MTF.

The effects of a public offer, including whether the public issue was successful, are to be reported to the Securities Commission by the issuer or person authorized to offer securities and they need to be publicly disclosed. If a public offer of securities was successful, securities are to be recorded in the Central depository through its members. After registration, securities can be (and in the case of public companies equity securities must be) introduced to trading on regulated markets or MTF (*see* below under VI).

### *C. Prospectus*

*107.* The prospectus is a document containing all information which, according to the particular nature of the issuer and of the securities offered to the public or admitted to trading on a regulated market or MTF, are necessary to enable investors to make an informed assessment of the assets and liabilities, financial position, profit and losses, and prospects of the issuer and persons providing guarantees (if any), as well as rights attached to securities.[196] Information contained in the prospectus must be accurate, complete and consistently presented. The prospectus needs to be presented in an easy and comprehensible way, while information contained must be easy to analyse.

Prospectus must contain a *summary*, indicating all necessary information on the issuer, guarantees and securities briefly and in a comprehensible manner. The prospectus can consist of *one or several documents*, whereby a prospectus containing

195. *See* in detail Arts 12 and 14 Law on Capital Markets.
196. *See* Arts 15ff Law on Capital Markets.

several documents must include a registration document including information on the issuer, a document containing information on the securities to be publicly offered or admitted to trading, as well as a summary. The prospectus for the issue of debentures and other debt (non-equity) securities is regulated by the Securities Commission act, but is to be made as a single document without summary.

The prospectus has to be *supplemented* if, during its validity (from the date when approved by the Securities Commission until the end of the public offer validity or admission to the market), important new information comes to light, or prospectus already includes information proven to be false or imprecise in a way that can influence the evaluation of the securities. The issuer or other person responsible for the public offer has to issue a prospectus supplement only upon the approval of the Securities Commission, within seven days, after which the supplement has to be published the next day. In cases of prospectus supplements, investors have the right to withdraw their purchase or subscription if it was made before supplement publication.

*Validity of a prospectus* for the public issue of securities or for the admission of securities to the regulated market or MTF is set for the period of twelve months after its publication if supplemented by a prospectus supplement with new information regarding the issuer and securities to be publicly offered for issue or admission to the regulated market or MTF.

A *submission of the application for approval of the publication of a prospectus* for the public issue of securities is made either by the issuer or other person responsible for the public offer (offeror), including all necessary documents. This application can also include an application for the admission to the market (*see* below under VI).

Publication of a prospectus for the public issue can be made only if approved by the Securities Commission. The Securities Commission shall make a *positive decision on the publication of a prospectus* for the public issue of securities or their admittance to the regulated market or MTF, including documents on registration and securities, as well as prospectus summary within ten working days (or additional twenty days for the initial public offers) of the application. The Securities Commission can reject the application on formal grounds. If no positive decision is made, or in other cases when all substantial requirements (regarding prospectus, information provided or the issuer) are not fulfilled, the Securities Commission shall refuse the application.[197]

Once approved, a *prospectus has to be published* by the issuer or other person responsible for the public offer within fifteen days of the receipt of the positive decision and no later than the public offer or admission of securities to the regulated market or MTF is made. Publication can be alternatively effectuated in several ways. First, it can be made in *paper form* in one or more general or financial media, distributed in the Republic of Serbia. It is also possible to make publication in *written form* and free of charge in the office of the regulated market or MTF, where securities have been admitted to trading; at the issuer's office and office of the investment company selling or providing other services for the public issue. Publication can be made *electronically on the issuer's web page*, and, if possible, on the

197. *See* in detail Arts 28 and 29 Law on Capital Markets.

web page of the financial intermediaries selling or providing other services for the public issue of securities. Finally, publication can be made *electronically on the web page of regulated market or MTF*, where securities are to be admitted. If publication is made in paper or written form, the Securities Commission can additionally require electronic publication by the issuer. Disclosure of information on the publication method, including where the prospectus can be found, is obligatory in a daily newspaper. Finally, all approved prospectus publication decisions made by the Securities Commission in the last twelve months are available on the Commission website, including, when possible, a hyperlink to the prospectus or information on other publication methods.

For all necessary information within the prospectus and its summary, including the case when information provided is false, inaccurate or misleading, *responsibility* is with the issuer, director and members of the board of directors (excluding when voting against a public offer), all persons making an offer (when different from the issuer); persons providing guarantees for securities (if any), the investment company acting as an agent or underwriter, an independent auditor (with respect to audited financial reports, included in the prospectus), or other persons who have taken the responsibility for the accuracy or completeness of any information in the prospectus (and in relation to this information).[198] Responsibility for the content of prospectus and its summary, when issued by foreign states, bodies, central banks and other international and supranational institutions, is exceptionally determined upon articles of incorporation or other act of that issuer.

The persons responsible have to be designated within the prospectus, and they need to make a statement on the information contained in the prospectus. The Law on Capital Markets has an explicit provision on the exclusion of the responsibility for the Securities Commission regarding authenticity and completeness of the information provided in the prospectus or its summary, approved by the Commission.[199]

## VI. Stock Exchange Introduction Requirements

*108.* Shares and other equity securities must be (and other debt securities can be) introduced to trading on the regulated markets in the Republic of Serbia under specific conditions, or alternatively, if conditions for introduction are not satisfied to the Multilateral Trading Facility (*see* below under section A). Shares are freely tradable only if exclusion condition requirements are not fulfilled (*see* below under section B).

198. On the responsibility for the prospectus *see* Zoran Arsić, 'Odgovornost za sadržinu prospekta' (Responsibility for the prospectus content), *Pravo i privreda (Law and Economy)* 9-12/2004, 75ff.

199. *See* critically on this issue: Nebojša Jovanović, *Berzansko pravo (The Capital Markets Law)*, Pravni fakultet Univerziteta u Beogradu, Beograd 2009, 218-219.

*A. Introduction Requirements*

*109.* Admission of securities to trading on the regulated market or MTF is conditioned upon the *publication of a prospectus* for admission of securities to trading on the market.

The publication of this prospectus is obligatory, but *exceptions when publication is not obligatory* apply in certain cases. They include the case when shares represent, over the period of twelve months, less than 10% of the total number of shares of the same class are already accepted to trading on the regulated market or MTF; shares issued in exchange for already issued shares, if there is no capital increase; securities offered as a compensation after a successful takeover bid based on the document equivalent to a prospectus; securities offered as compensation with regard to merger, and based on the document with information equivalent to prospectus; shares issued to existing shareholders upon capital increase from company's reserves or profits made or in other situations when issued to shareholders free of charge or as dividend payment, if they are based on the document containing information on the securities and issue conditions; in exchange or as a compensation to members of board of directors or employees with regard to securities of the issuer whose securities of the same class are already admitted to regulated market or MTF or to a connected company, if based on the document containing information on the securities and issue conditions; and finally, to shares converted from securities convertible to shares, or other rights conferring certain amount of shares, if shares of the same class are admitted to trading on the regulated market or MTF.

*Minimum content of the prospectus* includes information on the entire class of securities, including securities reserved for issuance in order to exercise the rights from securities or for conversion of issued securities, such as the case with options, warrants or convertible securities. A *submission of the application* to the Securities Commission for approval of the prospectus for admission of securities to trading on the regulated market or MTF has to be made by the issuer.

Public companies must submit applications for the introduction of *equity securities* to trading on the regulated market in the Republic of Serbia.[200] They are admitted to trading on the listing of the regulated market, or if all conditions for listing are not fulfilled to the non-listing segment of the regulated market. In the Republic of Serbia, trading is organized on the Belgrade Stock Exchange (Beogradska berza), organized as prime, standard, SMart listing and open market and upon Rules on Listing of the Belgrade Stock Exchange.[201] In the case when equity securities do not fulfil conditions to be admitted to the regulated market (listing and non-listing), they must be introduced to trading on the MTF. Free trade is allowed only for equity securities excluded from the regulated market or MTF (*see* below under section B). In certain cases (including merger and other statutory change, procedure on the basis of a takeover bid, reorganization in insolvency, for the realization of certain minority shareholders' rights, or in order to execute a court judgment; also, in other

200. *See* in detail Art. 46 Law on Capital Markets.
201. *See* further information on http://www.belex.rs/eng/ (accessed 24 Mar. 2022).

transactions involving equity securities when owned by the Republic of Serbia or in other special circumstances) financial transactions need not be performed on the regulated market, or MTF.[202]

For the issuer of *debt securities*, there is no obligatory application for admittance for trading on the regulated market, but they can be included either on the listing of the regulated market or, if no conditions are met, in the non-listing segment of regulated market or MTF. Admission to trading is not exclusive to the regulated market or MTF – therefore, debt securities are still freely tradable upon conditions of the Law on Capital Markets.

Admittance to the regulated market includes an approved prospectus for the admittance to the regulated market and other specific conditions, prescribed by the acts of the market operator, especially including public distribution of shares, financial information and results as well as other information on the issuer and its business operations. Additional conditions for the admittance on the listing of the regulated market include expected market capitalization (or capital and reserves) of at least EUR 1,000,000, disclosed and approved financial reports for at least three business years and public distribution of shares of at least 25%.[203]

### *B. Exclusion Requirements*

*110.* Financial instruments can be *excluded from the regulated market in order to be admitted to the MTF* if no trading occurred within a 180-day period, other conditions for admittance of the public company are not fulfilled, or in case of a breach of certain legal conditions (including public issue and obligations for public companies).[204]

Financial instruments can be *excluded from trading* either from the regulated market or MTF if the public company is in insolvency or liquidation or upon request of the public company terminating public company status. That will be the case if a public company decides on the withdrawal of issued shares admitted to trading on the regulated market or MTF from that market, redeems all dissenting shareholders and submits application for termination of the status (*see* above under section V.A.3.).

*Decision on the withdrawal* of issued shares admitted to trading on the regulated market or MTF can be adopted only by the general meeting with a majority of no less than three-fourths of the total number of voting shares, or a higher majority prescribed by the statute and if cumulatively certain conditions are fulfilled.[205] They

---

202. *See* Art. 48 Law on Capital Markets.
203. Article 121 Law on Capital Markets. For summary of general conditions of the Belgrade Stock Exchange *see* http://www.belex.rs/eng/trzista_i_hartije/uslovi as well as more detailed in the *Rules on listing of the Belgrade Stock Exchange*, available in English at http://www.belex.rs/eng/regulativa/pravilnik_listing (both accessed 24 Mar. 2022).
204. For the exclusion from the regulated market or MTF *see* Art. 122 Law on Capital Markets. On the problems with regard to going private in previous regime of financial market regulation *see* in detail: Nebojša Jovanović, 'Why going private is (was) prohibited in Serbia?', *Annals of the Faculty of Law in Belgrade* 3/2012, 113ff (in English).
205. *See* Art. 123 Law on Capital Markets.

include that there are less than 10,000 shareholders, also that market trade turnover of total number of shares to be withdrawn was less than 0.5% during three months before the decision was taken and within this period a one-month monthly market trade turnover was less than 0.05%. Decision can be taken only upon irrevocable statement of the company to purchase all shares from dissenting shareholders upon request, including shareholders neither present nor voting at the general meeting.

## VII. Forbidden Reductions of Capital and Acquisition of Shares by the Corporation Itself

*111.* As already stressed, Serbian company law pays special attention to legal capital with regard to all limited liability companies. Among principles related to the legal capital of a joint-stock company, especially important ones are related to capital maintenance. Apart from already discussed provisions related to capital increase and reduction (*see* above this chapter §4.II), an important capital maintenance mechanism is achieved through restrictions on payments to shareholders (*see* below under section A). Capital maintenance is also achieved by provisions on general meeting's duty to consult in the case of a serious loss (*see* above this chapter §4.I.D). Finally, provisions on acquisition of shares by the company itself have important impact on capital maintenance (*see* below under section B).

### *A. Restrictions on Distributions to Shareholders*

*112.* One of the main provisions to protect legal capital of a joint-stock company deals with various limits in making distributions to shareholders. Namely, Serbian company law provided general restrictions to all payments (not only dividend payment) upon satisfaction of two conditions. These conditions are similar to those provided in the former Second Company Law Directive, now Directive (EU) 2017/1132 relating to certain aspects of company law, and are based on tests of net assets and profits made. Previous Law on Commercial Companies (2004) had provisions on restrictions on distributions with a combination of these criteria with a solvency test, but the introduction and application of the solvency test were later abandoned.[206] Still, unlike the Directive (EU) 2017/1132 provisions containing restrictions to all distributions, if not all criteria are satisfied, Serbian law limits this provision significantly by providing *restrictions to payments* only.[207]

Based on these criteria, a joint-stock company is not allowed to make any payments to shareholders, if, according to recent financial reports, net assets are, or following such payment would become lower than the amount of the paid-up capital plus those reserves (if there are any) which may not be distributed under the law or the statute, except capital reduction (*balance sheet net assets test*).

---

206. *See* Art. 230 LCC 2004.
207. *See* Art. 275 LCC 2011.

The amount of payment to shareholders within a business year may not exceed the amount of profit at the end of the last financial year plus any profits brought forward and sums drawn from reserves available for this purpose, less any losses brought forward and sums placed to reserve (if any) in accordance with the law or the statute (*profit and loss account test*). Exceptions for the payments are applicable upon payments made to shareholders – natural persons on the basis of a work contract. It is obvious that this exception could lead to circumvention of the provision on payment restrictions, especially in small or family-type joint-stock companies.

Any payments made contrary to this provision must be *returned by shareholders* who received payments provided that they knew or should have known that payments were irregular, within a time limit of five years after the payment was made. Legal action can be brought by not only the company but also one or more shareholders in his own name on behalf of the company under conditions provided for in the derivative claim (*see* below under this chapter §5.II.C.8).

### *B. Acquisition of the Company's Shares by the Company Itself*

*113.* General provision that shares issued by the company *may not be subscribed by the company itself* (including controlled company and third party subscribing shares in his own name but on behalf of the controlled company) is included in Serbian company law.[208] In the case of a breach of this general prohibition, founders of the company or, in cases of capital increase, members of the board of directors or executive and supervisory board members (in the case of a two-tier system) will be responsible for payment or fulfilment of contributions. Still, it is possible that a company acquires its own shares from shareholders.

Generally, *acquisition of a company's shares* by the company itself is limited upon several conditions.

The most important include *general meeting's resolution* to authorize acquisition of own shares, including terms and conditions for the acquisition (especially the maximum amount and maximum and minimum price for shares acquired, as well as time limit for the acquisition, no later than two years, and further conditions of share disposal).

A further condition is related to the effects of acquisition and provides that *net assets* of the company may not be, as a result of share acquisition, lower than the amount of the paid-up capital plus those reserves which must be accumulated (if that is the case) under the law or the statute, except those available for the acquisition of own shares.

Also, *own shares acquired by the company itself must be fully paid* and, in the case of a public joint-stock company, that total nominal (or in the absence thereof, the accountable par) value of acquired shares, including shares previously acquired by the company *may not exceed 10% of the capital subscribed.*

---

208. Provision on the acquisition of own shares by the company are contained in Arts 281–290 LCC 2011. Zoran Arsić, 'Zabrana upisa akcija' ('Prohibition of Subscription of Shares'), *Pravo i privreda (Law and Economy)* 4–6/2017, 39ff.

Acquisition of own shares *without general meeting's decision* is possible, upon a decision of the board of directors or supervisory board (in a two-tier system) in the case of a public joint-stock company if necessary to prevent serious and imminent harm to the company. In such a case, the next general meeting must be informed by the board of directors or supervisory board (in a two-tier system) of the reasons for and the nature of the acquisitions effected, of the number and nominal value, or in the absence of a nominal value, of the accountable par value of shares acquired, their proportion to the subscribed capital, as well as consideration for these shares. Also, board of directors or supervisory board is entitled to decide on the acquisition of own shares for distribution to employees of that or connected company, or for remuneration of board of directors or executive or supervisory members (in a two-tier system) but only up to 5% of any class of shares during a business year, if this is provided by the statute and there are available reserves for this purpose.

In cases of *groups of companies*, general provisions consider these acquisitions as acquisition of own shares. Therefore, if a subsidiary (or third person on behalf of a subsidiary) acquires parent company's shares, provisions on own shares are applicable. If acquisition occurred before control was established, these shares held by subsidiary company are not considered as own shares, but are restricted in voting rights, and their nominal (or accountable par) value is included in the total value of the shares for the purpose of conditions relevant for acquisition of own shares.

*Conditions for the acquisition of own shares are not applicable* in case of shares acquired as a result of the rights of minority shareholders to withdrawal (*see* below under this chapter §5.I.D.1) when shares are acquired free of charge, when acquired as a result of a merger or other statutory change, upon execution of a court judgment or in order to carry out a decision to reduce capital.[209]

The procedure for the acquisition of own shares has to be performed upon general meeting's (or board of directors or supervisory board's) decision. All shareholders of a relevant class are proportionately entitled to a redemption offer, which must include all conditions of redemption (share type, class, number and price for redemption, date and terms of payment).

Shares acquired upon general conditions for their acquisition and exceeding 10% of the subscribed capital *must be disposed of* within no more than three years of their acquisition for the exceeding amount. The Law on Commercial Companies allows that a non-public company after the three-year period must not exceed the value of the subscribed capital by 20%. For the shares acquired in contravention of the procedure prescribed, the period for their disposal or cancellation is within one year of their acquisition. Finally, if shares are purchased in order to be distributed to employees or board members, their disposal has to be limited within one year of the acquisition. In all cases, share disposal provisions on the preferential right of purchase are applicable.

Shares acquired by the company itself are *suspended in certain rights* during their holding. They are suspended in their right to vote, as well as dividends and other payments except in the case of capital reduction. Finally, if a company acquires or disposes of certain amount of own shares, it must include this *information in the financial reports* in the year of acquisition or disposal, including conditions for

209. For the exceptions *see* Art. 284 LCC 2011.

acquisition, type and class, as well as nominal or accountable par value of own shares acquired or disposed and their proportion in the capital subscribed; purchase price or consideration for the shares disposed, and the type and class, as well as nominal or accountable par value of own shares at the end of business year, including their proportion in the capital subscribed.

## VIII. Classes of Shares

*114.* A joint-stock company can issue *shares as registered (nominative) shares in dematerialized form.* Their registration of issuance as well as other provisions dealing with share issue, transfer of shares or rights and other important issues is prescribed in the Law on Commercial Companies and especially Law on Capital Markets.

A joint-stock company can issue different *types of shares*, including ordinary and preference shares.[210] Every share type entitling shareholders to the same rights forms one *class of shares*, but ordinary shares must always represent one share class. This means that a joint-stock company can have various classes of preference shares apart from ordinary shares. Other share types are not prescribed in Serbian company law.

Shares can have either a nominal value or if there is none an accountable par value. All shares within one share class must have the same nominal value, or if classes are issued without a nominal value, all issued shares have to be without a nominal value.

*Nominal value* is the value determined by the decision on the share issue but it cannot be below RSD 100 (approx. EUR 0.85). Nominal value of preference shares must be above the nominal value of ordinary shares.

Determination of the *market value* for shares depends on whether the joint-stock company is a public company or not. For public companies, *market value is determined* as weighted average price at the regulated market or MTF within six months if market trade turnover of the total number of issued shares of that class was above 0.5% and within this period trading was achieved during at least one-third of trading days within a month.

*Market price can be evaluated* if this is accepted by general meeting's decision upon written request from the board of directors or supervisory board (in a two-tier system) and indicating price determined upon market turnover. Also, evaluation of market price is applicable if no required market turnover was reached or in each issue of shares. Evaluation of market price is also applicable to determine the share market value of a closed joint-stock company.

*Issue price* is the value at which shares are issued. It is determined by the general meetings' decision on the share issue. Issue price must be above market value, except in case of initial public offer, nor can it be lower than a nominal value, or if there is none, an accountable par value. For other details in determination of the issue price below the nominal value or above nominal value, *see* above under this chapter §4.IV.

---

210. *See* further provision on types and classes of shares Arts 250ff LCC 2011.

*A. Nominative shares*

*115.* In Serbian company law, a joint-stock company is allowed to issue *shares as registered (nominative) shares*. They are registered in dematerialized form in the Central depository. Therefore, a joint-stock company is not allowed to issue bearer shares.

Shares are registered in the Central depository, while to the company as well as to third parties according to Law on Commercial Companies, shareholders are considered to be persons subscribed as holders in this register.[211] A similar provision is contained in the Law on Capital Markets, providing that the legal holder of a financial instrument (including shares) is the person on whose name securities are registered in the Central depository, or in the case of custody bank – on whose behalf securities are held on the account in Central depository.[212]

Subscription of shareholding in the Central depository register is considered to be the day of the share acquisition.

*B. Ordinary and Preference Shares in particular*

*116.* Shares can be issued as different types of shares, including ordinary and (different classes of) preference shares.

*Ordinary shares* give their holders the right to be present and to vote in the general meeting on the one share–one vote principle, right to dividend payment, right to liquidation or insolvency distribution of the remainder, preferential right of subscription of ordinary shares and other financial instruments convertible to ordinary shares, as well as other rights stipulated by law or statute. Ordinary shares cannot be converted to preference shares or other financial instruments.

1. In General

*117.* Holders of *preference shares* have one or more preferential rights, determined by the statute and decision on the share issue. These *preferential rights* may include right to fixed dividend payment in the amount or percentage of nominal value, paid in priority to ordinary shares; right to cumulate unpaid fixed dividend payments to be paid in priority to ordinary shares (*cumulative preference shares*); right to participate in dividend payment to ordinary shares upon every payment or only upon certain conditions are met (*participating preference shares*); right to be paid in priority to ordinary shares for liquidation or insolvency distribution of the

---

211. *See* Art. 249 LCC 2011.
212. *See* Art. 2, para. 1 under 32 Law on Capital Markets. *See* critically on this concept Mirjana Radović, *Čuvanje i administriranje (depozit) hartija od vrednosti (Holding and administration (deposit) of securities)*, Pravni fakultet Univerziteta u Beogradu, Beograd, 2014, 294-305.

remainder; right to be converted to ordinary or other class of preference shares (*convertible preference shares*); right to be bought back by the company under predetermined price or on other conditions (*redeemable preference shares – see* below under §2).

Holders of preference shares also enjoy different *shareholders' rights*, including right to be present and participate in the general meeting, but without voting rights, although certain exceptions apply; preferential right of subscription of preference shares of the same class, and other general rights including the right to be informed by inspection of companies' documents and acts.

Shareholders of preference shares are entitled to vote in any general meeting within each class of shares on a certain issue on the one share–one vote principle. Cases when preference shareholders are entitled to vote include situations when the number of issued shares or shareholders of that class is altered (including increase or reduction of the total number of authorized shares of that class, rights given to holders of other securities for conversion to shares of that class, division or consolidation of shares within that class or conversion to other shares class), as well as variation or abrogation of already existing preference rights in each share class (such as the case of change of any preferential right, limitation or exclusion of the preferential right of subscription of that class, limitation or exclusion of the right to vote if provided, new share issue within same class or class of shares providing more preferential rights or changing other share class to provide equal or more preferential rights). Right to vote can also be prescribed by the statute for preference shares convertible to ordinary shares on certain or all issues, when their votes are equal to the number of votes attached to votes of ordinary shares to be converted. Also, the statute can give a right to vote to preference shares in proportion to ordinary shares if no declared dividend payment was made, and until full payment.

There is a limit in the total nominal value of issued and authorized preference shares, which cannot be above 50% of the subscribed capital. Preference shares can be issued only for contributions made in cash.

## 2. Redeemable Shares

*118.* Preference shares can be issued as redeemable. This possibility is based on the general meeting's decision on redeemable preference shares issue, with the specification of company's obligation or entitlement for share redemption and other conditions. The general meeting decision must be made upon explicit authorization within company statutes of the possibility and conditions for the issue of redeemable preference shares.

Share redemption is conditional upon full payment of shares, provided that payment in case of redemption is made out of reserves made for this purpose and that net assets are preserved as provided for in the case of acquisition of own shares.

### C. *Deferred*

*119.* Serbian law does not explicitly provide for deferred shares. Although general provisions on party autonomy are applicable, many restrictions in provisions on capital and shares, their imperative nature with important constraints on the organization and functioning of this company type and general provision to provide equal treatment of shareholders limits this autonomy significantly.[213]

### D. *Non-voting*

*120.* Serbian law does recognize different class of preference shares, which have different restrictions regarding rights to vote (*see* above under section B).

### E. *Multiple Voting*

*121.* As already mentioned, Serbian law adopts principle of one share–one vote for ordinary, as well as for preference shares.[214] Therefore, multiple voting is excluded and would also be against the general principle of equal treatment of shareholders.[215]

### F. *Certificate and Warrant Shares*

*122.* Serbian Law on Commercial Companies has explicit provisions on *warrants*.[216] They are considered securities entitling their holder to acquire a certain number of shares of a certain type and class at a predetermined price, on a specified date or within a certain period of time. For other provisions regarding their issue, conditions, value, etc., *see* below under section X.

---

213. *See* Art. 269 LCC 2011.
214. *See* Art. 251 para. 1 under 1: 'Ordinary shares give to their holders right to be present and to vote on the general meeting *on the one share – one vote principle...*' as well as Art. 255 para. 1: 'Holders of preference shares are entitled to vote on any general meeting within each class of shares on certain issues *on the principle one share one vote....*'
215. *See*: Jelena Lepetić, 'Jedna akcija – jedan glas: da li je vreme za promene' ('One Share – One Vote: Time for Change?'), *Zbornik radova Pravnog fakulteta u Novom Sadu (Collected Papers of Faculty of Law in Novi Sad)* 3/2018, 1195ff; Jelena Lepetić, 'Dodatni glasovi kao nagrada lojalnim akcionarima: predlog za reformu' ('Multiple Votes as a Reward to Loyal Shareholders: A Reform Proposal'), *Anali Pravnog fakulteta u Beogradu (Annals of the Faculty of Law in Belgrade – Belgrade Law Review)* 1/2019, 147ff.
216. Article 262 para. 2 LCC 2011.

## IX. Transfer of Shares

*123.* General provisions provide for free transfer of shares.[217] In the case of a public joint-stock company, transfer of shares not fully paid (or if no full consideration is made) is restricted upon full payment (or other consideration).[218]

Provision on free transfer of shares is fully applicable to public companies, but certain exceptions to this general provision are provided for closed joint-stock companies. Transfer of closed joint-stock company shares can be restricted by the statute either through preferential right of purchase of existing shareholders or upon previous approval of the company.[219] Reasons to refuse consent do not have to be indicated in the statute, when body in charge is free to decide on the reasons for refusal, taking into consideration the company and shareholders' interests. The statute may also provide for a two-level consent decision. However, since the restriction of share transferability is not an instrument for preventing shareholders from leaving the company, the consent could be refused only for important reasons – the decision should not involve the abuse of the right. The affected shareholder could seek judicial remedy and even claim damages. In any case, a transfer without consent is not legally valid, and where there is consent, it has an *ex tunc* effect.

Also, shareholders are free to transfer certain rights contained in shares of each class, except certain rights which are not transferable. These include the right to vote or other rights when transfer is limited or restricted by the statute or decision on the issue of shares of the closed joint-stock company.

### *A. Registration*

*124.* Share transfer in a closed joint-stock company requires a written contract, whereby certification of signatures by public notary is obligatory. Share transfer in a public company is prescribed by the Law on Capital Markets whereby trading of equity securities must be performed on the regulated market, if not otherwise prescribed (*see* below under section C). Because shareholding needs to be registered in the Central depository (*see* above on the registration of securities under this chapter §4.VIII.A.), all rights from securities are transferred upon that subscription. Therefore, the transfer must be performed through subscription in the Central depository based on a legal act and upon a transfer order, given by a member of Central depository in the name of the shareholder, his representative or based on a court order.[220]

217. *See* Art. 261 LCC 2011.
218. Article 252 para. 3 under 1 LCC 2011.
219. On these mechanisms in particular *see* in relation to the limited liability company (below under Ch. 2, s. 4. VI. II).
220. Article 229 para. 1 Law on Capital Markets. *See* critically Mirjana Radović, *Čuvanje i administriranje (depozit) hartija od vrednosti (Holding and administration (deposit) of securities)*, Pravni fakultet Univerziteta u Beogradu, Beograd, 2014, 300.

### B. Gift-Sale

*125.* In the case of a contractual obligation to share transfer without consideration (including as a gift), it is necessary that a contract is concluded in written form and certified by public notary.[221] Certification is not necessary in the case when the Republic of Serbia is a contracting party.

### C. Stock Exchange

*126.* As already explained (*see* above under §4.VI.A.), public company must submit the application for the introduction of equity securities to trading on the regulated market in the Republic of Serbia.[222] They are admitted to trading on the listing of the regulated market or if not all conditions for listing are fulfilled to the non-listing segment of the regulated market. In the case when equity securities do not fulfil conditions to be admitted to the regulated market (listing and non-listing), they must be introduced to trading on the MTF. Free trade is allowed only for the equity securities excluded from the regulated market or MTF. Also, in certain cases (including merger and other statutory change, procedure on the basis of a takeover bid, reorganization in insolvency, for realization of certain minority shareholders' rights, or in order to execute a court judgment; also, in other transactions involving equity securities when owned by the Republic of Serbia or in other special circumstances), financial transactions need not be performed on the regulated market, or MTF.[223]

### D. Protection of Shareholders in Case of Tender Offer

*127.* Particularities of protection of minority (of so-called external) shareholders in case of a takeover of control of an open joint-stock company are particularly emphasized because the capital acquired through takeover enables the new holder (if left without special protection) to abuse the rights of remaining shareholders.

Taking over a control block of a joint-stock company is especially relevant in providing a special procedure to introduce transparency, competitiveness and protection of rights of (minority) shareholders. While shareholders of a closed joint-stock company can be protected in restricting share transfer (*see* above under IX), a takeover of a controlling block becomes rather important for shareholders of public joint-stock companies. Serbian law has particular provisions contained in the Law on Takeovers of joint-stock companies, done under strong influence of Directive 2004/25/EC on takeover bids. Further on takeovers *see* below under this chapter §7.III.

---

221. Article 229 paras 1 and 3 Law on Capital Markets.
222. *See* in detail Art. 46 Law on Capital Markets.
223. *See* Art. 48 Law on Capital Markets.

*E. Insider Dealing*

*128.* Serbian legislation covers this institute in the Law on Capital Markets, again under a strong influence of EU law.[224]

1. Inside Information

*129.* In order to consider an information to be privileged or 'inside', the following cumulative conditions apply. First, the information should relate directly or indirectly to very specific facts regarding one or several issuers of financial instruments or one or more financial instruments. Therefore, it is not sufficient that the information on issuer or financial instrument be general in nature; they have to be of a particular nature (which is a matter of fact to be determined by courts). A second condition is that information should be non-public (undisclosed). Finally, if publicly known, information would be likely to have a significant effect on the prices of those financial instruments or on the price of related derivative financial instruments.

2. Prohibitions Related to Insider Dealing

*130.* The most general prohibition exists with regard to situations when *a person possessing inside information uses that information* directly or indirectly by acquiring or disposing of, or attempting to acquire or dispose of, for its own account or for the account of a third party, financial instruments to which that information relates.

Second, prohibition relates to *disclosure of inside information.* It is, therefore, prohibited to disclose inside information to any other person, except where the disclosure is made in the normal exercise of an employment, a profession or duties; or on the basis of insider information to disclose the recommendation or inducement to other persons in order to acquire or dispose of financial instruments to which that information relates.

3. Addressees

*131.* In cases of prohibition of dealing or disclosure of inside information, *a person possessing inside information* relates to persons acquiring this information as members of the management boards or supervisory boards of the issuer or public company, through holding in the capital of the issuer or public company, having access to the information through the exercise of an employment, profession or duties; or being involved in criminal activities. Where that person is a legal person, this includes natural persons who participate in the decision to carry out transaction

224. *See* Art. 2 para. 1 under 46, and Arts 75–84 Law on Capital Markets.

for the account of the legal person concerned. These persons are usually considered as *primary insiders,* who are presumed to have inside information.

Still, Serbian law also extends the prohibitions related to inside dealing and applies them to so-called *secondary insiders* – any person who possesses inside information under other circumstances, if that person knows or ought to know that it is inside information. Still, it is not presumed only upon the mere knowledge of the inside information by the legal person that they were used for trading or that trade was accomplished upon inside information if a legal person introduced, performed and maintained appropriate and efficient internal mechanisms and procedures for prevention of the abuse of insider information.

## 4. Information to Be Disclosed

*132. The issuer of financial instruments* has a duty to disclose immediately to public all inside information (and their changes, if any) directly concerning that issuer, in a manner which enables fast access and complete, correct and timely assessment of the information by the public. Issuer may, upon informing of the Securities Commission, delay the disclosure to the public of inside information on his own responsibility in exceptional cases, involving legitimate interests of the issuer and enabling confidentiality of the information without misleading the public.[225]

*The issuer* of financial instruments *or person acting on his name or on his account* is due to disclose publicly inside information, if that information was disclosed to a third party through the exercise of an employment, profession or duties, unless that person has a duty to confidentiality. Duty to public disclosure arises immediately if disclosed to third parties as intended to bring about, or without delay in the case when there was no intent to bring out inside information and must be publicly available for the period of five years.

Issuers or any person acting on their behalf or on their account shall *draw up a list* of all persons employed or engaged and having access to inside information of that issuer, including information on these persons. This list must be updated and stored, and must be provided to the Securities Commission upon request.

Finally, important disclosure requirements are provided for *management or other persons* having access to inside information, including connected persons (natural or legal). They are required to submit to the Securities Commission every acquisition or disposal for his own account of the issuer's securities, admitted to trading on the regulated market of MTF or other financial instruments in connection to shares, including detailed information on persons and their transactions.

Apart from disclosure, persons on the management positions within the issuer are prevented to perform any direct or indirect transaction for their own- or third-party account of any equity or debt securities or other related financial instruments within a period of thirty days before annual, half-yearly or quarterly reports of issuer are

225. *See* in detail: Jelena Lepetić, 'Public disclosure of inside information', *Annals of the Faculty of Law in Belgrade* 3/2012, 188ff (in English).

submitted. This restriction can be exceptionally excluded by the issuer. Specific provisions also apply to persons involved in market research when inside information is disclosed to potential investors before transaction.

## X. Debentures and Other Securities Which Do Not (Yet) Represent Capital

*133.* Serbian Law on Commercial Companies has explicit provisions on the convertible debentures and warrants.[226]

*Convertible debentures* entitle their holder, under conditions specified in the decision on the issue, to be converted to ordinary shares. As already explained above (under VIII. F), *warrants* are considered as securities entitling their holder to acquire a certain number of shares of a certain type and class at a predetermined price, on a specified date or within a certain period of time. All provisions with regard to these securities within Law on Commercial Companies are common for both types of securities.

They provide that convertible debentures and warrants convertible to ordinary shares are *limited in proportion* to the number of total number of authorized ordinary shares – including issued and already issued convertible debentures and warrants to ordinary shares – or must be preceded by a general meeting decision on the conditional capital increase. The same limit is applicable for warrants convertible to preference shares.

Convertible debentures and warrants are issued *upon a general meeting decision*. They must be subscribed and consideration must be made only in cash. Issuance of convertible debentures is conditional upon preferential right of subscription of ordinary shares holders, while preferential right of subscription of warrants is given to the holders of a share class to which warrants are entitling their holders to acquire.

Convertible debentures' and warrants' issue price is the value at which they are issued. It is determined by a general meeting decision on the securities issue. Issue price must be at least equivalent to nominal, or if there is none to an accountable par value, as well as market value of shares to which convertible securities can be converted.

## §5. Shareholders, Management and Control

*134.* As already explained, a joint-stock company is a typical form providing for *separation of ownership from management*. It usually has a professional management whereby owners are not necessarily involved in management of the company. Consequently, while keeping only some of the most important segments of the governance function in a joint-stock company, the general meeting creates the structure of other bodies to be in charge of the governance and supervisory functions and, indirectly, those responsible for the management of the company operations. In such

226. Articles 262–263 para. 2 LCC 2011. There are also some general provisions on securities and other financial instruments, including form, content, currency, etc., contained in Art. 2. para. 1 under 1ff, as well as Arts 6–9 Law on Capital Markets.

a way, company governance is separated from the company ownership, and this is one of the essential characteristics of this type of company, distinguishing it additionally from other company forms, where the functions, as a rule, are concentrated within a single body, and often in a single person. This is a way of establishing a professional and functional circle of joint-stock company bodies. Each of these bodies is sovereign and highest in the hierarchy within its own competences, since they are prescribed by law or statutes. That means that the hierarchy in this respect is only conditional and statutory (appointment, removal), rather than a functional one.

Regarding the legal nature of the scope of competence of joint-stock company bodies (applicable to other company forms as well) specified by law or statute, in former theory and legislative methodology a *mandate theory* prevailed, though this was later abandoned. According to this concept, the general meeting gives the mandate to the board of directors, and may at any time, and usually without good cause, take this mandate away. Later on, a model of *legislative or statutory powers* was promoted, whereby specified competences were exclusive to certain bodies and could not be revoked. However, it seems that contemporary legislation as well as theory is merging these concepts, introducing bodies with exclusive or (in some particular issues where expressly authorized) delegated competences, but still insisting on the appointment and removal of management or supervisory bodies at any time and even without good cause. Therefore, competences of different bodies, established by law (and in some issues in the statute), should be considered imperative so that each body may decide on matters falling exclusively within its scope of responsibility, as well as on the delegation of responsibility for such matters. This is especially required as far as decision-making delegation from the board of directors to the general meeting is concerned (*see* below under II.B.). In the case of delegating powers (and responsibility) from the general meeting to the board of directors, it can be concluded that in certain issues delegation of power is allowed only in cases expressly provided by law (such as decision on acquisition of company's own shares (*see* above under §4.VII.B.)), while certain other (statutory or administration) issues could be delegated in conformity with the statute (on the general meeting competence *see* under this chapter §5.I.C.1.).[227]

The Law on Commercial Companies (2011 as well as 2004) unlike some previous provisions on this matter (such as the Law on Enterprises 1996) does not specify in an explicit manner the so-called presumed competence of body within joint-stock company, which is not the case for the limited liability company where this presumption relates to the director, presumed to have competences falling outside those of the general meeting (or general meeting and supervisory board in a two-tier system).[228]

The dilemma of how to organize the internal structure of company bodies in Serbian law was resolved under the influence of the modernization process of company laws, especially within the EU. It is the reason for a modern concept introduced for corporate governance, which includes internal organization on a statutory basis either through a one-tier or a two-tier board structure with important features of

227. *See* in detail on these issues: Mirko Vasiljević, *Company Law (Law of commercial companies of Serbia and the EU),* Pravni fakultet Univerziteta u Beogradu, Beograd, 2006, 357ff.
228. Article 224 para. 4 and 5 LCC 2011.

modern corporate governance (*see* below under II). Independently of the board structure, a joint-stock company always has a general meeting of shareholders.

## I. Shareholders

*135.* As already mentioned (*see* above under §4.VIII.A.), according to the Law on Commercial Companies, shareholders are considered by the company as well as third parties to be persons subscribed as holders in the Central depository register, or according to the Law on Capital Markets, a person on whose name securities are registered in the Central depository, or in the case of a custody bank – on whose behalf securities are held.[229]

Legal holder of a share can be one or several persons, in which case provisions on the share co-ownership are applicable.[230] Generally, share co-ownership can be based on the law (such as in case of inheritance), contract or statutory changes. In each case, co-owners are considered by the company to be one shareholder and have a joint and several liability for all obligations based on shares. Voting and information rights to access company's acts and documents can be enjoyed only by a common legal representative chosen by signed and certified written agreement of all co-owners and inscribed in the Central depository register, until the right to vote is suspended.

### *A. General Principles*

*136.* A general provision of equal treatment of shareholders stipulates that all shareholders under the same conditions are to be treated in an equivalent manner.[231] Also, the Law on Capital Markets underlines that a public company whose equity securities are admitted for trading in the regulated market or MTF must provide for an equal treatment of all shareholders of the same class of shares.[232] The principle of equal position of shareholders implies that every shareholder may not be treated differently, even with the consent of other shareholders or if specified in the statutes. It applies to all rights and obligations of shareholders and is to be assessed by objective criteria.[233]

The principle of shareholder equality (equality under the same conditions) does not mean an absolute prohibition of unequal treatment. Rather, it is the interest of the company and not individual shareholders which must be taken into account in deciding upon rights and obligations of shareholders. This is how different provisions including share classes, preclusion in voting in certain situations, voting

229. *See* Art. 249 LCC 2011 and Art. 2, para. 1 under 32 Law on Capital Markets.
230. *See* Art. 256 LCC 2011.
231. *See* Art. 269 LCC 2011.
232. *See* Art. 64 Law on Financial Markets.
233. *See* in detail Ivica Jankovec, 'Načelo ravnopravnosti akcionara u akcionarskom društvu' (Principle of shareholders' equality in the joint-stock company), in: Slobodan Perović (ed.) *Pravni život (Legal life)* 9-10/94, 1047ff.

threshold, duty of loyalty for the controlling shareholders, etc., exist. Still, it is prohibited to preclude shareholders generally and in advance in their rights.

### *B. Shareholders' Rights*

*137.* Shareholders have many important rights, which can be seen either as various pecuniary rights or important administrative, statutory rights, including those related to the general meeting. The most important pecuniary right is the right to dividend payments (*see* below under section 1), but also important are preferential rights of subscription (*see* above under this chapter §4.III) as well as the right to liquidation or insolvency distribution of the remainder. The most important non-pecuniary membership rights involve information rights (*see* below under section 2), rights related to the general meeting (participation, convocation, proposal of the agenda, *see* below under section 3 and in detail in part C), as well as the most important non-pecuniary right – the right to vote (*see* below under section 4).

#### 1. Right to Dividend Payment and Annual Accounts

*138.* The right of dividend payment is the most important pecuniary shareholders' right and is in close connection to provisions on companies' capital and its maintenance. A dividend is a part of the profit which the annual general meeting (or, exceptionally extraordinary general meeting or the board of directors or supervisory board in a two-tier system, when authorized by the general meeting resolution or statute) decides to distribute to shareholders, according to their type and class of shares and in proportion of the shares held. Therefore, there are two essential *conditions for dividend distribution* – those related to profits made and conditions related to dividend declaration by a competent body (usually general meeting and exceptionally board of directors).[234]

The first condition confirms strict provisions on capital maintenance and requires that a company can declare a dividend only if certain conditions related to the profits realized are fulfilled. The basis for this decision is always *annual financial reports* (exceptions apply for the interim dividend – *see* below). If, according to these reports, profits were made, they need to be used to cover all losses made from previous years, as well as reserves (if provided by law). If upon covering of losses (and reserves), there is a profit to be distributed, general meeting can decide to cover statutory reserves (if any) or to declare a dividend. Distribution of profit can be also made to employees of the company. Exceptionally, and if not otherwise provided by the statute, there is a possibility for an interim dividend payment during the business year upon interim accounts made for this purpose. These accounts must show that financial results clearly demonstrate that the company made a profit and have sufficient funds for interim dividend payments. Still, the amount of the interim dividend must not exceed the total profits made since the end of the last financial year

234. For these conditions in detail *see* Arts 270–274 LCC 2011.

for which the annual accounts have been drawn up, plus any profits brought forward and reserves available for this purpose, less losses brought forward and sums to be placed to reserves according to law or statutes.

Dividend payments can be made only *upon declaration of a dividend* (including the amount and method of payment) at the annual general meeting. Exceptionally, declaration of an interim dividend may also be made by the extraordinary general meeting or decision of the board of directors or supervisory board in a two-tier system, when authorized by the general meeting resolution or statute.

Can shareholders compel a joint-stock company to pay out the dividend? This is especially important to the minority shareholder status since unreasonable distribution policy may considerably harm their interests. The greatest difficulty in extending the right to sue the company because of decisions not to distribute dividends is the lack of standards helping the court in determining possible abuse of such policy, i.e., how much to pay and how much to set aside for future growth? As a rule, judges are not businessmen and do not have much knowledge relating to these matters. Consequently, even where *mala fide* would be found in denying the dividend payment, the courts still have to be extremely cautious in determining the payment amounts.

After declaring a dividend, the shareholder becomes a creditor for the dividend payment amount. Once decided, dividend payment must be made within the period of six months after general meeting decision was made. The right to dividend payment is conditional upon types and classes of shares (whereby different privileges for dividend payments within the same share class are forbidden) and is *proportional to the amount of shares held* to total amount of companies' shares.

Dividend payment can be made either *in cash or shares* of the same class (if approved by the shareholders of that class of shares), or exceptionally of other type or class of shares if approved by the three-fourths majority decision of present shareholders of that class. In the case of an interim dividend payment upon the decision of the board of directors or supervisory board, dividend payment is available only in cash.

*Dividend record date* is determined by the statute, including the method of its determination. It is the day on which all shareholders subscribed have the right to a dividend payment (or for the purpose of capital reduction – payment upon capital reduction or in the case of liquidation – right to liquidation distribution of the remainder). In other cases, when not determined by the statute, dividend record date is determined upon decision on the dividend (interim dividend) payment and according to methods prescribed (if any), although dividend record date for public company must not be before shareholders record date (*see* below under section C). Any transfer of shares after this date does not affect shareholders' right to a dividend payment.

## 2. Information Rights

*139.* In terms of the Law, every joint-stock company has to keep and retain for a prescribed time period certain acts and documents, including articles of incorporation, statute and other internal documents, including their changes; minutes and decisions of general meeting, board of directors and supervisory boards; document setting up branches and agencies, documents confirming property and other related rights, annual financial and consolidated accounts, information on directors and supervisory board members, including transactions made by them or persons connected to them. All documents must be kept on the company registered office premises or at the place accessible and known to all directors and supervisory board members. Certain acts and documents are also accessible to shareholders, including all normative acts of the company, minutes and decisions of the general meeting and annual, consolidated and all other financial accounts. It can be noticed that shareholders' right for access is limited to only certain acts and documents, especially noticeable when compared to equivalent rights of members of a limited liability company (*see* below under Chapter 2, .5.I.B.2).

Shareholders are entitled to have access to acts and documents on written request, and they are also entitled to inspect and copy these acts and documents during business hours or to be able to access them on an Internet site, free of charge.

A shareholder who was prevented (or was not allowed) to access acts and documents can petition to court in a non-litigious procedure. Acts and documents acquired by exercising the right to access may not be disclosed in the way harmful for the company or its reputation.

### 3. Rights Related to the General Meeting

*140.* In principle, every shareholder, may personally or through a proxy, be present at the general meeting and take part in its work (raising questions, participating in the debate, demanding answers, and submitting proposals – with or without reaching a certain threshold), while a shareholder possessing ordinary shares is also entitled to vote, which is also the case in certain issues for the shareholders of preference shares. Exceptionally, there is no participation in the general meeting on the grounds of own shares redeemed from shareholders (since these shares actually have no holder).

Rights related to general meetings consist of several rights, including a certain number of rights exercised before or outside the general meeting, such as the case with convocation rights, those related to the agenda and submission of decision proposals. A shareholder also has the right to participate in the general meeting and to ask questions. Nevertheless, the most important right related to general meetings is their right to vote. While certain rights related to the convocation, agenda and decision proposals will be discussed below under C, here we will discuss the right to participate in the general meeting and to ask questions. Finally, the right to vote will be discussed next below under section 4.

*The right to participate in the general meeting* includes the right of every shareholder to be present during the general meeting and to take part in discussion in the general meeting, including his right to submit proposals.[235] Exceptions related to this right concern either security or reasons of functional organization of the general meeting. Statute can limit the minimum number of shares necessary for participation in person only for organizational (and security) reasons during a general meeting, not higher than 0.1% of the total number of shares of each class, when another participation system – either through proxy or distance participation must be provided.[236] Also, shareholders can be restricted in this right only to provide identification of shareholders and their proxies.[237]

Every shareholder with a right to participate in the general meeting is entitled to *ask questions* of directors and members of the supervisory board in the case of a two-tier system and these persons *must provide them with an answer.*[238] The right to ask questions is related only to those issues already on meetings' agenda as well as other issues related to the company if responses are relevant for the proper evaluation of the issue on the meetings' agenda. In the case of groups of companies, the right to ask questions in the parent company can be related to the controlled company or companies, included in the consolidated accounts, if they are on the meetings' agenda.

The answer must be provided during the general meeting, although it is possible to deny an answer in exceptional circumstances. They include damage to the company or other connected person(s), if answering would be a criminal act, or if information is available on an Internet site. If unanswered, shareholders can petition the courts in order to be provided with an answer, but only on the issue upon which the answer was denied.

### 4. Right to Vote

*141.* Voting is the expression of shareholders' opinion regarding a decision put to vote, and is one of the most important shareholder control mechanisms. *Every shareholder* is entitled to vote on all issues that his class of shares is entitled to vote on.[239] As already explained, Serbian law adopts the principle of one share–one vote

---

235. Article 328 LCC 2011. *See also* Zoran Arsić 'Pravo učešća u skupštini' (Right to participate at the general meeting), in: Mirko Vasiljević, Vuk Radović (eds), *Korporativno upravljanje: drugi deo – Zbornik radova (Corporate Governance: second part – Collection of papers),* Pravni fakultet Univerziteta u Beogradu, Beograd, 2009, 5ff.
236. Case law is also favourable to this principle and underlies that these restrictions do not restrict the exercise of the shareholders' rights. *See* High commercial court judgment Pž.9598/2007, 27.5.2009, published in *Sudska praksa trgovinskih sudova (Commercial courts case law)* 2/2009.
237. *See* Art. 350 LCC 2011.
238. *See* Arts 342, 343 LCC 2011. *See* in detail: Zoran Arsić 'Pravo učešća u skupštini' (Right to participate at the general meeting), in: Mirko Vasiljević, Vuk Radović (eds), *Korporativno upravljanje: drugi deo – Zbornik radova (Corporate Governance: second part – Collection of papers),* Pravni fakultet Univerziteta u Beogradu, Beograd, 2009, 11ff; Jelena Lepetić, 'Pravo akcionara na postavljanje pitanja' (Shareholders' rights to ask questions), *Pravo i privreda (Law and Economy)* 4-6/2013, 207ff; Vuk Radović, 'Uslovi za vršenje prava akcionara na postavljanje pitanja' (Conditions for exercising shareholders' right to ask questions), *Anali Pravnog fakulteta Univerziteta u Beogradu (Annals of the Faculty of Law)* 1/2014, 62ff.
239. On the general right to vote *see* Art. 328 LCC 2011.

for ordinary, as well as for preference shares.[240] Namely, the basic voting principle in the general meeting is the *principle of proportionality* – shareholders vote proportionally to the nominal or accounting par value of the shares. Voting *according to the share nominal value* (proportionality) involves a multiplier of the lowest nominal amount of share entitlement to vote in a given joint-stock company. This is also the reason of regularly prescribing by law the minimum nominal share value entitlement to a vote and higher nominal values divisible by a round divisible number. Serbian law prescribes (minimum) nominal value of a share of at least RSD 100 (approx. EUR 0.85).[241]

Shareholders have the right to vote in the general meeting of shareholders or within a special meeting of each class of shares (class meetings) if that was required by at least 10% of the voting shareholders within that class of shares (except when class meetings are excluded in the statute).[242]

*142.* The right to vote can be exercised either *in person* – in the general meeting, in writing (whereby his signature on the document provided has to be certified, or without certification if explicitly excluded by the statute) when a shareholder is considered to be present; or by use of electronic means, if provided by the statute or general meeting's rules of procedure. Electronic communication can be achieved either as real-time transmission of general meeting or real-time transmission providing possibilities for shareholders' addressing the assembly from a dislocated place, but also includes electronic voting before or during a general meeting.[243]

*143.* The right to vote can be exercised by a *proxy*, but is not transferable.[244] Namely, the Law on Commercial Companies recognizes the institute of a proxy which may be granted (or must be granted in the case there is a threshold of a specific number of shares for the exercising of shareholders' voting rights set forth by the statutes or constitutive document of the company) by a shareholder to one or more proxies.

Therefore, shareholders have an option not to vote in person, but be represented by *a proxy*, who can be authorized to participate, including the right to vote on the general meeting in the name of a shareholder, when this person has the same rights as the shareholder.[245]A shareholder can authorize several persons as proxy, when every one of them individually is authorized to vote.

Proxy voting must be authorized in written form with obligatory certification of signatures for natural persons (if not excluded by the statute), or in electronic form if provided by the company. Public companies must provide for electronic proxy voting authorization and must provide the appropriate form of communication of

---

240. *See* Art. 251 para. 1 under 1: 'Ordinary shares give to their holders right to be present and to vote on the general meeting *on the one share – one vote principle...*' as well as Art. 255 para. 1: 'Holders of preference shares are entitled to vote on any general meeting within each class of shares on certain issues *on the principle one share one vote....*'
241. *See* Art. 258 para. 3 LCC 2011.
242. Article 357 LCC 2011.
243. Article 341 LCC 2011.
244. *See* Art. 261 para. 4 LCC 2011.
245. On proxy voting *see* Arts 344ff LCC 2011.

the company of proxies made. Companies may require the use of a specific form for proxy voting, but this form must enable shareholders to issue their proxy with instructions for each particular item on the agenda.

Proxy voting may contain *instructions* or orders on the right to vote, when the proxy is bound by them upon every agenda item, or if there are no instructions he can vote in good faith and in the best interest of the shareholder, or is otherwise responsible for any damage caused. Special provision is provided for the *custody bank*, holding custody accounts, considered as a proxy when entered in the Central depository register as acting on its own name and for the account of its clients.[246] In this case, a bank may exercise the right to vote on behalf of each of its clients individually. A custody bank may vote upon clients' instructions, or if there are not any it must vote either upon its own proposals given to clients in connection to the exercise of the right to vote.

Proxy can be a natural or a legal person, but there are certain *restrictions for proxies* in public companies, especially including controlling shareholders, directors and members of the supervisory board, as well as these persons and employees of the parent company or subsidiaries.[247] One person can be a proxy for several shareholders and can vote separately upon each proxy. A proxy can be authorized for one or several meetings, or indefinitely when authorization is revocable. Proxy voting is not transferable.

*144.* Voting can be *public* (which is presumed) or *by a secret ballot* if provided by the statute or rules of procedure.

Shareholders must vote with all votes for one option on a certain issue, except in the case of cumulative voting (*see* below under II.A.2.). The right to vote on the basis of voting shares may not be exercised in the general meeting in cases where the shareholder's interest conflicts with that of the company. Such a shareholder may be temporarily *precluded from voting*, and this preclusion is also valid for other connected persons. Exclusion for voting is also valid for quorum, and is specifically introduced when deciding on the renunciation or reduction of obligation of a shareholder towards company, filing or dropping of a lawsuit against him; or in the case when deciding on related party transactions.[248] However, Serbian law does not expressly rule out voting in the case of deciding on electing such a shareholder or relieving him from office of a board of directors' member, director or supervisory board member, or liquidator.

Where shares are pledged, given to usufruct or to a depositary, membership rights are not forfeited since these are special contractual relations, in which the shareholder still exercises his right to vote. *Share co-owners* exercise their voting right in the general meeting through a joint proxy, since they are just a single shareholder

---

246. Zoran Arsić, 'Zastupanje akcionara od strane banaka koje vode zbirne ili kastodi račune' ('Representation of shareholders by banks that maintain collective or custody accounts'), *Pravo i privreda (Law and Economy)* 46/2014, 35ff.

247. For the complete list *see* Art. 345 para. 3 LCC 2011. On the proxies provided by the company *see* Zoran Arsić, 'Punomoćnik akcionara predložen od strane akcionarskog društva' (Proxy recommended by the joint-stock company), *Pravo i privreda (Law and Economy)* 4-6/2013, 71ff.

248. Article 362 LCC 2011.

vis-à-vis the company and are jointly and severally liable for their obligations (on the basis of the share indivisibility principle).

*Voting agreements* are agreements between all or several shareholders on voting in a specific way regarding a given matter.[249] The purpose of this agreement is to retain control in the company or establish maximum control by cumulative share voting whenever possible, or to attain other goals (as a rule, shareholders agree their positions before voting in the general meeting, while possible disputes are to be settled by arbitration or a decision by a person of common trust). Such agreement does not affect any other shareholder rights, except for the method of exercising the right to vote. Voting contrary to such agreement does not invalidate the vote and a given decision may not be avoided on those grounds. Since no one may be compelled to vote as agreed, only consequences could be of contractual nature, especially liability for damages due to the violation of the agreement. This is explicitly provided in the provisions on shareholders contracts, where voting agreements are explicitly mentioned. They have internal nature and are valid between contracting parties only.[250] Although generally allowed in Serbian law, they have important limitations.[251] First, they are null and void if provide for obligation for shareholder or proxy to vote in favour of a proposal or instructions of the company, directors or members of the supervisory body in the case of a two-tier system. Null and void are also voting agreements when the right to vote is to be performed in a certain manner or not to be used in exchange for some other privilege or entitlement by the company, director of member of the supervisory board in the case of a two-tier system.

## *C. General Meeting*

*145.* General meeting comprises all shareholders. Even in the case of single member company, a general meeting is obligatory, when only one shareholder shall perform powers of the general meeting. The date to determine shareholders having the right to participate at the general meeting – *record date* is set to be tenth day before general meeting is held on the basis of a register kept by the Central depository. Every transfer of shares occurring after record day is not affecting rights of shareholders to participate at the general meeting.

Usually, general meeting sessions are held at the company's registered office, but can also be held in another locations, according to board of directors or supervisory board (in a two-tier system) decision, when necessary for organizational reasons.[252]

249. Zoran Arsić, 'Ugovori o vršenju prava glasa akcionara' (Shareholder's voting agreements), *Pravo i privreda (Law and Economy)* 9-12/2003, 29ff; *see also*: Jelena Lepetić, 'Jedinstvo članskih prava i ugovori o glasanju akcionara' ('Unity of Membership and Shareholder's Voting Agreements'), *Pravo i privreda (Law and Economy)* 4–6/2019, 225ff.
250. *See* Art. 15 LCC 2011.
251. Article 359 LCC 2011.
252. Article 332 LCC 2011.

1. Powers of the General Meeting

*146.* The general meeting, as a company's body where shareholders are represented is usually considered the hierarchically highest body within the company. However, due to its infrequent meetings, prevailing indifference of shareholders (particularly of the minority ones) to day-to-day activities, as well as their partial professional ignorance it is transformed into a body controlling the board of directors, while protecting the shareholders' interests. Although the position of a general meeting as being a place where shareholders are represented, which would imply the need for widening its democratic character in terms of functioning and scope of powers, it is still possible to conclude that this body, formally speaking, in that area is not sovereign and is retreating before the need for increased business efficiency through the strengthening of the board of directors or supervisory board functions (in the case of a two-tier system).

According to the Law on Commercial Companies, the general meeting has many powers, which may be basically divided into several categories. They concern *legislative power* of the general meeting and are related to different normative acts of the company, including change of the company's statute.[253] General meeting powers include very important issues on the *capital and securities*, including capital alterations – increase or reduction and issue of securities, as well as change to any right or privilege given to any share class; and issues related to the *company's property*, such as the acquisition or disposal of substantial property above a certain threshold.[254] General meeting's power is also to decide on *business results* – it approves financial and auditors' reports and decides on the profit and loss distribution. Power of the general meeting includes *electoral function and control over management and supervision,* including appointment and dismissal of directors and members of the supervisory boards, approval of their reports and deciding on their remuneration or criteria to determine remuneration, remuneration policy; appointment of auditors and their remuneration. Important power of the general meeting relates to various *statutory issues*, including statutory changes and changes of legal form, liquidation and petition requesting the opening of insolvency proceedings; and finally, all other issues put on the agenda according to law or the statute.

*The legally specified scope of competence (including statutory)* should, in principle, be considered as imperative, so that only the body designated as competent in specific matters could decide on delegating its powers, unless the law or statutes preclude such possibility. Delegation of powers is exclusively provided for delegation from the board of directors (or supervisory board in the case of a two-tier system) to general meeting, possible only when explicitly decided upon by the board of directors (supervisory board), if not otherwise provided by the statute.[255] Also, delegation of responsibility from the general meeting to the board of directors is explicitly provided in certain cases by law (examples include acquisition of own shares if certain conditions are met).

---

253. For the exclusive list of general meeting's powers *see* Art. 329 LCC 2011.
254. On the obligation to consult general meeting in the case of substantial property transactions, including those over 30% of the property net value *see* Arts 470–473 LCC 2011.
255. *See* Art. 398 para. 2 under 2 and Art. 441 para. 2 under 2 LCC 2011.

## 2. Different Kinds of Shareholders' Meetings

*147.* Distinguishing between *an ordinary* (annual) and *extraordinary* meeting is explicitly set forth in Serbian law.[256]

*Annual or ordinary general meeting* is held annually, no later than six months after the end of the business year (which is end of June).[257] Failure to hold the general meeting in due time does not affect the validity of other acts (and decisions not dependent on the adoption at the annual general meeting) of the joint-stock company. On the convocation *see* below under section 3.

The most important powers of the annual general meeting include decisions on financial reports and auditors' reports (if they are obligatory), annual profit and loss distribution, as well as other issues within the power of general meeting. For the public joint-stock company annual meeting also discuss and adopts annual and consolidated (if applicable) management reports (board of directors or executive board in the case of a two-tier system), as well as report of the supervisory board. Annual reports of the public joint-stock company must include a statement on the application of the Corporate Governance Code, its availability, as well as other issues on the corporate governance, especially those not explicitly provided by law and possible exceptions with explanation for non-appliance of the Corporate Governance Code. Public joint-stock company must disclose on its Internet site accurate and updated information on professional qualifications and previous employment of the members of the board of directors (in a one-tier system of management) or members of the supervisory board (in two-tier system of management), and to include information on their participation in other boards or appointments in other companies.

*An extraordinary meeting* can be held if necessary or when prescribed by the law or statute.[258] On the convocation *see* below under section 3. The law requires an *obligatory extraordinary meeting* in cases when the company suffers serious losses. That is the case when net assets as set out in the company's annual or other accounts fall below 50% of the amount of the subscribed capital. Nevertheless, it is only stressed that a general meeting of shareholders must be called, including specification in the convening of the general meeting of the reason for its convening, and must include decision proposal, either to liquidate or to adopt other adequate measures (for consequences regarding capital of the company *see* above under this chapter .4.I.D.).

## 3. Convocation

*148.* The *power to call the general meeting* is within the competence of the board of directors or supervisory board (in a two-tier system). Nevertheless, it is expressly provided that an extraordinary meeting can be called and its agenda made upon request of shareholders holding at least 5% of the total amount of the capital

256. Article 330 LCC 2011.
257. For provisions on annual general meeting *see* Arts 364–370 LCC 2011.
258. Articles 371–375 LCC 2011.

subscribed or shares within class of shares entitled to vote on the issues proposed for the agenda, and having shareholder status at least three months before calling the meeting and until the decision is made; unless lower amount of capital or votes is specified by the statute. When in liquidation extraordinary meeting can be called upon liquidator's request.

*Meetings can be convened by the court* if no annual meeting was held within three months of the time limit prescribed by law (*see* above under section 2), or in the case if no meeting was called or held upon valid request of the (prescribed holding of) shareholders in the case of extraordinary meetings.[259] Every shareholder entitled to participate at the general meeting (irrespective of his shareholding and number of votes), as well as director or supervisory board members in the case of a two-tier system, can request that the annual meeting be convened by the court or person appointed by the court to convene the meeting, and, if necessary, preside over the meeting. The same right has a shareholder entitled to initiate convocation of the extraordinary meeting upon failing or refusal to do so of the board of directors or supervisory board within eight days of the request made. If in the next thirty days extraordinary meeting is not held, shareholder entitled to initiate this convocation has another thirty days to request that extraordinary meeting is convened by the court.

*Notice of (call for) meetings must be communicated* to shareholders no later than thirty days before the general meeting is held for the annual general meeting, or twenty-one days in the case of extraordinary meetings and must include all acts and documents related to the agenda (including proposal of every decision taken, every contract to be approved, etc.).

*Notice of meeting must include certain information and acts or documents*, including day of calling, shareholders record date, time and place of the meeting, agenda proposal including proposed decisions, including in particular decision on the acquisition or disposal of substantial property above a certain threshold; and class of shares and total number of shares having the right to vote, including necessary majority and voting procedure.[260] Notice must also include information on the rights available to dissenting or absent shareholders, forms and procedure for proxy voting.

Notice of meeting is communicated *to all shareholders having this status at the time of convocation* of the meeting decision and all materials must be available for shareholders either in person (including proxy) or via upload from web page of the company. Notice must be *in writing* (including electronic communication) *or by publication on the Internet site* of the company and must also be made in the Registration Agency and the Central Depository register with the exception for the non-public single member joint-stock company. For a public company publication on the companies' Internet site is obligatory and must also be followed by publication on the regulated market of MTF Internet page immediately after decision on the convocation is made, no later than next working day. Statute may provide for additional publication in daily newspapers.

259. Article 339 LCC 2011.
260. *See* in detail Art. 335 LCC 2011.

Strict provisions on the meeting convocation must be applied. The only *exception* possible is the convocation of the general meeting of a non-public company, only if all shareholders having voting rights on all agenda issues are present at the meeting and agree that meeting be held.[261]

### 4. General Meeting Chairman, Agenda, Rules of Procedure, Minutes and Other Miscellaneous Matters

*149.* The person to preside over the general assembly – chairman – has to be designated by the statute or voted for in each meeting, or for all forthcoming meetings, according to statute or rules of procedure.[262] If that is not the case, chairman is the person possessing or representing the highest number of ordinary shares votes in proportion to the total number of shareholders with ordinary shares present at the meeting. In the case of convocation of the meeting by the court, the chairman can also be appointed by the court.

General meeting must adopt *rules of procedure* to specify procedural issues of the meeting. Rules are adopted on the first meeting (and can be amended) upon proposal of the chairman or at least 10% of present shareholders if no higher majority is prescribed in the statute.[263]

*Agenda of the meeting* is determined by decision on the convocation of the general meeting by board of directors or supervisory board in the case of a two-tier system. General meeting is bound by the agenda adopted and can decide only upon issues contained in the agenda.[264] Apart from persons in charge to adopt the agenda, there is a possibility for minority shareholders holding at least 5% of voting shares to submit in writing to board of directors or supervisory board additional issues for the agenda to be discussed (if explained) or additional issues of the agenda for the session that they propose the general meeting should decide on (if explained and submitted the wording of these decisions), issue already existing in the agenda but with different decision proposed (if explained and submitted in written form). Additional items to be put on the agenda must be submitted at least twenty days before annual general meeting is held, or ten days for an extraordinary meeting. Public companies must publish these submissions the next day on their web pages. If adopted, the new agenda must be communicated to shareholders without delay and, if that is the case, must include text of the decisions proposed to be adopted. If the board of directors or supervisory board in a two-tier system refuse the agenda items proposed by minority shareholders, they are entitled to address the court, who can decide on the agenda amendments and their communication to shareholders.

Every decision taken during a general meeting must be recorded in writing in the *general meeting's minutes*. There are detailed provisions on the content and formal

261. *See* Arts 335 para. 14 and 375 LCC 2011.
262. Article 333 LCC 2011.
263. Article 334 LCC 2011.
264. On the agenda *see* Arts 336–338 LCC 2011.

requirements of the minutes, which are under the responsibility of the chairman, including its publication and further communication to shareholders.[265]

## 5. Quorum and Majority

*150. Quorum* necessary for the general meeting is set as a simple majority of the total number of votes within the class of shares entitled to vote on a certain issue, except if a higher majority is prescribed in the statute. Quorum cannot include own shares, held by the company, or other shares when voting is suspended. Quorum must include all shareholders present at the general meeting or voting in the absence or electronically.

General meeting can discuss issues only if there is a quorum prescribed for the class and number of shares for the issue on the agenda. If conditions for quorum are not fulfilled, meeting can be *adjourned* with the same agenda and within a time limit of fifteen to thirty days. If adjourned, the annual general meeting can be held without quorum prescribed. Quorum for the adjourned extraordinary general meeting is one-third of the total number of shares voting on certain issue, if higher majority is not prescribed in the statute, but not above the quorum requirement of the first (initial) convocation. If there is no quorum on the adjourned meeting, board of directors or supervisory board in a two-tier system must call for a new general meeting. General provisions on the majority are applicable on the adjourned meeting, but in the case of public joint-stock company, the majority must not go below one-quarter of the total number of votes of shares entitled to vote on the issue.

General meeting can adopt decisions by *a simple majority of shareholders present* (including voting in writing or electronically), entitled to vote upon certain issue, except when higher majority is required by law or statute. Such as the case of the prescribed *absolute majority* in the case of change of statute, or *qualified majority of three-fourths of shareholders present at the meeting* for decisions on statutory changes, change of legal form, substantial property change, directors' responsibility, decisions upon control contract, reduction of capital, shareholders agreements, dividend payment when payment is made in shares, as well as to limit or exclude preferential right of subscription.[266]

*Majority necessary for the adjourned meeting* is the same as prescribed by the law or statute, but, as already mentioned, in the case of public joint-stock company majority must not be below one-fourth of votes out of the total number of voting shares on each specific issue.

Person in charge of minutes and *poll committee,* comprised of at least three persons, can be appointed by the chairman, if not otherwise prescribed by the statute or

265. Article 363 LCC 2011.

266. There was only one case when two-thirds majority of total number of shareholders was prescribed for joint-stock company, probably by mistake and according to majority required for limited liability company. That was the case of the prolongation for the period for which company was established. Later amendments changed this majority to qualified majority of three-fourths of shareholders present at the meeting. *See* Art. 10 LCC 2011.

rules of procedure.[267] *Results of votes cast* are to be determined by the chairman, including the total number of votes cast, percentage of the capital represented, the total number of votes in favour and against, as well as the number of votes sustained. Chairman is entitled to determine only the majority required, in the case of public joint-stock company, if no other shareholder present at the meeting opposes determination of majority only. Results of the votes casted must be published for public joint-stock company on company's web page, or must be submitted to every shareholder upon his request.

## 6. Action for Avoidance

*151.* Action for avoidance is prescribed in very limited circumstances. It is the right of one or more shareholders having the right to participate at the general meeting, only while shareholders and if not voting in favour of the decision taken.[268] Apart from the shareholder, the action can be filed by a director or supervisory board member if he would be responsible for criminal act or damage incurred to company or third party by execution of the general meetings' decision. Action of avoidance can include compensation of damage incurred.

The law prescribes the time limit for the action, which is within thirty days after interested person knew about decision taken, but no longer than three months from the moment when the decision was made. If the law prescribes obligatory registration of the general meeting decision, action is limited by the period of thirty days after registration has been made.

Reasons for the action include violation of decision-making provisions (regarding meetings convocation, and also including absence of shareholders and other cases when the decision is illegal) or are in relation to the decision's content. It is especially interesting to remark that there is a possibility to prevent abuse of majority, bearing in mind that reason implied for the action could be 'decision made by a shareholder voting with intent to grant himself or other person advantage and causing damage to company or other shareholders. Although there are several reasons for avoidance, their scrutiny and rejection can be made if the breach of shareholders' rights was minor compared to the decision made or especially for the protection of third parties' interests, including if there was successful public offering of securities.

If successful, action for avoidance has the effects towards company, shareholders, as well as directors and members of the supervisory board, while third parties' rights, if acting in good faith, are not affected by the decision. In the case of registered general meeting decision, the court will inform register on avoidance decision made, while parties from the proceedings for avoidance are entitled to submit

267. For the provisions on the poll committee nomination, powers, etc., *see* in particular Art. 355 LCC 2011.

268. For the action of avoidance, *see* Arts 376–381 LCC 2011. On the arbitrability of corporate disputes regarding general meeting's decisions *see*: Tatjana Jevremović Petrović, 'Arbitrabilnost sporova u vezi sa pobijanjem odluke skupštine privrednog društva' ('Arbitrability of Corporate Disputes Regarding General Meeting's Decisions'), *Pravo i privreda (Law and Economy)* 4–6/2018, 223ff.

registration application in order to change data or information registered upon cancelled general meeting's decision, but only if those data or information are still registered on the date of registration application. If action for avoidance is related to the approval of annual financial reports, it is affecting the decision on the dividend payment and includes an obligation for shareholders to return all payments received.

### *D. Minority Shareholders' Rights*

*152.* As a rule, a joint-stock company has a considerable number of shareholders who do not know one another, so conflicts are inevitable. Although decisions are rendered in the general meeting by a prescribed majority, and are binding for all of them (including the ones not taking part or voting against), frequently, minority shareholders complain that majority shareholders abuse the majority principle to pursue their own interest rather than the interest of the company; this causes conflicts and requires protection of minority shareholders.

The protection of minority shareholders cannot by any means block the decision-making process within the company, so it is necessary to find a balance between the *majority principle*, as a fundamental philosophy of this type of companies, and the *minority protection principle*.[269] There are several measures designed for such protection, and they affirm the majority rule, at the same time preventing its abuse, on the one hand (the *majority abuse theory*) and providing, on the other hand, the protection of the minority. Two groups are known: preventive (extrajudicial) measures (powers of the minority in the general meeting and various forms of internal and external institutional control) and measures of judicial and administrative protection. A widest protection of minority is introduced in Serbian law by duty of loyalty of controlling shareholder to the company parallel to directors' duties (*see* further on this issue below under II.C.). Certain particular rights were already mentioned, especially those related to the general meeting (convocation, putting additional items on the agenda), while others will be discussed below (including derivative and other corporate suits with regard to duties owed by directors and other persons to the company). Here we discuss only several particular minority shareholders' rights, including withdrawal right, right to request special or extraordinary auditing control, squeeze-out and sell-out rights, as well as right to liquidate or to be protected through other minority oppression remedies.

269. On minority shareholders' rights *see* Sonja Bunčić, 'Zaštita manjinskih akcionara' (Protection of minority shareholders), *Pravni život (Legal life)* 11/2011, 137ff; Mirko Vasiljević, Vuk Radović, 'Teorijske osnove prava nesaglasnih akcionara' ('Theoretical Foundations of Shareholders' Right to Appraisal'), *Anali Pravnog fakulteta u Beogradu (Annals of the Faculty of Law in Belgrade – Belgrade Law Review)* 3/2017, 7ff.

1. Withdrawal Rights

*153.* Every dissenting *shareholder* has a withdrawal right when voting against or sustaining to vote, while deciding *on the issues regarding* amendments to the statute, if they are making less favourable the most important shareholders' rights, in the case of change of legal form or statutory changes (mergers, divisions); if there is a change of the time scope for which company was established, as well as in the case of approval of the substantial property acquisition or disposal.[270] This right is also granted to shareholders in other cases when his rights are amended, if that is provided by the statute, or when a public company decides to withdraw one or more share classes of issued shares admitted to trading from the regulated market or MTF. Withdrawal right grants dissenting shareholders the right to have their shares purchased by the company at the most favourable price, including market price for public joint-stock company in the case of market trade turnover prescribed (*see* above under §4.VIII). If there is no prescribed market trade turnover for public joint-stock company or in the case of non-public joint-stock company, the purchase price will be the highest between accounting and evaluation price.

Shareholders must be informed of the withdrawal rights through the general meeting notice, which includes the forms to be filled in the case when shareholders decide to use right of withdrawal, and information on the price of shares (market – for public joint-stock company in the case of market trade turnover, or accounting and evaluation – for public joint-stock company when there is not prescribed market trade turnover, or in the case of non-public joint-stock company), to be bought out by the company.

Shareholders are entitled to submit a request for their shares to be purchased by the company at the general meeting when deciding on the issue granting a withdrawal right or fifteen days after the meeting was closed. The company has to purchase all shares from dissenting shareholders within sixty days after shareholder had right to submit their request, or otherwise court action can be brought. A shareholder can ask the court for full payment of the share price, when determined unlawfully or when full payment was not made or to ask for full payment in the event of non-payment of the shares. If court decides in favour of the shareholder, all other dissenting shareholders of the same class can ask the company for full payment, irrespective of whether they brought action before a court.

2. Right to Request Special or Extraordinary Auditing Control

*154.* Unlike the previous Law on Commercial Companies (2004) to provide for special investigation, the current Law on Commercial Companies provides only provisions regarding special and extraordinary auditing control.[271]

---

270. *See* in detail Arts 474–476 LCC 2011. *See*: Vuk Radović, 'Uslovi za ostvarivanje prava nesaglasnih akcionara' ('Conditions for Exercising Shareholder's Right to Appraisal'), *Pravo i privreda (Law and Economy)* 4–6/2017, 49ff.

271. For the special investigation rights, including right of minority shareholders holding at least 20% of the capital subscribed to ask for special investigation on the financial results and business records

*Special auditing* may be requested to re-evaluate contributions in kind or value and other conditions in the case of acquisition or disposal of substantial property (exceeding 30% of the net value) only within three years of contribution or acquisition or disposal made.

*Extraordinary auditing* may include already audited financial reports only in the case when there is a doubt that auditing was unlawful or made against accountancy standards and procedures; or when financial reports do not contain all remarks according to accountancy standards, or they are incomplete. A request for extraordinary auditing may be submitted within three years since the adoption of audited financial reports.

Both procedures can be initiated in writing by minority shareholders holding at least 10% of voting rights to board of directors, or supervisory board in the case of a two-tier system, who is obliged to put this item on the next general meeting agenda (annual if there is less than six months to this meeting, or to extraordinary meeting in the case of a longer period of time) or can ask the court to convene an extraordinary general meeting. Decision on special or extraordinary auditing control is made by the general meeting decision by a simple majority of present shareholders, and shall include the person appointed to perform auditing control. This person cannot be the same auditor as in the case of evaluation of the contribution in kind, or the one performing auditing for financial results during acquisition or disposal of substantial property, or other financial results for which extraordinary auditing was requested. If voted against, the right to request special and extraordinary auditing control can be put in front of the competent court, if the court agrees with the request, it must appoint a person to perform the audit. All expenses from the special and extraordinary auditing control are to be met by the company, although for the damage caused by an unsubstantial request and all expenses made, there is a joint and several liability of all shareholders requesting such auditing.

The auditor must submit his report in writing including his conclusions and compatibility with opinion taken by the evaluation of the contributions in kind or value and conditions of the property acquired or disposed of. Only essential incompatibility with previous evaluation will make the request substantiated. Extraordinary auditors' report must also be submitted in writing and must contain explained opinion including compatibility with the previous auditing opinion. Auditing reports must be submitted to the board of directors or executive and supervisory board in the case of a two-tier system, to shareholders and court (if auditing was requested upon court's decision). In the case of substantial inconsistency or incompatibility with previous evaluations or audited reports, the board of directors or supervisory board (or if not – the court) must convene an extraordinary general meeting to discuss the report and must submit their written report on the findings of submitted auditor's report. If special or extraordinary auditor's report is not approved by the general meeting, dissenting shareholders have withdrawal right. If there are no substantial inconsistencies or incompatibilities with previous reports, auditors' report is to be submitted to the next general meeting.

---

in the last three years, *see* Arts 334–336 LCC 2004. For details on the right to request special or extraordinary auditing control, *see* Arts 455–463 LCC 2011.

3. Squeeze-Out and Sell-Out Rights

*155.* The Law on Commercial Companies has adopted a modern institute designated as a compulsory purchase (*squeeze-out*) and parallel to it an adequate institute to protect minority shareholders' rights (*sell-out right*). These rights were connected only with takeover bids for public companies, but were included in the current Law on Commercial Companies after 2011 as a general right of majority or minority shareholders and irrespective of the public offer.[272]

While the squeeze-out right entitles the majority owner, holding at least 90% of the capital subscribed and at least 90% of the total number of ordinary shares (including connected persons during last year) to initiate a decision of the general meeting on the compulsory purchase of all remaining shares from existing shareholders, and irrespective of the burdens, restrictions or third-party rights on these shares. Shares purchased compulsorily from shareholders must be made at the most favourable price during the last three months, calculated by the method prescribed for purchase of the shares by the company from dissenting shareholders in the case of their withdrawal (*see* above under section D.1). They include market price for public joint-stock company in the case of market trade turnover prescribed. If there is no prescribed market trade turnover for public joint-stock company or in the case of non-public joint-stock company, the purchase price will be the highest between accounting and evaluation price.[273] The decision can be executed only if decision on the compulsory purchase was registered within three working days in the Business Register and next five working days in the Central depository register, after which it is necessary to provide compensation for shares to be purchased in the next three working days on the special account in the Central depository. An action for avoidance may be made with respect to the decision on compulsory purchase during thirty days, but not on the grounds related to the share value. In that case, for the calculation of share value, every shareholder being purchased upon general meeting's decision on compulsory purchase can initiate court proceeding in order to re-evaluate the purchase price during the period of thirty days after decision on the compulsory purchase was registered at the Business Register. If price determined by the court is higher than the one determined by the company, the purchaser must provide and deposit the difference, including interest for all shares being compulsorily purchased, or otherwise the company is jointly and severely liable for the payment of the difference in price.

Next to the right of a majority shareholder to buy out all remaining shareholders, there is an equivalent right of minority shareholders. It entitles all minority shareholders upon their written request to sell shares to controlling shareholder, holding at least 90% of the capital subscribed and 90% of total votes of the ordinary shares. Minority shareholders must submit a request to the company, and it is considered to be submitted to the controlling shareholder as well. Purchase price must be determined as in the case of the withdrawal right – as the most favourable price. It

272. Arts 515–523 LCC 2011.

273. Special provisions exist in the case of majority ownership over 90% being acquired on the basis of voluntary public offer bid, when acquirer can squeeze out all remaining shareholders under conditions from the takeover bid. *See* Art. 523 LCC 2011.

includes market price for public joint-stock company in the case of market trade turnover prescribed. If there is no prescribed market trade turnover for public joint-stock company or in the case of non-public joint-stock company, the purchase price will be the highest between accounting and evaluation price. Purchase price must be determined by the company within sixty days, after which controlling shareholder has the obligation to make payment within thirty days to make transfer effective. If the purchase price is not calculated by the company, minority shareholders are entitled to initiate court proceedings in order that a purchase price be determined. Shareholders can also initiate court proceedings in the case of unlawfully determined price similarly to the proceedings provided for in the case of dissenting shareholders. The majority owner must pay the difference, including interest upon court's order if the court finds out that the purchase price is inadequate, or otherwise the company is jointly and severally liable for the payment of the difference in price, including interest.

### 4. Right to Initiate Liquidation and Other Minority Oppression Remedies

*156.* Exceptionally, and in circumstances that leave no other remedy, Serbian law leaves a possibility for the compulsory liquidation of the company upon court's decision. Shareholders holding at least 20% of the capital subscribed are entitled to bring a suit against the company in order to be liquidated.[274] Reasons leading to this decision involve serious obstruction of the company's bodies and inability to pursue normal business activities. This is understandable since there is a whole series of other rights intended to protect minority shareholders.[275]

They include that board of directors, executive or supervisory board cannot perform their functions either because of internal disputes or other reasons, and general meeting cannot solve this conflict, which is leading to the inability of the company to perform business activities in the interest of shareholders. Also, the important reason for liquidation might be inability of functioning of the general meeting during two consecutive meetings, which leads to inability of the company to perform business activities in the interest of the company; when directors or members of the supervisory board in case of a two-tier system are acting illegally, unfairly or in deceit and against interest of the shareholders bringing the suit; as well as in the case when company's property is wasted or diminished.[276]

According to the Law, the court may set a six-month time limit, following the filing of the petition, within which the situation should be settled where a shortcoming may be remedied; should that not be the case or should there be no such time limit, the liquidation proceedings have to be instituted, according to provisions on the compulsory liquidation. Instead of ordering that compulsory liquidation is to be

274. Article 469 LCC 2011.

275. *See* in particular: Mirko Vasiljević, *Privredna društva (Commercial companies),* Belgrade, 1999, 195-199 and 319-333.

276. *See*: Vuk Radović, 'Nevoljni prestanak privrednog društva' ('Involuntary Dissolution for Deadlock and Oppression'), *Revija Kopaoničke škole prirodnog prava (Review of the Kopaonik School of Natural Law)* 1/2020, 105ff.

proceeded, the court may order one or several alternative measures, including compensation for damages to shareholders. Alternative measures also include dismissal of directors or supervisory board members, appointment of provisional management until new management or supervision board is appointed, extraordinary auditing, dividend payment or other profit distribution decisions, as well as share purchases upon most favourable value of the shares (according to the provision of withdrawal rights, *see* above under section D.1) from shareholders who initiated proceedings.

As far as we know, there is no case in our case law ordering liquidation of a company of capital at the request of the minority shareholders or members of limited liability companies. With limited liability companies and close companies, it is a rule that the majority member (shareholder) is also the company representative, exercising management functions and signing all company documents which only increases the risk of minority shareholders' rights being violated, so that the issue of judicial protection becomes even more important as far as their right to demand company liquidation is concerned.

Before courts tried to justify such an approach by the character of liquidation (and insolvency) proceedings, by stating that these procedures are to quite a degree *extra-judicial*, where there is no enquiring into the forms of abuse as a possible ground for liquidation at the minority shareholders' request. This was later changed, and the courts now stand on the position that procedure upon request of minority shareholders to liquidate is a judicial procedure.[277]

However, the idea of preventing serious abuse must not be transformed into its extreme opposite – i.e., abuse by minority shareholders (members). And only a court practice which is as vital as business practice may find the balance between the two.

### *E. Long-Term Engagement of Shareholders in Public Joint-Stock Companies*

*157.* Under recent amendments, Serbian law introduced new chapter IVa in the Law on Commercial Companies on long-term shareholder engagement in public joint-stock companies.[278] It was done in order to harmonize Serbian Company Law with Directive (EU) 2017/828 as regards the encouragement of long-term shareholder engagement.[279] Provisions on long-term shareholder engagement will become effective after the Republic of Serbia joins the EU. Among the most important provisions are those introducing engagement policy and reports of institutional investors and asset managers and their disclosure obligations, inlcuding disclosure

277. *See* Decision of the Higher commercial court, Pž. 9464/2007, 11 Jun. 2008, published in *Sudska praksa trgovinskih sudova (Commercial courts case law)* 4/2008.
278. *See* Chapter IVa, Arts 469a-469j LCC 2011.
279. Directive (EU) 2017/828 of the European Parliament and of the Council of 17 May 2017 amending Directive 2007/36/EC as regards the encouragement of long-term shareholder engagement, *OJ* L 132, 20.5.2017.

obligations for voting advisors; company right to identify its shareholders and processing and correction of personal data in that case; provision of various information to shareholders and facilitating their exercise of voting rights. Also, intermediary costs, as well as provision of intermediary services of non-EU companies are briefly regulated.

## II. Management and Control: One-Tier System

*158.* The dilemma of how to organize the internal structure of company bodies is what every joint-stock company in any legal system is facing.[280] In determining how to organize internal structure of the joint-stock company, Serbian law has chosen to have an alternative system.[281]

A joint-stock company may be organized to have either a one-tier system, where the managing function is in the hands of one or several directors (board of directors), appointed by the general meeting of shareholders. The board of directors is comprised of persons permanently employed (executive directors) and may (and in certain cases must) comprise of persons not employed (non-executive directors) with the company. The other – *a two-tier system* is regulated alternatively to the first one. It has an obligatory supervisory board, appointed by the general meeting. Also, in the two-tier system, a company must have one or more executive directors (board of executive directors), appointed by the supervisory board. The choice between one or two-tier system is left to be made by the company's statute, with the possibility to change the internal organization through changes in the company's statute.

### *A. Board of Directors*

*159.* In the case of a one-tier system, the company must have one or more directors.[282] A board of directors exists if there are three or more directors. The number of directors is left to be decided by the statute. Still, an important restriction is provided for the public joint-stock company. It must have a board of directors with at least three directors.

---

280. There are several monographs and collected papers regarding corporate governance in Serbia. *See* in particular: Mirko Vasiljević, *Korporativno upravljanje: izabrane teme (Corporate governance: selected themes),* Udruženje pravnika u privredi, Beograd, 2013; Mirko Vasiljević, Vuk Radović (eds), *Korporativno upravljanje (Corporate Governance),* Pravni fakultet Univerziteta u Beogradu, Beograd, 2008; Mirko Vasiljević, Vuk Radović (eds), *Korporativno upravljanje: drugi deo – Zbornik radova (Corporate Governance: second part – Collection of papers),* Pravni fakultet Univerziteta u Beogradu, Beograd, 2009; Boris Begović et al., *Unapre enje korporativnog upravljanja (Fostering corporate governance),* Centar za liberalno demokratske studije, Beograd, 2003; D. Radonjić, *Organi društava kapitala (Bodies of the capital companies),* Podgorica, 1998.

281. Article 326 LCC 2011. *See also* Mirko Vasiljević, 'Corporate Governance of a Joint Stock Company (Models and Trends in Comparative Law and Practice)', *Pravo i privreda (Law and Economy)* 9-12/2003, 3ff.

282. *See* general provisions on board of directors in one-tier system in Arts 382ff LCC 2011.

1. General Conditions

*160.* Only few requirements exist for a person to be appointed as a director in a joint-stock company. *General positive requirement* is that a person must have full legal capacity – must be able to have rights and obligations and to exercise them. Further positive requirements are not prescribed by law, but can be introduced by the statute. This practically means that directors may be shareholders or other persons, company employees, Serbian or foreign nationals, with or without professional experience and education, etc., but these specific conditions could be specified in the statute.

Nevertheless, the law introduced several *negative requirements*, including inability to be a director for a person who is already a director or member of the supervisory board in more than five companies, but also if sentenced for criminal acts related to commercial activities in the last five years, or if he was sentenced to security measure of prohibition from practising a profession, activity or duty, which is related to the business activities of the company. In order to disclose as much information as possible in regard to directors and management, new provision of the Law of Commercial Companies requires that public joint-stock company must disclose on their Internet site accurate and up-to-date information on employment and previous employment of the members of board of directors, as well as supervisory board, including membership and position in boards of other companies.[283]

2. Appointment

*161.* General meeting appoints directors of the company. Board of directors' members are not elected as shareholders' representatives, which is particularly important for independent decision-making. Once appointed, all directors must be registered in the Registration Agency.

*Board members' nomination* can be made by director or board of directors (but only in a closed joint-stock company), nomination committee (if there is any) or shareholders entitled to put an item on the general meetings' agenda. *The appointment method* is direct, but may be cumulative if provided by the statute for public joint-stock company.[284]

*Mandate* is a period of time for which a director is appointed and is determined by the statute or general meeting's decision on the appointment. Nevertheless, it cannot be longer than four years, after which directors can be reappointed for a new

283. Art 368a LCC 2011.

284. Zoran Arsić, 'Kumulativno glasanje za izbor članova upravnog odobora direktora' (Cumulative voting for board of directors members), *Pravni život (Legal life)* 11/2004, 47ff; D. Radonjić, 'Pravni i matematički aspekti kumulativnog glasanja' (Legal and mathematical aspects of cumulative voting), *Pravo i privreda (Law and Economy)* 5-8/2003, 54ff; Vuk Radović, 'Kumulativno glasanje za izbor članova uprave: prvi deo' (Cumulative voting for election of board members: first part), *Anali Pravnog fakulteta Univerziteta u Beogradu (Annals of the Faculty of Law University of Belgrade)* 1/2008, 150ff; Vuk Radović, 'Kumulativno glasanje za izbor članova uprave: drugi deo' (Cumulative voting for election of board members: second part), *Anali Pravnog fakulteta Univerziteta u Beogradu (Annals of the Faculty of Law University of Belgrade)* 2/2008, 47ff.

mandate. If the statute or decision on the appointment fails to determine the period for which director is appointed, he will have a mandate for four years.

Mandate can be *terminated* by the expiration of time for which the person was appointed, but also in other cases. They include if director stops fulfilling necessary requirements for directors' position, or if general meeting fails to adopt annual financial reports during annual meeting. Director can also be *removed* from his position by the general meeting's decision at any time and without good cause. Finally, a director can *resign* from his position at any time. His written resignation must be submitted to remaining directors, or if there is only one director to the general meeting's chairman or shareholder holding the largest number of voting shares. If a company ceases to have a director and fails to make a registration of the new one, shareholders or other interested persons may petition in court for the appointment of a temporary representative.

In the event of board membership vacancy, remaining directors may appoint a person or persons to perform directors' obligations and duties until appointment by the general meeting. Although Serbian law allows for *co-optation*, it may be otherwise prescribed in the statute. Co-optation can be made of up to two directors, although co-optation is not allowed if the number of directors is below half of board members or is insufficient for decision-making or representation, when general meeting must be called in order to appoint vacant board member positions. The mandate for co-opted directors is restricted in time until next general meeting and cannot be more privileged than previous directors' mandate.

### 3. Composition of the Board of Directors

*162.* Directors can be executive or non-executive. If there is less than three directors, they all are executive directors. Nevertheless, public joint-stock company must have a board of directors with at least three directors, among which there must be non-executive directors, whose number must be higher than the number of executive directors.

*Executive directors* have the power of management and representation within limits set by the law, statute and the general meetings' and board of directors' decisions.[285] For all management and representation powers, all executive directors are authorized to act collectively, unless otherwise provided in the statute or a general meeting decision. Although all executive directors have the power of representation, it may be limited in the statute among them to one or more executive directors. Also, power of representation may be limited to all or some of them with additional signature requirement of the procurator (holding power of attorney and registered in the Business Register with a legal scope of representation powers). Further on management and representation, *see* under section B.

One of the executive directors who have the power of representation may be appointed to be *managing director (chief executive officer).*[286]Appointment is made by all other directors upon criteria or specific conditions for appointment which may

285. Article 388 LCC 2011.
286. Article 389 LCC 2011.

be introduced in the statute or through a general meeting decision. Powers of managing director include coordination of executive directors and organization of business operations of the company. Statue or general meeting decisions may regulate his powers and duties further in detail.

*Non-executive directors* cannot be employed by the company, but are engaged through a contract to provide services. In such a way, they exercise a specific controlling function regarding the executive directors.[287] Their most important power is not only to supervise executive directors, but also to propose business strategy and to be in charge of supervision for its execution. Important power of non-executive directors is to give consent in the case of related party transactions and conflict of interest of executive directors with the company (*see* below under section C).

Finally, Serbian law includes a requirement that a public company must have at least one *independent director*, being the non-executive director if he fulfils criteria for independence in terms of connection to directors or the company and its controlling shareholder(s).[288] A detailed list of criteria of independence include that person cannot be connected to the director. Also, he is considered to be independent only if in the past two years he did not hold the position of an executive director, or employee of the company or an associated company, did not hold more than 20% of the subscribed capital in that or associated company or employed or engaged in other company receiving more than 20% of its yearly income within a period of two years. Independence also includes that a person did not receive any payments or had claims from this person in value which is more than 20% of their yearly income during this period, in the past two years from the company or connected persons. Finally, independence excludes persons performing auditing in the company in the last two years.

A public company must have at least one independent director who must fulfil criteria of independence during whole period of his mandate. In cases when these conditions are not fulfilled, the director continues his mandate as a non-executive or executive director, or (if that is not possible) his mandate terminates. Remaining directors must co-opt other independent directors or call for an extraordinary meeting within thirty days since they found out about vacancy so that the general meeting can appoint another independent director.

Board of directors must choose one among them to be *chair of the board* with possibility to be removed at any time and without good cause. This person is registered in the Business Register. According to legal discussions as to whether a chairman of the board of directors' may and should be at the same time the managing director (chief executive officer – CEO), Serbian law took explicit position only for public joint-stock companies in preventing that chairman of the board of

287. Articles 390–391 LCC 2011.

288. Article 392 LCC 2011. *See* in detail: Dragan Radonjić, 'Nezavisni direktori' (Independent directors), *Pravo i privreda (Law and Economy)* 5-8/2004, 58ff; Vuk Radović, 'Put ka nezavisnom upravnom odboru' (Towards an independent board of directors), *Pravni život (Legal Life)* 12/2008, 73ff; Vuk Radović, 'Tri razloga neefikasnosti nezavisnih direktora' ('Three Reasons for Inefficiency of Independent Directors'), *Pravni život (Legal Life)* 11/2011, 99ff; Dragan Radonjić, 'Independent Directors and New Corporate Governance Paradigm – Pros and Cons of Independent Directors', *Annals of the Faculty of Law in Belgrade* 3/2012, 96ff (in English).

directors is also the executive director. His main powers include to call and chair the board of directors' meetings and to be responsible for minutes of the meetings. His task in public joint-stock company is to represent company towards executive directors according to the statute, general meeting decisions or unanimous decisions of the non-executive directors. In case of his absence, each director may call the board of directors' meeting when chair has to be elected among non-executive directors in a public joint-stock company, upon majority votes of directors present at the meeting.

### 4. Meetings and Decision-Making

*163.* Functioning of the board of directors may be regulated in the statute or through boards' rules of procedure which is obligatory for a public joint-stock company, according to law or the statute.

Board of directors of the public joint-stock company must have at least *four meetings* during each year upon summons of board's chairman or in case he fails to convene the board meeting upon directors' written request of any director personally. *Summons for the board's meeting* must be in writing and must include the agenda and all documents and information and must be communicated to all board members. Decisions made on the board in breach of provisions related to convening are null and void, except if all directors agree otherwise.

Meetings can be organized through the presence of board member in person, or in writing or electronically, by phone, fax or other audiovisual communication, if all directors agree and none objects in writing, and if otherwise is not prescribed in the statute or board rules of procedure. Absent members may vote in absentia in writing, when they are considered to be present for quorum determination. Board meetings can include not only board members but also other persons, including committee members or other persons if necessary. Auditors must be present at the meetings when financial reports are discussed.

*Quorum* for the meeting is set at the absolute majority of board members or higher majority prescribed in the statute or rules of procedure. Decisions are made by a simple *majority* of board members present at the meeting, if no higher majority is prescribed in the statute or rules of procedure. In the case of vote tie, the chairman of the board has a casting vote, if not otherwise prescribed in the statute or rules of procedure.

Meetings must be followed by *minutes*, including the most important information of the meeting (members present, agenda discussion and decisions made, including dissenting opinions of the board members). Minutes must be signed by the board chairman and communicated to all directors.

5. Remuneration

*164.* Every director is entitled to remuneration, including payment upon employment or provision of services contract.[289] He may also be entitled to a share-based incentive scheme, including share options, of that or another associated company.

Remuneration, including type and the amount or method of their determination, is to be determined in the statute or by a general meeting decision. Remuneration including share-based scheme may be an incentive with regard to business results, although profit distribution is not allowed.

Remuneration *in public joint-stock companies* is regulated by a new chapter in the last amendments of the Law of Commercial Companies.[290] Remuneration policy is obligatory in the case of two-tier management system. It has to be clear and understandable and must contain all relevant information. Remuneration report must be made on annual basis and must include exact, full and clear report on all remuneration made or stipulated by that company or other company from the same group of companies to each board of directors' member (present and past members included) in the last business year before report is made. The report has to be drafted by the board of directors or remuneration committee, if there is any. All relevant information on the board of director members, but also all information on the remuneration, changes in relation to their proportion, business results and average payments in the last five business years; remuneration types, including shares and share options received or stipulated and their price and other conditions; information on the return of the remuneration, etc., must be included in the yearly report. Remuneration report must be audited by the person entitled to audit annual financial report and submitted to the annual meeting of shareholders with the remuneration report. Remuneration report must be disclosed on the Internet site of the company and must be publicly available free of charge during ten days after its disclosure.

Remuneration policy must be submitted by the board of directors to the general meeting of shareholders at least every four years, upon which general meeting must vote. Remuneration policy voted by the general meeting decision must be respected in the remuneration of directors. If no remuneration policy is adopted, remuneration can be made according to the already existing practices in this respect.

Disclosure of the remuneration for each *director of the non-public (closed) joint-stock company* must be made upon shareholders' request if he holds at least 5% of the company's shares. Disclosure can be made alternatively through free access to information on remuneration on the Internet site of the company. If information on the remuneration is classified as a business secret, shareholder is entitled to have access to information upon signing of the confidentiality agreement, and is considered as a breach of duty not to disclose business secrets, if information is disclosed to public or third persons.

---

289. Article 393 LCC 2011. *See* on this issue Vuk Radović, *Naknada članovima uprave akcionarskog društva* (*Remuneration of directors of joint-stock company*) Pravni fakultet Univerziteta u Beogradu, Beograd, 2011.

290. *See* Arts 463a, b and v LCC 2011.

6. Committees

*165.* Board of directors may form different committees in order to facilitate functioning of the board of directors and provide professional service. Committees can also be formed in order to prepare or execute certain board decisions. Members of committees may be directors or other persons, with specific knowledge or experience in certain matters, but are not allowed to decide on the issues within board of directors' powers.

A public joint-stock company must have an audit committee (which must include at least one auditor or other professional of knowledge and experience), and may also have nomination, remuneration or other committees prescribed in the statute, according to company's needs and business organization.

Committees must have at least three members among which one must be a non-executive director in a public joint-stock company, and at least majority of them must be non-executive directors in the audit (including chairman), nomination or remuneration committee in the public joint-stock company. Nomination and selection of members of public joint-stock companies must also be made by non-executive directors only.[291] Voting majority is the absolute majority of committee members with casting vote of the chairman in cases of vote tie.

*B. Power of Management and Representation*

*166.* Serbian law regulates competence of the board of directors generally, but also contains provisions explaining in detail management and representation powers within a board of directors. Competences set for the board of directors are related to the board as a whole – as a body responsible, without possibility of delegation of those powers to the executive directors.

General provision defines competence of the board of directors (as body responsible) including various issues with regard to management and control of the company.[292] The main issues include *management of the joint-stock company*, including management of business and internal organization, business strategy and planning as well as internal control. Further issues are related to *business record keeping and risk management*, with their responsibility for the accuracy of all business and financial records and accounts, accounting practice implementation and financial reporting. Important competence of a board of directors is related to the *general meeting, including various proposals*. It is within their competence to convene a general meeting and to determine minutes and decision proposals, to determine the amount of dividend as well as interim dividend payments, including method and date of payment, to execute general meeting's decisions and to inform the general meeting. Issues falling into competence of the board are also related to proposals to

291. Further on powers and organization of work of audit, appointment and remuneration committee *see* Arts 411–414 LCC 2011.
292. Article 398 LCC 2011.

the general meeting with regard to *board management*, remuneration policy, assignment of board members and other issues related to their work or assignment contracts. Board of directors is entitled to *determine the issue and market share price*, as well as issue price for other securities, as well as to *decide on the acquisition of own shares* exceptionally under prescribed conditions.

According to a strict division of powers between the general meeting and board of directors, it is explicitly provided that competence of the board of directors *may not be delegated* to executive directors or general meeting, except when delegation to the general meeting is decided upon board of directors' decision, unless otherwise provided for in the statute.

As already explained under section A.3, all executive directors have the *power of (day-to-day) management and representation*, although representation may be limited in the statute among them to one or more executive directors. For all management and representation powers, all executive directors are authorized to act collectively, unless otherwise provided for in the statute or general meeting decisions. Legal acts executed or performed towards one executive director are considered to have the effect on the company itself.

Power of representation may be limited in the statute, general meetings or board of directors' decision to all or some of executive directors with additional signature requirement of the procurator (holding power of attorney and registered in the Business Register with legal scope of representation powers). It is within the power of board of directors to give authorization to a procurator to have the power of attorney, or to take it away.

### *C. Duties of Directors to the Company*

*167.* Under the Law of Commercial Companies there are several persons having duties *towards a company*. Therefore, Serbian law is clear in setting the principle according to which all duties are owed to a company, and not directly to other stakeholders, including shareholders, creditors or other interested persons. Even in the case of controlling shareholders duties are owed to the company only, and not to other shareholders. Although certain persons owe their duties to the company, the interest of the company itself is not explicitly provided for, but it is considered to be rather particular and not in correlation with any other individual interest. It is usually conceived as a specific interest comprising all individual interests in their totality.[293]

293. *See* further on this issue Mirko Vasiljević, *Company Law (Law of commercial companies of Serbia and the EU)*, Pravni fakultet Univerziteta u Beogradu, Beograd, 2006, 132ff; Miodrag Mićović, 'The Interest of a Commercial Company and the Liability of its Management in Serbia', *Annals of the Faculty of Law in Belgrade* 3/2012, 136ff (in English); *See* further on purpose of a company and basic theories on representation of different interests: Mirko Vasiljević, "Bermudski trougao' kompanijskog, stečajnog i prava preuzimanja akcionarskih društava (tri subjekta zaštite: kompanija, poverilac i akcionar' ("The Bermuda Triangle' of Company, Bankruptcy and Law on Takeover of Joint Stock Companies (Three Subjects of Protection: Company, Creditor and Shareholder'), *Strani pravni život (Foreign Legal Life)* 2/2021, 194ff; Vuk Radović, 'Cilj privrednog

## 1. By Whom Duties Are Owed

*168.* In the case of a joint-stock company, relevant persons owing duties to the company are set as following: shareholders having significant shareholdings, or controlling shareholders, directors, members of the supervisory board, legal representatives and procurists, as well as the liquidator. Other persons may owe duties if it is prescribed in the articles of incorporation or in the statute.[294]

A shareholder holding more than 25% of the voting rights in a company by himself, or acting in concert with another person is considered to be a *shareholder having significant shareholdings*. *Majority shareholdings* exist if a person (by himself or acting in concert with other persons) holds more than 50% of the voting rights. *Control* is considered to be the right or possibility of a person (by himself or together with other persons acting in concert) to control business activities of another person either through shareholdings or by contract or right to appoint the majority of directors or members of the supervisory board.[295] It is presumed that a person has control in the case of majority shareholdings.[296]

## 2. Duty of Care

*169.* General limits concerning the conduct of a director (including members of the supervisory board, legal representatives, procures and liquidator) define several duties, among which the most important one is duty of care.[297] This duty implies acting within limits of law and other provisions according to a certain standard of conduct. Duty of care requires a person to perform activities in good faith. Also, he must act with care of a diligent manager. This standard implies behaviour of a diligent and conscientious person with knowledge, experience and skills which can be expected of a person performing these kinds of activities (objective standard) but also include his personal abilities, knowledge and experience (standard with regard

---

društva sa osvrtom na aktuelnu pandemiju' ('Corporate Purpose with a Look on COVID-19 Pandemic'), *Revija Kopaoničke škole prirodnog prava (Review of the Kopaonik School of Natural Law)* 2/2021, 25ff; Borko Mihajlović, 'Cilj poslovanja privrednog društva – samo sticanje dobiti ili još nešto' ('The Purpose of a Company's Business Operation – Gaining Profits or Anything Else'), *Pravo i privreda (Law and Economy)* 4–6/2017, 140ff.

294. Because of the similar regime irrespective of the one or two-tier system of management, here we will discuss taking care of both of them, and pointing out difference between the regime of duties in one-tier system to two-tier system, if any.

295. Regarding the control and acting in concert in detail *see*: Tatjana Jevremović Petrović, *Grupe privrednih društava (Groups of Companies)*, Pravni fakultet Univerziteta u Beogradu, Beograd, 2014, 80ff; regarding the acting in concert *see also*: Vuk Radović, 'Nejedinstven pojam zajedničkog delovanja' ('Non-uniform Concept of Acting in Concert'), in: Vuk Radović (ed.), *Uskla ivanje poslovnog prava Srbije sa pravom Evropske unije (2019) (Harmonisation of Serbian Business Law with EU Law (2019))*, Pravni fakultet Univerziteta u Beogradu, Beograd, 2019, 27ff.

296. Persons who are considered to be connected persons include close relatives for natural persons or, in the case of legal persons involve different control mechanisms, especially shareholdings or management control. For complete list and details *see* Art. 62 LCC 2011. *See* Jelena Lepetić, 'Povezana lica u poslovnom pravu' ('Connected persons in business law'), *Pravo i privreda (Law and Economy)* 10-12/2015, 19ff.

297. Article 63 LCC 2011.

to specific person). Finally, a director (or other person owing duty of care) must believe to act in the best interest of the company. In the case of damage caused to the company, a director (or other person owing duty of care) is presumed to be responsible for the damage caused, but can prove that he acted according to this standard of conduct.[298]

## 3. Transactions with the Company

*170.* All persons owing duties to the company (not only directors and other persons involved in management but also shareholders having significant shareholdings and controlling shareholders) must inform the company, specifically the board of directors (supervisory board in case of a two-tier system), when transacting with the company if he or a connected person has a personal interest in the transaction.[299]

Transactions included are not only those between persons owing duties, and other connected persons, but also those with other interested persons if in existing or potential financial connection to the person owing duty (or other connected persons). Included are not only transactions, but also other legal acts, such as in front of the courts or other similar procedures, renunciation of rights, etc.

When there is a transaction with the company involving personal interest of the director owing duty, that person is due to inform the board of directors (supervisory board in case of a two-tier system) and gets approval by the simple majority of the board members (supervisory board in case of a two-tier system) who are not personally involved in the transaction. If there is a personal interest of the shareholder, decision is made by the simple majority of the board members (supervisory board in case of a two-tier system); or if the member of the supervisory board has personal interest – by a simple majority of the supervisory board members who are not personally involved in the transaction. If there is no necessary quorum or otherwise decision cannot be made, residual decision is on the simple majority of all shareholders present at the meeting and not personally involved in the transaction.

If a transaction is approved by the board, it will inform shareholders at the next general meeting, including all information and details on the transaction and personal interest involved. Joint-stock company must disclose all information on the transaction and approval on its Internet site, or the Internet site of the Business Register. Disclosure of all transactions must be also made within the annual financial reports and it must include all relevant information.

Exceptions to the approval requirement are applicable in the case of personal interest of a single shareholder or all shareholders of the joint-stock company, in the case of the preferential right of subscription of shares, or acquisition of own shares

---

298. Further on this issue and in relation to the business judgment rule *see* in detail: Mirko Vasiljević, 'Civil law and business judgment rule', *Annals of the Faculty of Law in Belgrade* 3/2012, 7ff (in English).

299. Articles 67-68 LCC 2011. *See*: Borko Mihajlović, 'Promene u pravnom regulisanju dužnosti prijavljivanja poslova i radnji u kojima postoji lični interes' ('Changes in Legal Regulation of the Duty to Report Businesses and Acts in which Exists Personal Interest'), *Glasnik prava (Herald of Law)* 2/2018, 53ff.

by the company if made according to law. Also, when entering into a transaction or undertaking a legal action if the value of the subject matter of that transaction or legal action is less than 10% of the accounting value of the total assets of the company shown in the last annual balance sheet; when a member of a company that owns significant participation in the company's share capital or a controlling member of a company is the Republic of Serbia, an autonomous province or a local government unit; as well as when concluding an employment or some other appropriate contract to hire a director, i.e., member of the supervisory board. Prior to approving the conclusion of the legal transaction or undertaking of the legal action, in the event that the value of the subject of the transaction or legal action is 10% or more than 10% of the carrying amount of the total assets of the company shown in the last annual balance sheet, the competent body which received the notification shall appoint a person which shall make an assessment of the fair value of the objects or rights that are the subject matter of the legal transaction or legal action, and make a report about it. This report, alongside the notification, is an integral part of the decision whereby transactions are approved. The fair value of objects or rights shall be determined in accordance with International Financial Reporting Standard 13 - Fair Value Measurement.

In cases when approval was not granted or a competent body was not adequately informed on all relevant issues of the transaction, including also when transaction was not made under fair conditions, company may bring legal suit and ask for annulment of the transaction, including claims for damage from the person acting in breach of his duties. Jointly and severally liable to the company are: a person owing duty, as well as connected persons, if involved in transaction as contracting (or beneficial) party, or third person when he was aware or must have been aware that personal interest existed in the transaction. Upon court's judgment that a person was acting in breach of duties, that person is disqualified from acting as a director, procurist or representative of the company for a period of twelve months.[300] Disqualification must be registered in the Central disqualification register, which is held by the Business Register Agency.

A person owing duty can prove that there was no breach of his duty, including approval requirement if transaction was in the company's interest or when there was no personal interest while transacting with third parties.

## 4. Conflicts of Interest

*171.* Persons owing duties to the company (including controlling or significant shareholders) must act in the interest of the company when their interest or interest

300. *See*: Borko Mihajlović, 'Diskvalifikacija člana uprave privrednog društva: nova sankcija za povredu dužnosti prijavljivanja poslova i radnji sa ličnim interesom u srpskom pravu' ('Disqualification of the Company's Member of Management: New Sanction for the Breach of Duty to report Businesses and Acts in Which Exists Personal Interest in Serbian Law'), *Glasnik prava (Herald of Law)*, 2/2019, 81ff. Arguments in favour of accepting directors' disqualification in general *see*: Vuk Radović, 'O opravdanosti prihvatanja instituta diskvalifikacije direktora' ('Necessity of Accepting Directors' Disqualification'), *Pravo i privreda (Law and Economy)*, 1–3/2010, 26ff.

of other connected persons exists.[301] This is particularly the case when he used company's property, private information or corporate opportunities (irrespective of the fact whether the company could have used those opportunities) or when he abused his position within the company.

As an exception, a person owing duty towards the company may use property, private information or corporate opportunities if that was approved before or after the conflict arises by the board of directors (supervisory board in case of a two-tier system) as in the case of transactions with the company, including exceptions for the approval (*see* above under §3).

If there was a breach of duty of loyalty, a company may bring a legal suit against a person owing duty (as well as connected persons) and claim damages or transfer of any benefits received by the person owing duties or other connected persons to the company.

### 5. Duty of Confidentiality Regarding Business Secrets

*172.* All persons owing duties towards the company, as well as employees, have a duty of confidentiality with regard to corporate business secrets.[302] They must keep that information secret not only during employment or position of a person owing duty but also for two years afterwards. Nevertheless, important prolongation of this duty is possible in the articles of incorporation, statute, company's decision or upon contract up to five years.

Business secret is considered to be information whose publication to a third party could induce damage to the company, or having economic value because of its confidentiality and could benefit third parties if used or communicated. It encompasses different production, technical, technological, financial, commercial data, study, research, or document, formula, drawing, object, method, procedure, information or internal instruction, etc. Business secrets must be protected by the company in order to have confidentiality status, and be declared to be confidential information, or if this status of confidentiality is granted by the law or other act.

There is no breach of duty of confidentiality if communication is required by the law or necessary for carrying out business or to protect company's interests, or made to authorities or public in the case of a criminal act.

In case of a breach of the duty of confidentiality, the company may bring a legal suit against a person owing duty and claim damages or exclusion of the shareholder (if that is the case).

301. *See* in detail on this and other duties in Serbian law: Jelena Lepetić, *Kompanijskopravni režim sukoba interesa: Dužnost lojalnosti (Conflict of Interest in Company Law: Duty of Loyalty)*, Pravni fakultet Univerziteta u Beogradu, Beograd, 2015.

302. Articles 72–74 LCC 2011.

## 6. Duty Not to Compete with the Company

*173.* All persons owing duties to the company (except liquidator) are not allowed to have the same or any position of a person owing duties, towards a joint-stock company performing the same or similar business activities – competitor company; or be employed or engaged, founder or member in that company. Other persons can be also subjected to this duty by provisions in the statute, or may owe this duty for a certain time after holding a position in the company, but no longer than two years. Also, the statute can exclude certain activities, method or place of their performance as those not representing breach of duty.

When there is a duty not to compete with the company, there is a possibility of approval upon the same requirements as in the case of transactions with the company (*see* above under §3).

In the case of a breach of duty not to compete, the company may bring a legal suit against a person owing duty and claim damages, transfer of all benefits gained by the person owing duties as a consequence of breach of duty, or exclusion of the shareholder (if that is the case).

## 7. Individual Suits

*174.* In the case of a breach of duties owed by persons owing duties, every shareholder is entitled to bring a legal suit against him in order to claim damages caused to him personally by the breach of duties. The suit can be brought during six months since the shareholder found out about breach of duty, but no longer than five years since the breach was made.[303]

## 8. Derivative Suits

*175.* Serbian law also allows for one or more shareholders to bring a legal suit against person owing duties or other persons prescribed by law (connected or third person in connection to transaction) in their name and on behalf of the company. Shareholders are entitled to bring a legal suit if holding at least 5% of the subscribed capital in time of bringing the legal suit, irrespective of the time when the breach of duty took place.

The Law on Commercial Companies does not extend the right of so-called multiple derivative suits with the possibility of shareholders to bring suit for breach of duty not in his but other connected company (companies).

In order to bring derivative suit, shareholders must first address the company in writing and claim that the company brings legal suit against persons owing duties (or other persons). If the company fails to bring a legal suit within the time limit of

303. *See* in detail and critically on this: Jelena Lepetić, 'Pravo akcionara na individualnu tužbu' (Shareholders' personal action), *Annals of the Faculty of Law in Belgrade* 1/2014, 187ff; Add: Mirko Vasiljević, 'Privredna društva i privredno sudstvo' ('Commercial Companies and Commercial Courts'), *Pravo i privreda (Law and Economy)* 3/2020, 19–24.

thirty days from the shareholders' request, shareholders are allowed to bring a legal suit in their own name but on behalf of the company.

Time limits for this legal suit are the same as in the case of the individual suit (*see* above under §7). Nevertheless, the importance of derivative suits, as an expression of minority shareholders' right, is diminished in Serbian law by the high costs of a legal suit, falling upon minority shareholders with relatively small chances of success.

### *D. Liability of Directors*

*176.* In Serbian law, there is only one explicit provision for civil responsibility of members of company bodies, including members of the board of directors, as well as executive or supervisory board members. This liability exists for directors towards the *company* (but not creditors with whom they do not stand in a direct relationship) for all damages made by their decision-making in contravention of legal and statutory provisions or general meeting decisions.[304] Nevertheless, this responsibility will not be established if the director acted in accordance with a general meeting decision. Previous Law on Commercial Companies contained detailed provisions on responsibility, among which special cases of responsibility, including unlawful payments, distribution of dividends, purchase of company's own shares, etc., were recognized, which is not the case anymore.[305]

The liability exists for all board members voting for the board's decision, if damage was caused by this decision. It is presumed that board members voted for a decision in the case when sustained or absent, except when an absent member opposed the decision in writing. Company can claim damages only within a time limit of three years since damage was caused. This right cannot be renounced, except on the basis of a general meeting decision taken by a three-fourths majority of shareholders present, but not if opposed by shareholders holding at least 10% of the capital subscribed.

In comparison to the regime of directors' liability in a limited liability company, including provision on special responsibility for unlawful payments, as well as directly to creditors in case of a breach of duty of information of the general meeting which decided on profit distribution, liability regime for directors of a joint-stock company is general and relates to acts against the law, statute or decisions of the general meeting.

Since the directors' liability for damage relates to management fault, which is an issue of opportunity more than legality – the discussion is still ongoing as to its

---

304. *See* Art. 415 LCC 2011. *See* in detail: Tatjana Jevremović Petrović, 'Directors' Responsibility to Creditors in Company Law', *Annals of the Faculty of Law in Belgrade* 3/2012, 149ff (in English); Nataša Petrović Tomić, 'Odgovornost direktora za štetu po Zakonu o privrednim društvima' ('Liability of Directors for Damage According to Companies Act'), *Pravo i privreda (Law and Economy)* 4–6/2014, 130ff.

305. *See* Art. 328 of LCC 2004.

genuine nature (contractual or extra-contractual liability). This is a rather mild and inefficient sanction, compared to criminal liability, prescribed by the Criminal Code.[306]

## III. Management and Control: Two-Tier System

*177.* In the case of a two-tier system, company must have one or more executive directors (board of executive directors) and supervisory board.[307]

### *A. Supervisory Board*

*178.* Supervisory board is an obligatory body in the case of a two-tier system. It must have at least three members; there must be an odd number of members, although their exact number is defined in the statute. One person cannot be a member of the supervisory board and executive director or procurist. Every member of the supervisory board must be registered in the Business Register.

#### 1. General Conditions

*179.* General conditions for a person to be appointed as a member of supervisory board are the same as those prescribed for the appointment of directors in a one-tier system (*see* above under II.A.1).

#### 2. Appointment

*180.* General meeting appoints members of the supervisory board of the company. Supervisory board members' nomination can be made by other members of the supervisory board, nomination committee (if there is any) or shareholders entitled to put an item on the general meetings' agenda.

For other issues regarding co-optation, mandate, termination, resignation and removal, the same provisions apply as for directors in a one-tier system (*see* above under II.A.2).

---

306. *See* in particular Arts 234–241 of the Criminal Code (Krivični zakonik) *Official Gazette of Republic of Serbia (Službeni glasnik Republike Srbije),* 85/2005 and further amended; available in English at: https://www.mpravde.gov.rs/files/Criminal%20%20%20Code_2019.pdf (accessed 24 Mar. 202 2).
307. Arts 417–447 LCC 2011.

3. Composition of the Board of Directors

*181.* A public joint-stock company must have at least one member of the supervisory board who fulfils criteria for independence. For the position, conditions and other provisions related to the independent member of the supervisory board same provisions apply as for an independent director (*see* above under II.A.3).

4. Meetings and Decision-Making

*182.* All issues with regard to supervisory board meetings, resolutions, chairman, minutes, etc., as well as committees, are the same as in the case of board of directors in a one-tier system (*see* above under II.A.4 and 6).

5. Remuneration

*183.* All provisions regarding remuneration are the same as for directors in a one-tier system (*see* above under II.A.5).

*B. Executive (Board of) Director(s)*

*184.* In the case of a two-tier system, the company must have one or more executive directors and a supervisory board. If there are three or more executive directors, they form the executive board of directors, which is obligatory with at least three members in a public joint-stock company. The number of executive directors is left to be defined in the statute.

1. General Conditions

*185.* General conditions for a person to be appointed executive director are the same as those prescribed for the appointment of directors in a one-tier system (*see* above under II.A.1.).

2. Appointment

*186.* Supervisory board appoints executive directors of the company. *Executive directors' nomination* can be made by nomination committee (if there is any) or any member of the supervisory board. Once appointed, all executive directors must be registered in the Registration Agency. Issues related to the mandate of executive directors, including termination, resignation and removal, are the same as for directors in a one-tier system, although removal is made by the supervisory board (*see* above under II.A.2.).

## 3. Composition of the Executive Board of Directors

*187.* If there are three or more executive directors, they form the executive board of directors. One of the executive directors who has the power of representation may be appointed to be *managing director (chief executive officer)*.[308] There must be a managing director if there is an executive board of directors. Appointment is made by the supervisory board upon criteria or specific conditions for appointment which may be introduced by the statute or general meeting or supervisory board decision. Powers of the managing director include coordination of executive directors and organization of business operations of the company, including chair in the case of executive board meetings and agenda proposals. If absent, all other executive directors may convene an executive board meeting and appoint a chairman among them with a majority of votes of directors present at the meeting. Statue or general meeting or supervisory board decisions may regulate his powers and duties further in detail.

## 4. Meetings and Decision-Making

*188.* Executive board of directors is independent in the management of company's affairs. It can decide and act without meetings, but they can be convened either if needed or in the case when the managing director decides it is necessary. If there is a meeting, all decisions are adopted by the majority of executive director's votes, with the casting vote of the managing director. Other issues are the same as in the case of board of directors' meetings in a one-tier system (*see* above under II.A.4.).

## 5. Remuneration

*189.* All provisions regarding remuneration are the same as for directors in a one-tier system (*see* above under II.A.5.). Specific for this case is that remuneration may be determined not only in the statute or general meeting decision but also by a supervisory board decision.

## *C. Power of Management and Representation*

*190.* Competence of the board of directors in a one-tier system is in a two-tier system basically divided between two boards, so that certain issues mainly dealing with management and control in general belong to the supervisory board, while other issues, especially with regard to internal organization, are entrusted to the executive (board of) directors.

*Competence of the supervisory board* includes issues related to *business strategy and planning* and *internal control*, including *control of executive directors*. Further

308. Article 423 LCC 2011.

issues are related to *accounting policy* and *risk management*, with their responsibility for financial report and business report making and submission to the general meeting. Important issues related to *general meeting, including various proposals*, are also within the competence of the supervisory board, including to convene the general meeting and to determine minutes and decision proposals, to determine the amount of interim dividend payments when authorized. Issues falling into the competence of the supervisory board are also related to the proposals to the general meeting with regard to *executive board management*, their employment contracts and conditions for employment; and proposed policy for their remuneration if not stipulated by the statute. Supervisory board is entitled *to determine the issue and market share price*, as well as issue price for other securities, as well as to *decide on the acquisition of own shares* exceptionally under prescribed conditions. Finally, it approves acts of executive directors when prescribed and acts in various issues and decides upon the law, statute or general meeting authorization and gives approval in the case of related party transactions or conflict of interest of executive director(s) with the company.

According to the strict division of powers between company's bodies, it is explicitly provided that the competence of the supervisory board *may not be delegated* to executive directors or general meeting, except when delegation to the general meeting is decided in a supervisory board decision, unless otherwise provided for in the statute.

Following issues fall within the *competence of the executive directors*: *management of the joint-stock company*, including management of business and internal organization, issues related to *business record keeping and* responsibility for the accuracy of business and financial records and accounts. Important powers of executive (board of) directors are related to the *preparation of the general meeting,* including proposals to the supervisory board. It is within their power to determine the amount of dividend payments, including method and date of payment, to execute general meeting's decisions and to perform other activities entrusted to them by the law, statute, general meeting or supervisory board decisions. According to division of powers between supervisory and executive board of directors, it is explicitly provided that powers of the executive (board of) directors *may not be delegated* to the supervisory board.

Executive directors have the same powers of management and representation as executive directors – members of the board of directors in a one-tier system (*see* above under II.B.).[309] Still, certain powers are restricted by the supervisory board approval (except where otherwise prescribed by the statute or supervisory board decision for certain acts or acts above certain value) including acquisition, disposal or burden on stakes and shares in other companies or of immovable property; borrowing and lending agreements, security bonds on company's assets, guarantees or warranties for third-party obligations, as well as other acts prescribed to be within supervisory board powers, or for which the statute or supervisory board require approval.

309. Article 422 LCC 2011.

*Powers of management* of executive directors are restricted by necessary approval of the supervisory board or general meeting if prescribed by the law, statute, general meeting or supervisory board decisions.

### *D. Duties of Directors to the Company*

*191.* For duties of executive directors and members of the supervisory board, *see* above under the general regime of duties owed to the company (this chapter §5.II.C.).

### *E. Liability of Directors*

*192.* The same rule of directors' liability for the members of the board of directors in a one-tier system is applicable to executive directors and members of the supervisory board in a two-tier system.[310]

## IV. Company's Secretary

*193.* A joint-stock company may have a secretary, if provided by the statute. Secretary may be employed by the company and is appointed by the board of directors or supervisory board in a two-tier system.[311] His mandate is for four years, if not prescribed otherwise in the statute or appointment decision.

Competence of the secretary is prescribed by the law but may be otherwise provided for in the statute or appointment decision. The most important competences of the secretary include preparation of general meetings and responsibility to draw up minutes from the meeting, preparation of the board of directors, executive board of directors, or supervisory board meetings. He is in charge of all documents and minutes and must keep them during time limits and in place provided by the law. Secretary has the responsibility to communicate with the shareholders and provide them with all necessary documents and acts according to law.

## V. Internal Audit

*194.* The Law on Commercial Companies prescribes obligation of a joint-stock company to provide in internal acts the organization and management of business activities, including internal control. Nevertheless, a public joint-stock company must have at least one person responsible for internal control who fulfils criteria to be an internal auditor. The person in charge of internal control cannot be engaged in other positions, must be employed, while other professional and competence requirements may be introduced by the statute or other internal acts of the public

---

310. *See* Arts 430 and 447 LCC 2011.
311. Articles 448–450 LCC 2011.

joint-stock company. He cannot be a director or member of the supervisory board in the case of a two-tier system. His appointment is made by the board of directors or supervisory board in case of a two-tier system, upon audit committee proposals.

Competence of the internal audit is particularly related to control of business activities, according to law, statute and other acts, supervision of accounting policy and with regard to financial reporting, control of risk management and implementation of the corporate governance code, etc.[312]

## VI. External Audit

*195.* External audit for a joint-stock company is prescribed by the Law on Commercial Companies and the Law of Capital Markets for public companies, but the most important provisions are in the Law on Auditing and the Law on Accounting.[313]

### *A. Principles of Accounting and Bookkeeping*

*196.* General principles defining accounting and bookkeeping are prescribed by the Law on Accounting. International Standards of financial reporting form an integral part of the law when prescribed upon official translation by the Ministry of Finance. Large companies, a parent company preparing consolidated accounts and public companies must prepare their financial reports in application of the IFRS.

All legal persons (companies included) are divided into micro, small, medium and large legal persons according to the number of employees, yearly income and assets value.[314] They have an obligation of keeping business records and books.[315]Also, their obligation is to prepare annual financial reports for each business year (equivalent to calendar year), consolidated accounts for the legal persons having control (parent company) over one or more dependant legal persons, as well as other reports when prescribed by law.[316] Finally, there is an obligation of preparation of the yearly business reports, including corporate governance report; yearly consolidated business reports for parent company.[317] There are also provisions on non-financial reporting, as well as consolidated non-financial reporting.[318] Financial

312. For details on the internal audit competence *see* in particular Art. 452 LCC 2011.
313. For details with regard to these Laws *see* General Introduction s. 4. II. A.
314. While *micro companies* do not exceed at least two of the following criteria: average number of employees of ten; business income of EUR 700,000 and average assets value up to EUR 350,000. Small companies have at least two criteria above micro companies, but not above two criteria in the average number of employees of fifty, EUR 8,000,000 income and average assets value up to EUR 4,000,000. Medium-size companies have at least two criteria above small companies, but not above two criteria in the average number of employees of 250, EUR 40,000,000 income and average assets value up to EUR 20,000,000. Large companies have at least two criteria above medium-size companies. *See* Art. 6 Law on accounting.
315. *See* Arts 8ff Law on accounting.
316. *See* Arts 29ff Law on accounting.
317. Articles 34ff Law on accounting.
318. *See* Arts 37ff Law on accounting

reports must be submitted to the Registration Agency by 31 March the latest (30 April for consolidated accounts) for publication in the Public Register of financial reports of the Registration Agency, accessible on its Internet site.

### *B. Auditing*

#### 1. In General

*197.* Annual financial reports of large and medium-size companies, public companies (independent of the size) and other companies whose yearly income is above EUR 4,400,000, including consolidated annual accounts for parent company must be audited according to Law on auditing.[319] In addition to that, the Law on Capital Markets has additional financial reporting requirements. According to them (as explained before in this chapter §4.V.A.2), financial results, including an independent expert report, need to be disclosed *annually* for all public companies, *half-yearly* for all public companies whose securities are traded on the regulated market and *quarterly* for the companies whose securities are traded and quoted on the listing of the regulated market during the period of listing.[320] Auditing is in other cases voluntary.

#### 2. Auditors

*198.* Serbian law allows that auditors can be organized as an *Audit Company – company performing audit* (under general provisions of the Law on Commercial Companies) and employing at least one full-time certified registered auditor; or as *independent auditor* (certified registered auditor) registered as sole proprietor.[321] While *registered auditor* is a natural person who passed required exams, he is a *certified registered auditor* only upon getting a valid licence – certificate (and during its validity) which entitles him to perform audits. Auditing of annual and consolidated accounts for a large-scale company must be performed by an Audit Company with at least four certified registered auditors employed by the company.

Finally, the law recognizes certified internal auditors to perform internal audits in the company (*see* above under section V).

#### 3. Appointment

*199.* Auditors are appointed by a general meeting decision or decision of other competent body by at the latest the 30 September for each business year. The

319. *See* Art. 26 Law on auditing. *See also* Art. 453 LCC 2011.
320. *See* Arts 50–56 Law on Capital Markets.
321. *See* in detail Art. 4 Law on auditing. For other conditions for audit company *see* Arts 12ff Law on auditing.

appointed auditor (auditor company) must conclude an audit contract in writing, including the most important information on the auditors and audit to be performed.[322]

The auditor must be independent from the company. Therefore, it is especially provided that auditor company, certified registered auditors and physical persons in a position to influence, directly or indirectly on the auditing process, must be independent from the company where auditing is performed and must not participate in the decision-making in the company where auditing is performed. Auditing company and certified registered auditors must take all reasonable steps in order to provide their independence while performing auditing, including existing or possible conflict of interest, business or other direct or indirect relationship. Other provisions on independence also insist on economic, material and other independence, as well as all forms of physical or psychological treats, or other treatments which could endanger independence of the auditor.[323] LCC also provides that the auditor must submit to the audit committee of a public company all details with regard to his independence.[324]

A certified registered auditor may not perform audits in a company where it is a shareholder or has important financial influence in the company or other important interest in the connected person to the company; if a director, or member of the company's management or supervision bodies, procurist or representative of that company or legal person with a significant interest in the company; if director, or member of the company's management or supervision bodies, procurist or representative is his relative or spouse. Also, certified registered auditors may not provide auditing services for that year or the year for which auditing is performed if he or other connected person(s) already provided auditing services, including bookkeeping and preparation of financial reports, evaluation of the property or capital; represented the company in financial, accounting or tax matters, internal control or provided other services which could imperil his independence. Similar conditions apply to auditing company.[325]

Law on Auditing has a general provision to prevent the same certified registered auditor in the Audit Company from performing an audit after ten consecutive years in the same company if the company is of the public interest, after which he may again perform audits after four years. There is also obligation for an Audit Company to change a certified registered auditor in auditing of other companies where auditing is performed by the same registered auditor for a maximum of seven consecutive years, after which there must be a pause of at least three years.[326] Additionally, the Law on Capital Markets limits the period of auditing by one Audit Company in order to provide independent position of auditors engaged. Therefore, an Audit Company may perform audits of annual financial reports for five consecutive years in the same public company.[327]

---

322. *See* Arts 32–33 Law on Auditing for details.
323. *See* for details Art. 29 Law on Auditing. Additional provisions on the independence criteria for auditors are also provided for public companies. *See* Art. 54 Law on Capital Markets.
324. *See* Art. 453 LCC 2011.
325. Arts 44-45 Law on Auditing.
326. Article 50 Law on Auditing.
327. *See* Art. 54 Law on Capital Markets including all other relevant details.

4. Powers

*200.* Auditor has *information rights* with regard to the company, its documents, acts and information. Therefore, the company where audit is performed must submit all information, documents, reports, programmes and electronic data; provide all necessary information, allow access during business hours, and make available equipment and employees to the Audit Company. Also, the auditor has a right to be informed and be present at the general meetings of shareholders, and meetings of the board of directors or supervisory board in case of a two-tier system when deciding on financial reports.

His position is *safeguarded* when his opinion is not accepted by the company. Therefore, a company may not end the contract with the auditor (audit company) because of his opinion on financial reports he was in charge of audit.[328] Auditor has to be *compensated*, according to contract provisions.

5. Duties

*201.* Auditing must be carried out in the interest of all shareholders, with due diligence, competence, honesty, good faith and independence that could be expected from a professional. Auditors perform their duties under the requirements and provisions provided by the law and international standards and codes of conduct (including International Standards on Auditing (ISA) as well as IFAC Code of Ethics for Professional Accountants). His disqualification is possible, but it should be based on fault (lack of competence, violation of confidential information, etc.). The objective standard of conduct should include increased duty of care according to professional knowledge and experience (when required).

They must *keep as secret* (including not only certified registered auditor but also auditor) all information, data and facts gained or acknowledged during auditing.

Auditor must *draw a report* upon ISA, which must include financial reports which were audited, aim and scope of audit, including Standards applied, his opinion of whether financial reports represent true and fair view of the financial position of the company in accordance with the law, as well as whether they are in accordance with special laws (if that is the case). The auditor may have a positive opinion, opinion with reserve or negative opinion. As an exception, he can abstain from expressing an opinion due to an inability to take a position.[329] The auditor may have additional observations and remarks, and he will also express his opinion on the coordination of yearly business reports with financial reports for the same business year.

It is obligatory for the audit company, as well as for an independent auditor, to have *professional indemnity insurance* for damage caused to the company where auditing was performed and to third parties with regard to damage caused by breach of contract or breach of other standards of conduct.[330]

328. *See also* Art. 454 LCC 2011.
329. *See* in detail Art. 39 Law on Auditing.
330. *See* Art. 22 Law on Auditing.

### VII. Workers' Participation

*202.* As already mentioned in the General Introduction §6, the Law on Commercial Companies has no particular provisions with regard to employees' participation in company's management and control. The controversial nature of labour position was seen from the perspective of the concept of labour involvement in company's affairs in the past decades of socialist Yugoslavia. Therefore, after the period of overemphasizing the concept of labour in corporate management through the self-management model, which produced an evident negative effect in the sphere of working discipline and economic effectiveness, new commercial legislation in Serbia has chosen to leave the position of labour to the Labour Law and limit employees' rights to information and consultation.

Under the Law on Labour, employees are granted with certain rights, including right to associate with labour unions (syndicates) while emphasizing their right to be informed.[331] There are several other possibilities of employees' involvement in the companies' affairs, including their involvement in the adoption and application of collective agreements. Law on Labour specially introduces protection of employees in the case of statutory changes, and adopts the concept of acquired rights and continuation of contracts.[332]

Finally, the most important provisions for the involvement of employees in the management of the company are provided by the possibility for employees to be organized as a separate body – employees' council in the case of a company having more than fifty employees. In the case where this body is organized, its main task is to promote consultation rights and to be involved in decision-making in the case of decisions affecting employees' rights.[333] Nevertheless, it must be emphasized that these provisions are optional and not obligatory in nature.

## §6. Liquidation of the Company

*203.* The dissolution of a solvent commercial company is known as voluntary winding-up, regular winding-up or just–winding-up (liquidation).[334] Since winding-up as an institute is connected to solvent commercial companies, it is logical that it is regulated by laws governing the status of commercial companies, beginning with their setting up and up to the termination as solvent. In our case, this is the Law on

---

331. General provisions on employees' rights are particularly regulated under the Art. 13 Law on labour. Further rights concerning labour unions and their information rights are stipulated in the Arts 206ff Law on labour.

332. *See* Art. 147–151 Law on labour. More on participation of employees: Vuk Radović, 'Participacija zaposlenih u upravljanju privrednim društvom – aspekti korporativnog upravljanja' ('Employee Participation on Companies' Boards – Corporate Governance Aspects'), *Pravo i privreda (Law and Economy)* 46/2016, 98ff; Ljubinka Kovačević, 'Participacija zaposlenih u odlučivanju o restrukturiranju kompanija' ('Employees' Participation in the Decision-Making in the Event of Restructuring of Companies'), *Pravo i privreda (Law and Economy)* 4–6/2016, 651ff.

333. *See* Art. 205 Law on Labour.

334. Nataša Cvetićanin, 'Prav(n)i značaj i mesto dobrovoljne likvidacije u sistemu prestanka privrednih društava' ('Legal Significance and Position of Voluntary Liquidation within Companies' Cessation System'), *Pravo i privreda (Law and Economy)* 10–12/2014, 91ff.

Commercial Companies.[335] Insolvency is, however, regulated by special law – Law on Insolvency – and includes insolvency proceedings as well as reorganization.

## I. Liquidation upon Decision of the General Meeting (Voluntary Liquidation)

*204.* Under Serbian company law winding-up may be a result of a decision of its members – shareholders in a general meeting decision (*voluntary winding-up/liquidation*), while in the case specified by law, it may be carried out by competent authority (*compulsory winding-up/liquidation*). It should be noted that both voluntary and compulsory winding-up should relate to a solvent company. The essential difference between these two procedures is that voluntary winding-up requires a decision of the company's competent body (or members, depending on the form of the company) and is voluntary, whereas compulsory winding-up is initiated by the competent authority if certain conditions are met, and is, therefore compulsory. Also, Serbian company law has special provisions for winding-up without liquidation in the case of statutory change (*see* below under this chapter §7.I.).

### A. *Grounds for Winding-Up*

#### 1. Entering into a Liquidation

*205.* Liquidation can be carried out upon a general meeting decision, taken by a simple majority of shareholders present at the meeting.[336] Registration of the liquidation decision taken by the general meeting is obligatory, as well as publication of the fact that company is to be liquidated, after which *effects of the winding-up procedure* take place. These include denomination 'in liquidation' after registration of the liquidation decision in the Business Register. Also, all procedures (against or in favour of the company) continue, including possibility of execution of a judgment or other decision on the assets of the company. Liquidation procedure does not affect applicability of provisions related to the filing for the opening of the insolvency proceedings. Finally, a company cannot make dividend payments while in liquidation, or make any asset distribution before all creditors are completely satisfied.

#### 2. Winding-Up Procedure

*206.* Winding-up procedure starts after the *liquidation decision registration* in the Business Register, after which *publication of the fact that the company is to be liquidated* must be made.[337] This publication, which must be made within ninety

335. Arts 524–548 LCC 2011.
336. *See* Arts 525–528 LCC 2011.
337. *See* in detail Arts 533–535 LCC 2011.

days on the Business Register Internet website, is the first and the most important mechanism introduced to protect the company's creditors. It must contain information on the company and its registered seat address or correspondence address; it must call all creditors to submit their claims including notice that their claims must be precluded if submission of the claims is not made thirty days from the publication end date, at the latest. Apart from information made to all creditors, the law prescribes for the *individual notification* of creditors by the liquidator within fifteen days of winding-up procedure start, at the latest. Individual notification must contain the same information as a general publication of the liquidation procedure.

All creditors must submit their claims until the prescribed time date. Still, creditors holding writ of execution, or creditors with claims upon which legal action against the company was brought in front of the court, are considered to have already submitted their claims to the company. Also, all claims which do not antedate winding-up procedure start date must be compensated, but need not be submitted.

All claims received must be listed, including undisputed and disputed claims. If disputed, the company must communicate this to the creditor, who must file legal action within fifteen days and inform the company; or otherwise, his claim will be precluded.

Liquidation can be prevented if shareholders decide by a simple majority of shareholders present at the meeting to *bring to an end winding-up procedure* and continue regular business operations, but only if the company fulfilled all creditor claims, disputed as well as undisputed, and if all contracts with employees are still valid and liquidation remainder was not distributed to shareholders. General meeting decision must include appointment of the legal representative. In order to be a valid decision, it must also include liquidators' (joint – when there is more than one liquidator) statement that the company fulfilled all creditors' claims and that it did not make any payments to shareholders. The decision to bring an end to winding-up procedure must be registered with the Business Register.

### 3. Liquidation Financial and Other Reports

*207.* Since liquidation requires an exact evaluation and records of the assets and liabilities, the liquidator must draw up and submit an *opening liquidation balance sheet* to the general assembly for approval. He must submit this report within thirty days of winding-up procedure start at the latest, while the general assembly must approve this report in the next thirty days.[338]

The liquidator must also submit an *opening liquidation report*, including list of all claims submitted, undisputed and disputed, information on the assets of the company and whether they can cover all claims submitted, including disputed ones, acts to be performed in order to liquidate company, time when liquidation can be completed and other information important for liquidation. This report must be drawn up and submitted to the general assembly within a time limit of 90 to 150 days since winding-up procedure started, while a general meeting must approve this report in

338. *See* in detail Arts 536–537, 539–540 LCC 2011.

the next thirty days, after which registration must be made with the Business Register within fifteen days after its approval by the general meeting. Until registration, the liquidator is not allowed to make any payments to creditors or shareholders, except payments made in regular course of business.

If opening liquidation balance sheet or opening liquidation report shows that assets of the company are inadequate to fulfil all creditors' claims, the company is insolvent and the liquidator must file for the opening of insolvency proceedings within fifteen days and is not allowed to make any payments to creditors, except in the regular course of business.

During winding-up procedure, the liquidator must submit to the general meeting *yearly liquidation reports* including the most important information on the winding-up procedure six months after the end of each business year, at the latest. These reports must also be registered with the Business Register fifteen days after their approval of the general meeting.

The liquidator must submit a *closing liquidation balance sheet* and a *closing liquidation report*, as well as a *written statement* that all known creditors were informed according to law, and that all submitted claims were fulfilled. Finally, the liquidator must draw a *proposal of the decision on the distribution of the liquidation remainder*. All documents must be submitted and adopted in a general meeting decision, taken by a simple majority of shareholders present at the meeting. If not adopted by the general meeting, the decision can be substituted by a written report of the liquidator that documents submitted to the general meeting were not adopted within sixty days of submission being made.

### 4. Liquidator

*208.* Liquidator is *appointed* through a liquidation decision, taken at the general meeting. If liquidator is not appointed by a general meeting decision, all legal representatives with the power of representation upon their position are considered to be liquidators.[339]

The liquidator has *representation power* which, by his appointment, has been taken away from all other representatives of the company. Since there can be one or more liquidators, in this latter case, all of them have joint power of representation, unless otherwise provided by the appointment decision.

Once appointed, a liquidator can be *dismissed* by a decision of the general meeting taken by a simple majority of shareholders present at the meeting. The decision on liquidator dismissal must also include a new liquidator appointment. The liquidator may *resign* under the same conditions as a director in a joint-stock company (*see* above under this chapter §5.II.A.2.). Irrespective of the appointment method, the liquidator, including dismissal or resignation, must be registered with the Business Register.

The liquidator has important *powers*, including representation power and responsibility for the legal functioning of the company and its business activities. He is

339. *See* Arts 529–532, 542 LCC 2011. Đor e Perišić, 'Likvidacioni upravnik privrednog društva' ('Liquidator of the Company'), *Pravo i privreda (Law and Economy)* 1–3/2018, 124ff.

also empowered to perform current business activities which need to be completed; to prepare liquidation, including sale of company's assets, fulfilment of creditors' claims, as well as collecting payments or other performance obligations from company's creditors; and perform other activities necessary for liquidation.

The liquidator owes special *duties* towards the company, including duty of care and duty of loyalty (as already explained under this chapter §5.II.C.1). He is also liable to company's shareholders and creditors for damage made during his assignment within three years of company being deleted from the Business Register.

The liquidator has the right to be compensated for all expenses made during the winding-up procedure, as well as to be remunerated for his work. Remuneration and compensation are to be defined in a general meeting decision, or if that is not the case, by the court. For the remuneration and compensation payment, the liquidator has the position of a creditor of the company.

### *B. The Effect of Winding-Up: Liquidation*

*209.* 204.1. Winding-up procedure ends by the adoption of a general meeting decision, or if that is not the case, through a written report of the liquidator that documents submitted to the general meeting were not adopted within sixty days of submission (for these documents, *see* above under section I.A.3.). Liquidation is registered with the Business Register after which the company is dissolved, including loss of legal personality.[340]

Liquidation involves *distribution of the liquidation remainder* to the shareholders according to a distribution decision, taken at the general meeting upon liquidators' proposal. Liquidation remainder represents all assets available after all liabilities upon creditors' claims were fulfilled.

Distribution is made according to a general meeting decision, if not otherwise prescribed in the statute. Preferential shareholders have priority in distribution of remainder, after which distribution is made to all other shareholders holding ordinary shares in proportion of their shares to the total number of ordinary shares. All payments received must be returned by shareholders receiving them in good faith, if that is necessary to fulfil creditors' claims.

*Company's books and records*, including documents of the liquidated company, must be kept on the territory of the Republic of Serbia, and must be available to third parties. They are kept according to provisions on the archives and their storage, and are held by the person registered with the Business Register, while all interested persons have the right to inspect these documents (while covering expenses of this inspection by themselves). Interested persons are authorized to request from a court to appoint a liquidator if there are unresolved issues with regard to assets or other matters.

Shareholders have joint and several liability for all company's liabilities after the company is dissolved, but limited by the amount received from the liquidation remainder during three years of the company being deleted from the Business Register (dissolved).

---

340. *See* Arts 541–545 LCC 2011.

## II. Compulsory Liquidation

*210.* Liquidation can be initiated by a competent authority if certain conditions are met. In this case liquidation is compulsory.[341]

Compulsory liquidation is performed *by the registrar of the Registration Agency*, upon fulfilment of prescribed conditions. Different conditions upon which compulsory liquidation can be initiated deal with non-performance of various imperative requirements with regard to company, its business activities, members, representatives, etc. For the sake of clarity, they can be divided according to time limits after which compulsory liquidation is obligatory.

In that sense, compulsory liquidation is initiated if *during thirty days*: company *fails to change business activity* when sentenced to discontinue to pursue any or registered business activity or when necessary approval, licence or permission to perform certain activities was repealed; *company fails to change its registered address* if registration of address was refused; if *company was founded for a limited time* and does not make prolongation of that time or decide to be wound up in voluntary liquidation; if *liquidation was ordered by the court decision* upon request of shareholders holding at least 20% of the capital subscribed and if no voluntary liquidation was decided upon.

Also, compulsory liquidation is initiated if *during three months* the company *fails to register a new legal representative or liquidator* after the former one is deleted from the register. The same time frame is provided if *company fails to register partner or limited partner* in the partnership/limited partnership, when there is no minimum partners registered. Compulsory liquidation is also initiated if *during six months* the buyer of the company sold in the insolvency proceedings does not fulfil his obligation of payment of a minimum capital requirement.

Finally, compulsory liquidation will be initiated if the company *fails to submit financial reports* by the end of the previous business year for two consecutive years or fails to submit an *opening liquidation balance sheet or opening liquidation report*; when courts' decision was made upon *nullity* of articles of incorporation or registration was pronounced null and void; as well as in other cases prescribed by law. Such cases, mentioned in the Law on Commercial Companies, include situation when upon courts judgment company must change its registered seat or business name but fails to do so within thirty days. In these last two cases, but also when company has been sentenced to discontinue any activity and be liquidated; when liquidation was ordered by the court decision upon request of shareholders holding at least 20% of the capital subscribed; or must be liquidated upon courts' judgment on the nullity of articles of incorporation or when registration was pronounced null and void liquidation; as well as in the case when the company fails to submit its financial annual reports, it is considered that compulsory liquidation is unavoidable, because the *reasons for compulsory liquidation cannot be remedied.* Other reasons are considered to be remediable.

---

341. *See* Arts 546–548 LCC 2011. Ljubiša Dabić, 'Postupak prinudne likvidacije privrednih društava u Republici Srbiji' ('Procedure for the Compulsory Liquidation of Companies in the Republic of Serbia'), *Pravo i privreda (Law and Economy)* 4–6/2019, 62ff.

If reasons for compulsory liquidation cannot be remedied, registrar has to publish information on the Internet site of the Business Register that company has fulfilled conditions for compulsory liquidation which cannot be remedied. This information has to be published within thirty days. In other cases, if conditions for compulsory liquidation are remediable, the Business Register will publish on its Internet site information that company has fulfilled conditions for compulsory liquidation, while allowing additional ninety days to remedy reasons for compulsory liquidation and make all necessary changes through obligatory registration. After that, registrar announces its decision on the beginning of procedure of compulsory liquidation and publishes it on its Internet site for sixty consecutive days. Publication should include date, name and identification number of the company, and fulfilment of necessary conditions for compulsory liquidation. Compulsory liquidation is completed after the expiration of thirty days, when Business Register is authorized to delete company from the register, which has for the effect that a company ceases to exist.

During the procedure of compulsory liquidation, its effects involve special legal capacity of the company, followed by the denomination 'in compulsory liquidation' within its business name. Legal capacity of the company in the compulsory liquidation is limited to the existing business affairs of the company, which can be liquidated, while all debts can be paid, including payment to the employees of the company. Company bodies continue with their competences, even though it is forbidden to register any changes to the Business Register or Central Depository Register. Company's property cannot be divided among the members before company is deleted from the register, and members of the company are not allowed to dividend payments. All proceedings involving company in compulsory liquidation are suspended, including court or other administrative proceedings with the exception of the insolvency proceedings, which can be initiated. If there were proceedings suspended during compulsory liquidation, they can be continued after company has been deleted from the register, by the request of shareholders or creditors.

The assets of the company become assets of shareholders in proportion to their shareholding in the company. Shareholders have joint liability for company's debts, limited by the amount received from the liquidation remainder during three years of company being deleted from the Business Register. Additionally, it is interesting to underline that controlling shareholder has a joint and several unlimited liability for the liabilities of the joint-stock company after company was dissolved, also during three years of company being deleted from the Business Register. This exception to the limited liability has been particularly underlined by the new amendments to the Law on Commercial Companies, and stands together with the exception on liability for the company's debts in the case of piercing the corporate veil.

Provisions of the Law on Commercial Companies, as can be seen, provide inadequate and incomplete legal regime for the compulsory liquidation, leaving important issues, such as the protection of creditors and fulfilment of their claims, open. This is especially the case even though provisions on the compulsory liquidation have been changed several times since the adoption of the Law on Commercial

Companies. Provisions introducing unlimited liability of the controlling shareholder while limiting protection of creditors to their individual claims after compulsory liquidation is completed and company deleted from the Business Register remain problematic and much disputed in the legal theory and practice.[342]

## §7. Mergers and Takeovers

*211.* While mergers and other statutory changes are prescribed by the Law on Commercial Companies, a special law with regard to takeovers of joint-stock companies was introduced in 2006.

## I. Mergers and Other Statutory Changes

*212.* Serbian law defines several statutory changes, for which common provisions with regard to procedure, protective measures and effects are prescribed. In these provisions, a strong influence of the provisions of the European Company Law, including Directive (EU) 2017/1132 relating to certain aspects of company law in regard to national, as well as cross-border mergers and national divisions are evident.[343] There are still no provisions on the cross-border divisions, following recent Directive (EU) 2019/2121 of 27 November 2019 amending Directive (EU) 2017/1132 as regards cross-border conversions, mergers and divisions.[344]

### *A. Regulation*

*213.* Statutory change is considered to be every change during which one company (transferor) transfers to the other (acquiring) company all its assets and liabilities, while shareholders become members of the acquiring company in proportion to their shareholdings, unless all shareholders agree otherwise.[345] Shareholders can also receive cash payment not exceeding 10% of the nominal or accounting par value for shares issued to shareholders of the transferor company. Statutory change

342. *See* in detail: Mladen Nikolić, 'Prinudna likvidacija društva sa ograničenom odgovornošću i odgovornost članova za obaveze društva' ('Compulsory Liquidation of a Limited Liability Company and Liability of Members for the Obligations of the Company'), in: Tatjana Jevremović Petrović (ed.), *Zbornik radova sa onlajn konferencije Udruženja pravnika u privredi Srbije i časopisa „Pravo i privreda" (21. decembar 2021. godine) (Collected papers from the On-line conference of the Association of Business Lawyers and Journal „Law and Economy" (December 21st 2021))*, Belgrade, 2021, 21ff.
343. On different issues of mergers in Serbian law and the influence of the former Third Company Law Directive, now Directive (EU) 2017/1132 relating to certain aspects of company law, *see* in detail: Tatjana Jevremović Petrović, *Prekogranična spajanja društava u pravu EU* (*Cross-border mergers in the EU Law*), Faculty of Law University of Belgrade, Belgrade, 2010.
344. *See* Tatjana Jevremović Petrović, 'Harmonizacija prekograničnih kretanja privrednih društava u pravu EU' ('Harmonization of EU Law on Cross-border Movement of Companies'), *Pravo i privreda (Law and Economy)* 3/2020, 81ff.
345. Arts 483–484 LCC 2011.

may result in the foundation of a new company, where provisions with regard to company formation must be applied. Statutory change can involve one or more companies of the same or different form. Although legal provisions from the Law on Commercial Companies usually have in mind statutory change of a joint-stock company, they are also applicable to all other company forms.

Nevertheless, statutory changes are not possible when a company is in liquidation or in insolvency, except when applying provisions on the reorganization within insolvency. In the case when statutory change involves a public company, provisions on the change of status from public to closed companies must be satisfied (*see* above under this chapter §4.VI.B.), if applicable. Also, statutory changes must be performed only if in compliance with the provisions of the competition law.

### *B. Different Kinds of Statutory Changes*

*214.* Law on Commercial Companies recognizes four different kinds of statutory changes.[346] They include merger by acquisition, merger by foundation of a new company, division and separation. There is also a separate chapter on the cross-border mergers by acquisitions and cross-border mergers by foundation of a new company, even though their application is postponed by the 1st of January 2025.[347] This time frame could be further postponed and is, in fact, related to the potential membership of the Republic of Serbia to the EU.

*Merger by acquisition* is the operation whereby one or more companies are wound up without going into liquidation and transfer to another all their assets and liabilities.

*Merger by the formation of a new company* is the operation whereby two or more companies merge and are wound up without going into liquidation and transfer all their assets and liabilities to a company they found.

*Division* is the operation whereby a company is divided and wound up without going into liquidation by the simultaneous transfer of all its assets and liabilities to two or more companies it founds (division by the formation of the new companies) or two or more already existing companies (division by acquisition) or one or more companies it sets up and one or more already existing companies (division by combination).

*Separation* is the operation whereby company continues to exist and transfers part of its assets and liabilities to one or more companies it founds (separation by the formation of a new company) or one or more already existing companies (separation by acquisition) or one or more companies it founds and one or more already existing companies (separation by combination).

346. Articles 485–489 LCC 2011.
347. *See* Arts 514a–514m LCC 2011.

### *C. Regular Procedure on Statutory Change*

#### 1. Acts and Documents Which Are to Be Prepared

*215.* Certain acts and documents are to be prepared for every statutory change in order to inform interested persons – shareholders, creditors and others – of the statutory change which is going to take place.[348]

Board of directors or supervisory board in the case of a two-tier system must draw up the following documents: *(draft) terms of merger or division*, *audited financial reports* (including existing annual financial reports or semi-annual financial reports) drawn up in the last six months before general meeting is deciding on the statutory change – except when all shareholders of the participating companies agree they are not necessary; *auditors' report* on the statutory change – except when all shareholders of the closed joint-stock company of the participating companies agreed this is not necessary, *board of directors' report or board of executive directors' report* in case of a two-tier system – except when all shareholders of that company agree this is not necessary, as well as *proposal of the decision on statutory change* to be made at the general meeting. Also, the board of directors or supervisory board shall draw up a proposal for the statute change or articles of incorporation and the statute (in the case of newly formed company).

*(Draft) terms on the statutory change (or division plan)* are to be drawn when two or more companies participate in the statutory change.[349] It must have obligatory content, especially including information on the participating companies (name, registered seat), conditions and goals of the statutory change, value of the assets and liabilities to be transferred and their description, share exchange ratio, including proportion and cash payment if any (which is not applicable for the case when transferor company is a wholly owned subsidiary of the acquiring company), the terms of the allotment of shares and date from which the holding of such shares entitles the holders to participate in profits, the rights conferred by the acquiring company to the holders of shares to which special rights are attached, the date from which business activities of the acquiring company end (if that is the case), the date from which the transactions of the company being acquired shall be treated for accounting purposes as being those of the acquiring company, any special advantage granted in the acquiring company to the members of the board of directors, executive or supervisory board of participating companies, conditions on which employees continue their employment in the acquiring company, as well as other issues important for the statutory change.

Draft terms include proposals for decision on the statute change of the acquiring company or draft articles of incorporation and the statute (in the case of newly formed company), as well as financial balance sheet for division or separation (if

348. *See* Art. 490–494 LCC 2011.

349. *See*: Tatjana Jevremović Petrović, 'Ugovor o statusnoj promeni: trenutak zaključenja, kontrola i drugi povezani problemi' ('Terms on Statutory Change: Moment of Conclusion, Control and other Related Issues'), in: Vuk Radović (ed.), *Uskla ivanje poslovnog prava Srbije sa pravom Evropske unije (2015) (Harmonisation of Serbian Business Law with EU Law (2015))*, Pravni fakultet Univerziteta u Beogradu, Beograd, 2015, 94ff.

that is the case), list of all shareholders of the transferor company, including nominal value of their shares in the acquiring company and number of shares to be issued to them (not applicable when transferor company is a wholly owned subsidiary of the acquiring company), and list of all employees of the transferor company who will continue to be employed by the acquiring company.

Draft terms must be in written form and signed by all participating companies. Certification of signatures by public notary is obligatory, or in the case of transfer of immovable property solemnization must be performed.

Draft terms of merger, division or other statutory change must be *audited by the auditor*, appointed by the court for each of participating companies, upon their request. As already explained, an audit is not necessary if all shareholders of participating closed joint-stock companies agree so.

Court can appoint one auditor for all participating companies upon their joint request. The auditor must draw up his report for each company (or jointly, if appointed for all participating companies) and communicate it to all participating companies no longer than two months since his appointment. *Auditors' report* must be in writing and must include his opinion whether the share exchange ratio is fair and reasonable. He must state which methods of evaluation were applied for the share exchange, whether they are adequate, or another ratio could be achieved by application of other methods, and whether there were any other evaluation difficulties. The auditor is entitled to obtain any act or document from all participating companies necessary to prepare the report and to carry out all necessary investigations.

*Board of directors' report or board of executive directors' report* in case of a two-tier system must be also drawn in each of the participating companies, containing at least an explanation of goals and economic effects of the statutory change, legal consequences and share exchange ratio, as well as major changes in relation to the terms of merger, division or other statutory change or on the assets and liabilities of the participating companies (if any). Board of executive directors' report in case of a two-tier system must be submitted to the supervisory board for approval before its submission to the general meeting. Board of directors' report or board of executive directors' report is not necessary if all shareholders of that company agree it is not necessary.

### 2. Publication of Acts and Documents and Shareholders' Information Rights

*216.* Company must *publish draft terms of the merger, division or other change* on its Internet site and submit to the Business Register for publication sixty days before a general meeting is to decide on the statutory change, at the latest.[350] Publication of draft terms has effects for creditors also, who are also considered to be informed.

The company must also publish information to shareholders on time and date when inspection of all documents and acts prepared for the statutory change is possible, except for a closed joint-stock company, which can fulfil this obligation by personal notification of all shareholders.

350. *See* Arts 495ff LCC 2011.

Shareholders have *inspection right and right to obtain copies*, free of charge, at the registered office of their company with regard to all acts and documents related to the proposed statutory change (unless published), including annual financial reports of all participating companies for the last three years with auditor's report (if audited), at least one month before general meeting is to decide on the statutory change.

#### 3. General Meeting's Decision

*217.* General meeting must decide on the draft terms of merger, division or other statutory change, or already signed terms of merger or other statutory change by a three-fourths majority of shareholders present at the meeting, if no higher majority is prescribed in the statute. The general meeting decision shall also include statute change or articles of incorporation and statute adoption (in the case of newly formed joint-stock company). The decision can be valid only if the chairman of the board of directors or supervisory board in the case of a two-tier system signed a declaration that all dissenting shareholders are satisfied in full (*see* on this issue above under this chapter §5.I.D.1.).

### *D. Simplified Procedure on Statutory Change*

*218.* A simplified procedure can be applied when the acquiring company holdings at least 90% of the capital subscribed or at least 90% of the voting shares of the transferor company. If that is the case, provisions imposing a decision of the general meeting of the acquiring company need not be applied if publication of draft terms was made at least one month before the general meeting of the transferor company, deciding on the statutory change was held and inspection right and the right to obtain copies were allowed, while none of the shareholders of the acquiring company holding at least 5% of its capital subscribed ask that a general meeting must decide on the statutory change.

Transferor company is also not required to draw up and submit for approval reports of the auditor and board of directors or board of executive directors in case of a two-tier system.

When the acquiring company holds all shares of the transferor company, draft terms of statutory change cannot include information on the share exchange ratio.

### *E. Protective Measures*

#### 1. Creditors' Protection

*219.* Creditors of each participating company are informed on the proposed statutory change by the publication of draft terms of merger or other change in the Business Register (as explained above under section C. 2). Still, company must inform in person all known creditors with claims above RSD 2.000.000 (approx.

EUR 17.040) on the day of publication of the proposed statutory change at the latest thirty days before a general meeting is to decide on the statutory change. Declaration on the personal notification must be signed by the chairman of the board of directors, or supervisory board in case of a two-tier system.

Once notified, all creditors of the company participating in statutory change (except creditors who have a privileged position in insolvency or when already secured) whose claims antedate registration of the statutory change can *claim for security* thirty days from the publication of the terms of statutory change.[351] Creditors can be protected by providing security, by changing or ending their contract, separate management of the assets of the transferor company until all creditors are satisfied or by other acts in order to protect the same position of a creditor that was held before statutory change took place.

Creditors can request security from the transferor or acquiring company if the financial situation of the companies participating in statutory change makes such protection necessary and when it is necessary to safeguard their claims in order to provide the same position creditors held before statutory change. If no adequate protection is provided for within fifteen days of request being made, creditors can bring a legal suit in order to have their claims secured and must prove that their claims will be at stake because of the statutory change. The court may even decide to bring to a temporary halt statutory change, if that is necessary for the protection of creditors who filed for adequate protection.

The same level of protection is prescribed for debenture and other security holders of the transferor company, except if otherwise prescribed in the decision on the issue of securities or arranged with their holders. Holders of convertible debentures, warrants and other securities to which special rights are attached of the transferor company which cease to exist must have at least equivalent rights in the acquiring company unless otherwise provided by the decision on the issue of securities or arranged with their holders, or when acquiring company according to terms of statutory change must redeem securities for their market price (which must be confirmed by the auditors' report) upon request. If unsatisfied with the market price, determined by the terms of statutory change, holders of these securities are entitled to file for legal action in front of a competent court in order to determine the market value of their securities.

## 2. Shareholders' Protection

*220.* In the case of a share exchange ratio determined unlawfully, every shareholder is entitled to submit a legal suit against the acquiring company within thirty

351. *See* in detail Arts 509–514 LCC 2011. Mirjana Radović, 'Pravo poverioca da zahteva dobijanje odgovarajuće zaštite u slučaju statusne promene privrednog društva – dužnika' ('Creditor's Right to Obtain Adequate Safeguards in Case of a Merger or a Division of his Debtor'), *Pravo i privreda (Law and Economy)* 4–6/2016, 645ff.

days of publication of the (draft) terms of statutory change and demand to be *compensated in cash.*[352] In deciding on the case, the court will take into consideration and compare market values of shares of the transferor and acquiring company. When this value is lower in the acquiring company, acquiring company must make compensation in cash not exceeding 10% of the nominal value of the shares exchanged in the transferor company to all shareholders of the transferor company.

*Dissenting shareholders have the right for their shares to be purchased by the company* (*see* above under this chapter §5.I.D.1.) at the price determined by the statutory change decision. If this price is below market price, or when not received, dissenting shareholders can file a legal action for determination or payment of the price. Shares purchased by the company become own shares, except in the case of division by the formation of the new companies, when they are distributed to members of the companies that are being incorporated.

Finally, shareholders are protected by the provision on the responsibility of directors and members of the supervisory board in case of a two-tier system of the company participating in the statutory change for damage caused to them intentionally or with gross negligence in preparing or implementing statutory change. The only exception provided exists in the case of a merger by acquisition of a wholly owned subsidiary, when persons provided will not be responsible. Legal action can be brought during three years of statutory change registration publication being made.

### *F. Effects and Avoidance of Decision*

*221.* Serbian Law on Commercial Companies prescribes that terms of statutory change *take effect* when approved by general meetings of all participating companies, or when the draft terms were signed (if later), unless a later day is provided for in the draft terms. Taking effect of the articles of incorporation and the statute are set as the same date.[353] Nevertheless, according to general principles of registration in Serbian Company Law, effects of the statutory change are dependent on the registration performed at the Business Register, which is obligatory for all participating companies, but not before terms of statutory change take effect. Registration of the statutory change is conditional upon the payment of all dissenting shareholders.

Statutory change may imply *capital increase* for the acquiring company, when provisions on the capital increase will be applicable. In the case of capital increase, cross-shareholdings will not give rise to a share exchange, but are considered as shares owned by the company itself. Any capital increase is also registered with the Business Register.

Finally, in the case of statutory change, *one or more companies may cease to exist* (merger by acquisition or foundation of the new company or division) when

352. *See* Art. 507 LCC 2011. On shareholders' protection *see*: Vuk Radović, 'Prava članova u slučaju statusnih promena sa posebnim osvrtom na neke neusaglašenosti srpskog prava sa pravom EU' ('Rights of Companies Members in Mergers and Divisions with a Particular Emphasis on Certain Discrepancies Between Serbian and EU Law'), in: Vuk Radović (ed.), *Uskla ivanje poslovnog prava Srbije sa pravom Evropske unije (2018) (Harmonisation of Serbian business law with EU law (2018)),* Pravni fakultet Univerziteta u Beogradu, Beograd, 2018, 27ff.

353. Article 499 LCC 2011.

deleted from the Business Register. If that is the case, the company is dissolved without going into liquidation. All liabilities are transferred to the acquiring company, but if there are more than one acquiring company, they are transferred according to the division (or other statutory change) plan with secondary liability for other company's liabilities. This secondary liability is limited to the value of assets and liabilities transferred.[354]

A *statutory change has following consequences* after registration: transfer of all assets and liabilities from the transferor to the acquiring company according to the terms of statutory change (and upon inscription in the public register or conditional upon approval or authorization when prescribed); acquiring company is jointly and severally liable with the transferor company for all liabilities not transferred, but limited to the amount of the assets and liabilities transferred, except otherwise agreed with creditors; shareholders of the transferor company become shareholders of the acquiring company according to share exchange ratio set in the terms of statutory change while their exchanged shares in the transferor company are cancelled (third-party rights on cancelled shares or giving right to share subscription are transferred as well); employees of the transferor company continue to be employed in the acquiring company if that is provided for in the terms of statutory change and according to terms conditions.[355] All permission, concession, other privileges granted or obtained are transferred as well, unless otherwise is prescribed. Directors and members of the supervisory board in a two-tier system as well as legal representatives suffer the loss of their duties and powers.

If certain assets are not transferred to any of the acquiring companies, nor this can be determined, every company shall have a proportionate part of the assets according to total value of the assets and liabilities transferred. Liabilities not transferred according to terms of statutory change or when determination on the transfer is not possible will impose joint and several liability of all companies, limited by the value of assets and liabilities transferred.

Decision on the statutory change cannot be declared null and void, but *action for avoidance* can be filed under general conditions for avoidance of general meeting decisions (*see* above under this chapter §5.I.C.6.), although the decision cannot be avoided on the grounds of the exchange share ratio.[356]

---

354. Mirjana Radović, 'Odgovornost društva sticaoca za obaveze društva prenosioca kod statusnih promena podele i izdvajanja' ('Liability of the Acquiring Company for Liabilities of the Transferor Company in Case of Division and Separation'), *Uskla ivanje poslovnog prava Srbije sa pravom Evropske unije (Harmonisation of Serbian Business Law with EU Law (2017)),* Pravni fakultet Univerziteta u Beogradu, Beograd, 2017, 145ff.

355. *See* Art. 505 LCC 2011.

356. *See* on avoidance of decision on statutory change and nullity of merger: Tatjana Jevremović Petrović, 'Pobijanje odluke skupštine o statusnoj promeni' ('Avoidance of General Meeting's Decision on the Statutory Merger'), *Uskla ivanje poslovnog prava Srbije sa pravom Evropske unije (Harmonisation of Serbian Business Law with EU Law (2017)),* Pravni fakultet Univerziteta u Beogradu, Beograd, 2017, 91ff; Tatjana Jevremović Petrović, 'Ništavost statusne promene nakon registracije' ('Nullity of Merger after Registration'), *Anali Pravnog fakulteta u Beogradu (Annals of the Faculty of Law in Belgrade – Belgrade Law Review)* 2/2016, 79ff.

## II. Change of Legal Form

### *A. Regulation*

*222.* A joint-stock company may change its legal form to any other form provided by the Law on Commercial Companies and vice versa: any other company form may be changed to the joint-stock company form. Change of legal form does not affect legal personality and is considered to be legal continuity of the same company.[357] Change of legal form requires application of provisions with regard to company formation. Change of legal form is not possible when company is in liquidation or in insolvency, except when applying provisions on the reorganization within insolvency. In the case when change of legal form involves a public company, provisions on the change of status from public to closed companies must be satisfied (*see* above under this chapter §4.VI.B.).

### *B. Change of Legal Form Procedure*

#### 1. Acts and Documents Which Are to Be Prepared

*223.* Every case of change of legal form requires certain acts and documents to be prepared, similarly to statutory change.[358]

One or more directors, board of directors or executive board of directors in case of a two-tier system must draw up and submit to the general meeting the following documents: *proposal of decision on the change of legal form*, *proposal of decision on the articles of incorporation or statute change or adoption* (depending on the legal form); *proposal of decision on appointment of members of bodies* (depending on the legal form), and *report* on the goals and legal and economic reasons and consequences of the change of legal form, including share (or stake) exchange ratio, as well as *notification of the rights of dissenting shareholders* (or members) for their shares to be purchased by the company.

*Decision on the change of legal form* must include information on the company (name, registered seat), legal form to be taken, share (or stake) exchange ratio depending on the form, as well as other information.

#### 2. Publication of Acts and Documents and Shareholders' Information Rights

*224.* The company must publish a proposal of the decision on the change of legal form. All provisions in respect of this publication are applicable according to provisions on the statutory change.

---

357. *See* on the legal nature of change of legal form: Tatjana Jevremović Petrović, 'Pojam i pravna priroda prekograničnе konverzije' (Notion and legal nature of the cross-border conversion), *Annals of the Faculty of Law in Belgrade*, 2/2013, 110ff.

358. *See* Arts 479–482 LCC 2011.

3. General Meeting's Decision

*225.* A general meeting must decide on the change of legal form by a three-fourths majority of shareholders present at the meeting if no higher majority is prescribed in the statute. The general meeting decision shall also include articles of incorporation and statute adoption or change, depending on the legal form and decision on the appointment of members to company bodies. When changing from another company form to the form of a joint-stock company, general provisions on the decision taking including majority will be applicable.

### *C. Effects of the Change of Legal Form*

*226.* Change of legal form must be registered with the Business Register when all legal effects take place. Effects of the change include transformation from stakes to shares or vice versa, holders of convertible debentures, warrants and other securities to which special rights are attached must have at least equivalent rights in the company with new legal form unless otherwise provided for in the decision on the issue of securities or specifically arranged with their holders.

If the company is changing form into a joint-stock company, it must register its shares in the Depository Agency. In the case of change of legal form into or from a public joint-stock company, other provisions on the acquisition or loss of status of the public company must be applied.

## III. Takeovers

*227.* Taking over a control block of a joint-stock company is especially relevant in providing special procedures in order to introduce transparency, competitiveness and protection of rights of (minority) shareholders. Serbian law has specific provisions contained in the Law on Takeovers of joint-stock companies, done under strong influence of Directive 2004/25/EC on takeover bids.[359]

---

359. For the Serbian takeovers regime before Law in 2006 was enacted *see* critically in: Nebojša Jovanović, 'Manjkavosti srpskog pravnog režima preuzimanja akcionarskih društava (Disadvantages of the Serbian takeover regime)', *Pravo i privreda (Law and Economy)* 9-12/04, 84ff. *See also*: Zoran Arsić, 'Javna ponuda za sticanje značajnog i većinskog učešća kapitala u akcionarskom društvu' (Takeover bid in the joint-stock company), *Pravni život (Legal Life)* 11/1996, 111ff; Vuk Radović, 'Obavezna javna ponuda za kupovinu akcija ciljne kompanije' (Mandatory bid rule), *Pravni život (Legal Life)* 11/2004, 103ff; Vuk Radović, *Mere odbrane akcionarskog društva od preuzimanja kontrole* (*Defensive measures in the joint-stock company during takeover bid*) Pravni fakultet Univerziteta u Beogradu, Beograd, 2008.

*A. Equal Treatment of All Shareholders*

*228.* Several rules have to be adhered to in the event of a takeover of controlling participation (holding).[360] First, *equal treatment of all shareholders* of the offeree company, including protection and equivalent position in selling their shares to offeror of other shareholders in the case when a person acquires control of a company.

*B. Mandatory Takeover Bid*

*229.* In order to protect shareholders of a public joint-stock company (whose shares are traded on the regulated market or MTF in the Republic of Serbia and having more than 100 shareholders during the last three months, and with subscribed capital to at least EUR 3.00.000 equivalent in RSD), the law provided the obligation for the person who acquires control of more than 25% of the total number of voting shares (with already existing holdings represents controlling threshold), acting independently or in concert, directly or indirectly to make a *mandatory bid*.[361] Further acquisition of additional 10% of the total number of voting shares (additional threshold) obliges another mandatory bid up to the final shareholding of 75% of the total number of voting shares (final threshold). Mandatory bid needs to be made after publication of the takeover bid intent within two working days, following which *submission of the application for approval of the publication of a takeover bid* to the Securities Commission is necessary during the next 15 working days.

It is allowed to make a *voluntary takeover bid*, which can be conditioned upon acquisition of the minimum number or percentage of shares offered. In the case of a voluntary takeover bid, all conditions, including submission of the application for approval of publication of a takeover bid to the Securities Commission, need to be fulfilled.

*C. Information for Shareholders*

*230.* Shareholders of the offeree company *must be informed* completely, accurately and on time on the takeover bid, in order to have sufficient time to make a proper decision on the bid, and to define their interest and reach a decision to accept or refuse the takeover bid. All provisions with regard to publication of the takeover bid intent and, especially, approved publication of the takeover bid serve this purpose. Publication must be made in daily newspapers and can be followed by intent publication on the offeror's website.

Takeover bid must include important *information and documents*.[362] They specifically include information on the offeror (including all persons acting in concert) and offeree company, issued, already acquired and shares intended for acquisition

360. *See* in particular general provision in Arts 3ff Law on Takeovers of Joint-stock companies.
361. For the exceptions *see* Art. 8 Law on Takeovers of Joint-stock companies.
362. *See* in detail Art. 20 Law on Takeovers of Joint-stock companies.

(including type, class and number and percentage of votes), price including compensation method and conditions, information on the financing of the bid, time allowed for acceptance, goals of offeror with regard to the offeree company in case of a successful takeover bid and other information with regard to investment company, acceptance of the bid and other important information. Documents on the legal base for share acquisition within last year, documents providing information on the financing of the bid, evaluation of the fair price of the company if shares are not liquid which must be audited by independent auditor; necessary approvals and other documents are also to be included in the takeover bid.

General provision on the price offered for shares during takeover bid depends on their liquidity (market turnover). Shares of the joint-stock company are liquid if there was market turnover within six months before it was necessary to make publication of takeover bid with at least 0.5% of the total number of issued voting shares and if within three months of this period trading was achieved above one-third of trading days within a month with market trade turnover of total number of issued voting shares above 0.05%.

If shares of the target company are liquid offeror has the obligation to offer at least the highest price from: *average weighted market* (regulated market or MTF) *price* of voting shares in the last six months before offeror had the obligation to make publication of takeover bid, or the *highest price by which voting shares in the target company were acquired* in the last twelve months by the offeror or other person acting in concert, including acquisition by which offeror has the obligation to make takeover bid. If the shares of the target company are not liquid or are not traded on the regulated market of MTF, offeror has the obligation to offer at least the highest price from: the *highest price by which voting shares in the target company were acquired* in the last twelve months by the offeror or other person acting in concert, including acquisition by which offeror has the obligation to make takeover bid; or *accounting value* of the voting shares (based on the last annual financial accounts); or *evaluated fair price* of the voting shares (based on the date when offeror has the obligation to make takeover bid).[363]

Further protection of shareholders must be achieved by the obligation of the offeree to provide for necessary *compensation for shares* to be purchased, which can be either in cash, financial instruments (regulated by the Law on Capital Markets) or debt securities issued by the Republic of Serbia or National Bank of Serbia.

### *D. Obligations of the Offeree Company*

*231. The board of directors* of an offeree company *must act in the best interest of shareholders* of the offeree company during a takeover procedure. They also need to respect the interest of employees and are obliged to inform them in writing of the takeover bid.

During the takeover bid, the board is *entitled to* seek alternative bids, but apart from that is *not allowed to* act or make certain decisions from the moment when the takeover bid intention was disclosed until the end of the takeover bid procedure

363. *See* further details in Art. 22 Law on Takeovers of Joint-stock companies.

except with prior approval of the general meeting of shareholders by a simple majority. Decisions which the board is forbidden to make include authorization for share issues in order to increase subscribed capital; decisions which do not form part of the normal course of the company's business, including contracts which substantially change assets or obligations of the offeree company. Also, board of directors is prohibited from making decisions with regard to acquisition or disposal of company's shares by the company itself, and is prohibited from publishing a takeover bid of another company.

After informing the employees of the offeree company, who are allowed to express their view on the takeover, the board of directors of the offeree company must draw up and publish a statement on the takeover bid, including explained views on the offer in general, and especially on price offered, intentions and goals of the offeror. The board has to take its own position on the takeover bid, either in support or to oppose. If employees' representatives expressed their opinion, it shall be published simultaneously with the board's opinion on the offer. Joint and several liability for the accuracy of information is with all persons involved in drafting of the board of directors or employee's opinion to shareholders for any damage they incurred if these persons knew or should have known that information contained in the opinion is false or misleading.

*E. Other Provisions*

*232.* Offeror and the offeree company must ensure that the takeover procedure is conducted *no longer than necessary* so that offeree company is not hindered for longer periods in conducting its affairs. Therefore, time allowed for bid acceptance must be at least twenty-one days and no longer than forty-five days since takeover bid publication, although this period can be prolonged if an alternative bid is made but no longer than seventy days.

Finally, an offeror and other persons involved in a takeover must not act in such a way that the rise or fall of the prices of the securities becomes artificial and the *normal functioning of the markets is distorted.*

The most important sanctions provided for a breach of mandatory takeover bid include voting restrictions with regard to all shares of the offeree company until submission of the application for approval of the publication of takeover bid to the Securities Commission.[364] There is also a possibility for the shareholder to petition in front of the competent court that offeror purchases his shares, if offeror fails to apply for approval of the publication of a takeover bid or fails to publish takeover bid (or procedure of takeover is suspended by the Securities Commission) under conditions provided for obligatory takeover bid.[365]

Although in the beginning the Law on Takeovers of Joint-stock companies contained provisions on the sell-out and squeeze-out rights, they were abolished after their inclusion in the Law on Commercial Companies in 2011 granting these rights to all minority or controlling shareholders (*see* above under this chapter §5.I.D.3.).

364. *See* in particularly Art. 41a Law on Takeovers of Joint-stock companies.
365. Art 41b Law on Takeovers of Joint-stock companies.

§8. Holding Companies and Subsidiaries

## I. In General

*233.* Serbian Law on Commercial Companies has a section dealing with different forms of groups of companies. These provisions are rather simplified and general in nature, except for contractual groups of companies (*see* below under II).[366]

General provision allows for the companies to be affiliated (connected) by capital (holding of stakes or shares), contractually or in both ways.[367] The concept of affiliated companies is a generic term for a parent (controlling) and a subsidiary (controlled) company. When affiliated, companies may form a group of companies, holding or they can be mutually connected – when each has substantive shareholding in the other company (the case of cross-shareholdings).

Affiliate companies make vertical or horizontal concentrations, as well as the so-called conglomerates (the activities of affiliated entities are diverse and most often not relating to one another). Several objectives are attained through affiliation of companies: fiscal advantages, risk distribution, rationalization, more efficient and flexible management, market conditions, elimination of mutual competition, etc.

*Groups of companies* exist when a controlling company has one or more commercial activities, unlike a *holding company* which controls one or more subsidiaries and whose only activity is to manage and finance its subsidiaries. Groups of companies exist either as *factual* – involving controlling and one or more controlled companies when a controlling company has effective control (manages) controlled companies; *contractual* – when a controlling company has control and management agreement with one or more controlled companies or *group with equivalent position of its members* – when they are not dependent of each other if having central management. As previously mentioned, these provisions are only general in character. Therefore, apart from the classification presented, all other provisions dealing with groups of companies basically deal only with contractual groups.

For factual groups, all provisions of the Law on Commercial Companies are applicable, including those imposing a duty of loyalty of the controlling shareholder to its company. Nevertheless, case law is not very familiar with this concept. Further, the separate nature of legal entity status of the parent company and that of subsidiary companies is present in the case law and does not provide for an adequate regime for frequently diverse and conflicting interests of parent and subsidiary companies, including their shareholders, creditors and other interested persons.

366. On the groups of companies in Serbian law *see* in detail: Tatjana Jevremović Petrović, *Grupe privrednih društava (Groups of companies),* Pravni fakultet Univerziteta u Beogradu, Beograd, 2014. *See also*: Vrleta Krulj, *Pravni režim i oblici koncentracija u privredi (Legal regime and forms of commercial concentrations),* Savremena administracija, Beograd, 1978.

367. On general provisions on affiliation of companies, as well as groups *see* Arts 549–553 LCC 2011.

## II. Contractual Groups

### *A. Control and Management Contract*

*234.* Under a major influence of German law, Serbian law introduced contractual groups on the basis of control and management contract. Although previous Law on Commercial Companies recognized not only control and management but also profit transfer contract, the only contract to be expressly provided for at this moment is the control and management contract.[368]

Nevertheless, unlike all other national laws under German influence, to include German provisions on the factual and contractual group, Serbian law tried to take over only several conceptual provisions of the German system, including provisions on control and management agreement, while preserving certain issues to be dealt with in original manner.[369]

Control and management agreement (contract) grants the right to a controlling company to manage and control business activities of another – controlled company. There are no explicit provisions on the form of companies which form contractual groups, so it must be taken that it can be concluded by a company in every form prescribed by the Law on Commercial Companies.

Control and management agreement must be *drawn in writing and must be approved* by a general meeting decision taken by a three-fourths majority of shareholders present at the meeting of all companies, if no higher majority is prescribed in the statute. It must be registered and effects can take place only after registration and publication on the Business Register website within at least the next ninety days.

*Board of directors or supervisory board* in the case of a two-tier system must draw up a *report* for shareholders and submit it with the proposal of the control and management contract. It must include financial information of all companies involved, as well as legal and economic reasons for the agreement conclusion, including its contents, as well as shareholders' compensation or its determination method. Boards of directors or supervisory boards of companies involved can make a joint report for all companies – parties to the agreement.

Provision of the control and management contract can be altered through the same procedure necessary for contract approval. If not otherwise provided, the contract is concluded for an indefinite period of time, with right of each party to end the contract at the end of a business year or other financial period by written notification to the other party in the contract. End of control and management agreement must be registered and published with notification to creditors that can ask for adequate protection from the controlling company with regard to their claims towards the controlled company.

---

368. For LCC 2004 provisions *see* in particular Arts 373–376.

369. *See* provisions on the *Behherschungsvertrag* in Arts 291–310 German Law on Joint-stock companies and compare with Arts 479–495 of the Croatian Law on Commercial Companies or Arts 533, 535–544 and 549–553 of the Slovene Law on Commercial Companies.

*B. Rights and Obligations*

*235.* Control and management agreement (contract) grants the right to a controlling company to manage and control business activities of another – controlled company by obligatory instructions given to controlled company bearing in mind the interest of the group.[370]

If for realization of certain instructions a decision or the approval of board of directors or supervisory board in a two-tier system of the controlled company is necessary and is denied, the director or executive board of the controlled company must inform the controlling company without delay, if otherwise is not provided by the control and management agreement, when instruction may be repeated only with approval of the board of directors of controlling company or supervisory board in case of a two-tier system.

Directors of the controlling company must give instructions to the controlled company with care of a diligent manager and by the application of controlling company directors' duties towards the controlled company. Directors or supervisory board members of the controlled company are not responsible for damage made by the breach of their duties if following obligatory instructions of the controlling company.

Controlling company is responsible for damage caused to the controlled company if it is incurred following obligatory instructions of the controlling company. Therefore, it is clear that the main protection of the controlled company is based on damage caused, for which proof of damage and causal link need to be established, while burden of proof rests with the controlled company. This system provides for inadequate protection of the controlled company.

*C. Protection of the External Shareholders and Creditors*

*236.* Control and management contract grants minority (external) shareholders of the controlled company *adequate compensation* during a business year. It must be determined upon future expected dividend payments for three consecutive years, as if the company was not party to a control and management agreement but not below average dividend payments for the previous three years, except when the controlled company is a fully owned subsidiary. In the case of control and management contract change or end, approval of minority shareholders as a separate class of shares is necessary. Although conceptionally adequate, further provisions, providing that compensation cannot be made if the controlled company made a loss, change the whole system of shareholders' protection. Still, compensation can be made for previous years if the controlled company made a profit. It is, therefore, plausible that external shareholders will not be compensated because of the losses

370. Mirko Vasiljević, 'Subjektivitet grupe društava ('interes grupe' – stvarnost i/ili fikcija)' ('Subjectivity of a Group of Companies ("Interest of the Group" – Reality and/or Fiction)'), in: *Uskla ivanje poslovnog prava Srbije sa pravom Evropske unije (2015)* (*Harmonisation of Serbian Business Law with EU Law (2015)*), Pravni fakultet Univerziteta u Beogradu, Beograd, 2015, 11ff.

made. Provisions on capital maintenance are fully applicable in the case of a control and management agreement and provide for minimum protection of controlled company capital. Still, they do not provide any additional protection to external shareholders.

Minority shareholders claiming that compensation is inadequate can file a legal action in front of the court in order to determine an adequate compensation within three months of contract or contract changes being registered. In case higher compensation is determined by the court, the controlling company may end the contract during the next three months.

External shareholders are entitled through the control and management agreement *for their shares to be purchased* by the controlling company at the market price. The contract may provide for alternative exchange rights for the shares of the controlling company, upon proportion set by contract provisions, and which must be determined as in the case of merger by acquisition with the possibility of unsatisfied shareholder to file legal action in order that court determines the adequate price or exchange ratio. Alternative share exchange may provide for additional cash compensation, whereby provisions as in the case of statutory change are applicable. If shareholders are not entitled for their shares to be purchased or exchanged for shares of the controlling company, the contract can be pronounced null and void.

The only provision to *protect creditors* provides that in the case when control and management contract ends, the controlling company must provide adequate protection for creditors' claims made before termination of the control contract. It is provided for creditors of controlled company upon their written request within six months after contract termination date. Secured creditors of the controlled company or those having privileged position during insolvency are not entitled for adequate protection from the controlling company.

## §9. Taxation of Corporations and Shareholders

*237.* The most important issues in relation to company taxation are contained in the Corporate Profit Tax Law.[371]

Companies or other legal persons formed in the Republic of Serbia or having their real seat or control in the Republic of Serbia are considered to have *tax residence* and must pay tax on profits realized on the territory of the Republic of Serbia or abroad. *Non-resident companies* must also pay tax on all profits realized upon activities of the permanent business unit in the territory of the Republic of Serbia, if otherwise is not prescribed by law or provided upon application of international contracts introducing provisions on double taxation.[372]

Taxable profit, determined from the fiscal balance sheet, is the *corporate profit tax base*. In determination of taxable profit, expenditures declared can be recognized, excluding certain expenditures, such as gifts, interest rates, fines, penalties

371. Corporate Profit Tax Law (Zakon o porezu na dobit pravnih lica), *Official Gazette of RS* (*Službeni glasnik RS)* 25/2001, further amended.

372. Articles 2–5 Corporate Profit Tax Law.

and similar expenditures.[373] Also, determination of taxable profit must be made upon revenue declared in the fiscal balance sheet in conformity with the IAS and/or IFRS and regulations dealing with accountancy and audit, or if that is not the case with a comparable method determined by the competent authority. Tax base does not include income accrued from dividends or participation in the profit of other taxpayers, or other income from interest on the debt securities issued by the Republic of Serbia, autonomous province, other territorial unit or Central bank, as well as revenue generated on the basis of long-term reservations.

*Capital gain*, calculated as the difference between purchase price, determined by the law and sell price, is included in taxable profit and represents all income from selling or other transferring with compensation (but not including statutory change) of the following assets: real estate, industrially property rights, stakes or shares and other securities except bonds issued by the Republic of Serbia for economic development loans, foreign exchange personal savings and debt securities issued by public bodies; as well as investment units.[374] Capital gain of the non-resident taxpayer also exists in case of sales or other transfers of real estate, stakes, shares and other securities, as well as investment units. Any capital loss, which exists if the difference between purchase and sell price is negative, may be offset with capital gains made during the same year, or with future capital gains over the next five years. Taxable are also profits realized during liquidation or insolvency proceedings, and liquidation remainder is considered as dividend.

Profit tax is *determined on a yearly basis* for a business year, which is the same as one calendar year, except in special circumstances, upon submission of a tax return and fiscal balance sheet within ten days of the end date for financial reports. *Tax return* and financial accounts must be submitted within 180 days of the end of the period of taxation.[375]

Corporate profit uniform and proportional *tax rate* is 15%.[376] In the case of a non-resident taxpayer and if not otherwise provided by international treaties on double taxation, tax after deduction shall be charged and paid at the rate of 20% (or exceptionally 25% in the case of a resident of a preferential tax jurisdiction) on the income earned from dividends and profit share, copyrights and related rights, as well as industrial property rights, interests and rent from leased immovable or movable property on the territory of the Republic of Serbia. The same rate is applied in the case of non-resident company for profits made on capital gains from another resident company, other non-resident legal or natural person, or resident or non-resident, as well as alternative investments fund on the territory of the Republic of Serbia. Tax declaration must be made within thirty days of profit made.

Law stipulates various *tax stimulations*, including stimulations for investment and *tax exemptions* for non-profit organizations, as well as legal persons employing disabled or other categories of employees.[377] There are provisions aimed with regards at *avoiding double taxation*, including dividends within groups of companies. An

373. For details *see* Arts 7–22v Corporate Profit Tax Law.
374. Articles 27–30 Corporate Profit Tax Law.
375. Article 63 Corporate Profit Tax Law.
376. *See* Arts 39ff Corporate Profit Tax Law.
377. Arts 41ff Corporate Profit Tax Law.

important part of the Law is dedicated to group taxation, whereby *tax consolidation* is possible for parent and subsidiary companies when holding at least 75% of shares or stakes only upon transfer prices for intra-group transactions.[378]

378. Arts 59ff Corporate Profit Tax Law.

# Chapter 2. Limited Liability Company

*238.* Limited liability company (*društvo sa ograničenom odgovornošću* – abbreviation d.o.o. or doo) is defined as a company with one or more members having stakes in the capital of the company, whereby members are not responsible for company's debts, except in case of lifting the corporate veil and other cases prescribed by law.[379]

## §1. Characteristics

*239.* Limited Liability Company is a company having all the major characteristics of a capital company, although it usually combines them with several characteristics typical of companies of persons. This combination explains the popularity of this form in comparison to all others.[380] Although suitable for the greatest number of activities, some of them are only available to a joint-stock company (*see* above under General Introduction §3.IV.D.).

It has *legal personality* upon registration and is responsible for all debts incurred during business operations. Members of the limited liability company only bear the business operation risk up to the amount of their subscribed contributions, and are not responsible for companies' debts, except in the case of lifting the corporate veil (*see* General Introduction under §3) or in the case of compulsory liquidation when controlling member have unlimited liability towards creditors (*see* below under §6).

Most often, this is a company with small capital and small number of members (appropriate to a family business). Limited liability companies can have either *one or more members* – natural or legal persons. An important implication of this is the possibility of this form, as is the case of the joint-stock company, to have only *one member* – natural or legal person (single member limited liability company), while still applying provisions on limited liability.

As underlined before, only joint-stock companies have their capital divided into shares which can be issued to the public. Limited liability company has its capital divided into stakes, according to contributions of the members, which cannot be offered publicly. Still, members' amounts of contributions are not necessarily equal.

The most important provisions on this company form also include principle of *fixed legal capital* and *minimum and capital protection requirements.* A limited liability company has similar provisions as a joint-stock company with regard to capital, although it has different provisions on minimum capital requirements and several other simplified provisions on capital formation (including evaluation of contributions). Provisions on capital maintenance are, on the other hand, in certain issues stricter, including those on restrictions of payments to members. Still, the possibility of owners being employed by the company influence importantly the legal regime of the payments made lawfully.

379. *See* Art. 139 LCC 2011 as well as Art. 548 for additional liability of controlling member in the case of compulsory liquidation.
380. For statistics *see* General Introduction, s. 1. V.

While a joint-stock company is generally strictly organized according to a prescribed structure, a limited liability company has, as the most important feature, *party autonomy in relation to all internal issues between company and members, as well as among members themselves.*[381] This far-reaching party autonomy to accommodate this form according to individual needs has many important consequences to internal organization, as will be seen below. Still, while possible to organize a limited liability company to suit the interests of a small-size company, usually managed by its owners, the law allows a possibility for this company form to have separate management and even a supervisory board. Although similarly organized, these forms usually differentiate between owners management (and supervision), or indirect management in close connection with members to directors in limited liability companies to professional management and independent supervision like in joint-stock, and especially public companies. Because of the flexibility, this form can be more attractive to members than a joint-stock company, which has many imperative provisions with regard to its organization.

A limited liability company is a closed company coupled with *intuitu personae* elements. Therefore, its legal capital is relatively static, while the structure of members is relatively stable with strict control on entry or exit and recomposition of positions within company. Therefore, an important distinction between a limited liability company and a joint-stock company is in *limited transferability of stakes* with important restrictions including pre-emption and other priority rights or restrictions. This distinction can also be made with regard to *exit rights* of members, as well as exclusion of a member in specific cases.

## §2. Formation

### I. Formal Requirements and Minimum Contents of Articles

*240.* A limited liability company is formed simultaneously in the same formal procedure including obligatory registration as is the case with a joint-stock company (*see* above under Chapter 1, §2.I.). Same as a joint-stock company, a limited liability company is founded on the basis of articles of incorporation (or unilateral decision if there is only one founder). Nevertheless, a limited liability company has only one obligatory document although internal organization can be regulated through a contract between some or all members, but only with internal character (agreement between members of the limited liability company).[382] Therefore, articles of incorporation must include the most important issues on the management of the company.

*Articles of incorporation* have to be in written form, signed by all founders, and their signature has to be certified. Registration is obligatory for this document, including all further amendments. Articles of incorporation can be drafted as an electronic document, when company members can apply their qualified electronic signature, when there is no need of additional certification of the document by the

381. *See* in particular Art. 140 LCC 2011.
382. Article 15 LCC 2011.

public notary, with the exception of the transfer of immovable property. If articles of incorporation are in electronic form or are digitalized by a person entitled to digitalize document with his qualified electronic signature, this document is registered in the Business Register in electronic form.

Articles of incorporation have *obligatory minimum content*, including identification of the company (name and seat) and its founders (name, identification number and domicile or seat of the natural or legal person), objects clause including principal activities, the total amount of subscribed capital, contributions in cash and in kind (including their value and content) and when these contributions are due, for each member, including percentage of their participation in the legal capital of the company.[383] Articles must also regulate the internal organization of the company, including bodies and their powers, or if there are no particular provisions on powers, dispositive provisions will be applicable. Here, it is important to underline vast party autonomy with regard to powers of the bodies, which is the most important difference between a joint-stock company in issues related to internal organization of the company.

Articles of incorporation can be *amended* if decided on by an absolute majority of votes of all members if no higher majority is prescribed. In case rights of members are less favourable after amendments, they must vote in favour of them, including limitations or exclusion of preferential rights of subscription or purchase of stakes, change of the majority necessary for general meeting decisions, introduction or increase in the right to additional payment, changes with regard to withdrawal and cancellation of members' stakes, exclusion of members, as well as the appointment of a director and members of the supervisory board in case of a two-tier system, with regard to nominations of these persons.

All amendments must be signed by all members who voted for them. Decisions on amendments to the articles of incorporation must be certified only if that is prescribed in the articles of incorporation and registered in the Business Register. The same provisions as in the case of a joint-stock company apply if articles of incorporation are to be pronounced null and void (*see* above under Chapter 1, §2.I.).

## II. Notification, Registration, Incorporation and Publicity

*241.* Registration procedure is regulated by the Law on Registration procedure in the Business Agency Register for all companies, irrespective of the form. Therefore, all provisions with regard to registration, incorporation and publicity apply as in the case of a joint-stock company (*see* above under Chapter 1, §2.II.). The same is the case with regard to contracts made on behalf of a company in formation (*see* above under Chapter 1, §2.III.).

383. *See* Arts 11–14 and 141 LCC 2011.

## III. Number of Subscribers

*242.* Limited liability company is a commercial company whose capital is divided between one or more members, owners of the stakes. Members can be natural or legal persons. Therefore, there is no limitation on the minimum number of subscribers. The current legal regime does not provide for a maximum number of members (or subscribers) in a limited liability company.

## IV. Initial Capital

*243.* A limited liability company has a minimum capital requirement of RSD 100 (approx. EUR 0.85), unless a higher amount is prescribed for certain activities.[384] The initial capital amount and its modifications have to be registered and published.

Principle of fixed capital adopted in the Law on Commercial Companies is equally applied to a limited liability company, same as for a joint-stock company. These provisions include duty to contribute. As already explained, contributions in all closed companies must be made in time, prescribed in the articles of incorporation (or other decision on the capital increase), within a time limit set by law, which must be no longer than five years.[385]

Contributions must be provided, although it is possible to allow changes of obligations only, upon approval of the general meeting by decision taken with the two-thirds majority of all members of the company, or other higher majority prescribed in the articles of incorporation.

In the case of non-provision of the obligation to contribute, the company may offer additional time to members to fulfil their obligations, which must be at least thirty days. After expiration of the additional time for provision of the contribution obligation, a limited liability company may decide on the exclusion of the member from the company.

In the case of stake transfer, there is a joint and several liability of the previous member as well as a person who acquired the stake to the company.[386] In this case, a lawsuit can be brought either by the company itself or its members holding at least 5% of the total amount of capital subscribed.

Initial capital is protected by the provisions of responsibility in the case of stake transfer; those on prohibitions of return of paid or performed contributions, including payment of penalties, as well as of prohibition on direct and indirect financial assistance (loans, guarantees, providing for securities) by the company for the acquisition of its stakes by members, employees or third parties.[387]

384. Article 145 LCC 2011.
385. Article 46 LCC 2011.
386. Article 49 LCC 2011.
387. *See* in particular Arts 60, 154 LCC 2011.

## V. Contributions in Kind

*244.* According to general provisions on contributions, they can be either in cash or in kind, and their value must be expressed in RSD. Contributions in kind may consist of different tangible assets (immovable and movable) as well as intangible and financial assets (different kinds of rights).[388] In a limited liability company, contributions cannot consist of obligations to perform work or provide services. Many controversial issues remain for the courts to decide regarding contributions in kind, especially with regard to certain rights (for example, whether grant of a loan or credit without interest by a member is a contribution expressed in the amount of interest, or how to assess the goodwill).[389]

The value of contributions in kind can be determined either by members or by evaluation. With regard to evaluation, all general provisions are applicable (*see* above under Chapter 1, §2.VI.).

## VI. Other Material Formation Requirements

*245.* Formation of a limited liability company is usually followed by several technical and administrative requirements. They include opening of bank accounts, making of a company's seal (even though it is no longer required the use of the company's seal in pursuing business activities) and obtaining a tax identification number from the tax authorities (which is obtained at the moment of registration, organized as a one-stop shop). Pursuing certain activities requires applying with competent inspection agencies or other authorities (market, sanitary, labour, building inspection authorities, etc.) in order to obtain necessary certificates and approvals on meeting necessary requirements for performing registered activities.

These approvals and certificates are dependent on company's activities. Therefore, it is prescribed as a general provision in the Law on Commercial Companies that registration or pursuit of a certain activity may be, under specific laws, conditioned upon approval, permission or other authorization of the competent authority.[390]

# §3. Essential Elements of the Legal Person

*246.* All general provisions on the essential elements of the legal person, including seat, name, objects clause, commercial character of activities and identification

388. Article 45 LCC 2011.

389. *See* in detail: S. Šogorov, 'Predmet uloga u društvo sa ograničenom odgovornošću' (Contributions to the limited liability company), *Pravni život (Legal life)* 11/2003, 17ff; *See also*: Vladimir Marjanski, 'Podobnost nenovčanog uloga kao predmeta obaveze unošenja uloga u društvo s ograničenom odgovornošću' ('Eligibility of a Contributions in Kind as a Subject of an Obligation to Invest in a Limited Liability Company'), *Zbornik radova Pravnog fakulteta u Novom Sadu (Collected Papers of the Faculty of Law in Novi Sad)* 3/2019, 909ff.

390. *See* Art. 4 LCC 2011.

number are the same for all company forms. In this respect, *see* provisions explained with regard to joint-stock companies (*see* above under Chapter 1, §3).

## §4. Capital and Stakes

### I. Capital of a Limited Liability Company

*247.* As already underlined above (under Chapter 1, §4), legal capital in Serbian Company law is defined as nominal (also registered) capital as the total value of the subscriptions of its members. All general provisions in relation to legal capital of a joint-stock company are also applicable, and include capital formation with various limits with regard to contributions (*see* above under this chapter §2.IV and V), capital maintenance, especially distribution of profits (and other payments) and possible capital reorganizations, including capital increase or reduction. These mechanisms are also intended to protect creditors, here even more important than in the case of a joint-stock company. Reason for this special protection lies in the recent modernization of the capital minimum requirements, reducing it to a symbolic amount of RSD 100 (approx. EUR 0.85).

Therefore, a limited liability company can be incorporated with a symbolic amount of capital subscribed, or higher subscription, if that is provided in the articles of incorporation. Although the duty to contribute is unconditional, performance of this obligation is prescribed in the articles of incorporation and within time limits set by law – no longer than five years. This is the reason why Serbian Company Law pays special attention to mechanisms for capital maintenance, especially (un)lawful distributions to members with regard to limited liability companies (*see* below under IV.A.).

### II. Alteration of Capital Requirements

*248.* Maintenance of legal capital is a fundamental principle of Serbian law governing not only joint-stock but also limited liability companies. Therefore, there are important provisions on capital increase and capital reduction.[391]

391. Tatjana Jevremović Petrović, 'Zaštita poverilaca putem pravila o kapitalu društva' ('Creditor Protection Through the Rules of Company's Capital'), *Uskla ivanje poslovnog prava Srbije sa pravom Evropske unije (2011)* (*Harmonisation of Serbian Business Law with EU Law (2011)*), Pravni fakultet Univerziteta u Beogradu, Beograd, 2011, 114ff.

### *A. Capital Increase*

*249.* Legal capital of a limited liability company can be increased by new subscriptions of existing or new members, from the company's reserves or profits, through conversion of debt to equity, including additional payments, and finally, as a result of statutory change.[392]

Capital increase can be made only upon a general meeting decision. The resolution of the general meeting on the increase in the share capital can be passed even before the full payment, i.e., the entry of the contributions of the existing members of the company, provided that the member who joins simultaneously with the accession fully pays, i.e., enters his contribution. The most important special provision in relation to capital increase of a limited liability company introduces an obligatory preferential right of subscription of existing members in proportion to their stakes if capital is increased by new subscriptions.[393] This provision is nevertheless of the dispositive nature and makes other regimes possible if provided in the articles of incorporation.

### *B. Capital Reduction*

*250.* The most important provisions on capital reduction include limited cases when capital reduction can be made (including when company covers its debts or build a reserve), the principle of equal treatment of members, as well as various provisions introduced to protect creditors.[394] The prescribed majority for decision on the capital reduction is two-thirds votes of all members of the company, if no other majority is prescribed, even though it cannot be lower than an absolute majority of all members who have a right to vote on this issue. Decision on the capital reduction must be registered within three months, whereby registration has constitutive effect.

---

392. Vladimir Marjanski, 'Odluka o povećanju osnovnog kapitala društva s ograničenom odgovornošću novim ulozima' ('The Resolution on Capital Increase through New Contributions in Limited Liability Company'), *Zbornik radova Pravnog fakulteta u Novom Sadu (Collected Papers of Faculty of Law in Novi Sad)* 3/2017, 753ff.
393. Article 146 LCC 2011.
394. *See* Art. 147-147v LCC 2011. *See also*: Vladimir Marjanski, 'Vrste, cilj (svrha) i načini smanjenja kapitala društva s ograničenom odgovornošću' ('The Type, the Purpose (Goal) and the Ways of Capital Reduction of the Limited Liability Company'), *Zbornik radova Pravnog fakulteta u Novom Sadu (Collected Papers of Faculty of Law in Novi Sad)* 3/2018, 1025ff.

## III. Preferential Right of Subscription

*251.* It is the right of existing members to have preferential right of subscription of stakes when a limited liability company increases its capital by new subscriptions. Preferential right of subscription must be proportional to the existing members' stakes, but it may be provided for in another proportion in the articles of incorporation.[395]

## IV. Forbidden Reductions of Capital and Acquisition of Stakes by the Corporation Itself

*252.* As already stressed, Serbian company law pays special attention to legal capital maintenance with regard to all capital companies, but in particular to limited liability companies. Apart from already discussed provisions related to capital increase and reduction (*see* above this chapter §4.II.), an important capital maintenance mechanism is achieved through restrictions on payments to members (*see* below under section A), as well as provisions on the acquisition of stakes by the company itself (*see* below under section B).

### *A. Restrictions on Distributions to Members*

*253.* One of the main provisions to protect legal capital of a limited liability company provides for various limits in making distributions to members. As already explained, these provisions are of particular importance, bearing in mind that there is no significant minimum capital requirement (only RSD 100, approx. EUR 0.85).

General provision for a limited liability company limits all payments, including profit distribution, return of the amount additionally paid up by the members, return of the loans made by members, as well as all other payments conditional upon provisions of the articles of incorporation and restrictions introduced by the Law on Commercial Companies.[396]

All general provisions with regard to payment restrictions applicable to a joint-stock company – including balance sheet net assets test and profit and loss account test (*see* above under Chapter 1, §4.VII.A.) are also applied to limited liability companies. Exceptions for payments made to members – natural persons, on the basis of the work contract are also applicable. There is an even higher probability of circumvention of the provision on the payment restrictions in the case of a limited liability company because of the usual size and family character of this company

395. Article 146 para. 3 LCC 2011.
396. *See* Arts 182–185 LCC 2011. Vladimir Marjanski, 'Raspodela dobiti članovima društva s ograničenom odgovornošću i razlike u odnosu na druge isplate korporativno-pravnog karaktera' ('Allocation of Profit to Members of Limited Liability Company and Differences in Relation to Other Corporate Legal Payments'), *Zbornik radova Pravnog fakulteta u Novom Sadu (Collected Papers of Faculty of Law in Novi Sad)* 1/2020, 215ff.

form, where members prefer to be employed and compensated by the company for their work, than to distribute profits made.

Although all general requirements for payments restrictions for a joint-stock company are also applicable to a limited liability company, there are some other additional provisions. They introduce additional obligations to directors and members of the supervisory board in a two-tier system, who knew that since the end of the last financial year until general meeting's decision on approval of annual accounts, company's financial situation worsened seriously and permanently (loss or significant change of value of the subscribed capital) to inform the general meeting, after which general meeting cannot distribute profits in the amount equivalent to the value of reduction of the company's assets. Otherwise, a director or a member of the supervisory board will be responsible for damage occurred upon profit distribution to the members, as well as to company's creditors.[397] This is the only provision in Serbian Company Law to introduce directors' (or member of the supervisory board) direct responsibility to creditors.

Provisions with regard to persons responsible for unlawful payments are different to those applicable to a joint-stock company, where unlawful payments must be returned by the shareholders who received payments provided that they knew or should have known that payments were irregular and within the time limit of five years since payment was made.[398] In case of unlawful payments in a limited liability company *every member* who received any payment against general payment restrictions must return them to the company, and otherwise cannot be arranged with the company. Still, members who received payments in good faith must return them only if necessary for fulfilment of creditors' claims.[399]

Also, *members* who voted for unlawful payments, as well as *directors and members of the supervisory board* in case of a two-tier system if approving payments when they knew or should have known that payments were unlawful have unlimited joint and several liability for the return of unlawful payments to the company, and otherwise cannot be arranged with the company. Finally, all other members, directors and members of the supervisory board in the case of a two-tier system if proved to act intentionally or with gross negligence and contributed to these payments also have unlimited joint and several liability for return of unlawful payments to the company. Time limit for responsibility is five years, except for members receiving payments if company proves that they knew or should have known that payments were unlawful when time limit is ten years.

---

397. Article 184. para. 2 and 3 LCC 2011.

398. Tatjana Jevremović Petrović, 'Zaštita poverilaca putem pravila o kapitalu društva' ('Creditor Protection Through the Rules of Company's Capital'), *Uskla ivanje poslovnog prava Srbije sa pravom Evropske unije (2011) (Harmonisation of Serbian Business Law with EU Law (2011)),* Pravni fakultet Univerziteta u Beogradu, Beograd, 2011, 129–131.

399. *See* Art. 185 LCC 2011.

*B. Acquisition of the Company's Stakes by the Company Itself*

*254.* Although not regulated in detail as is the case for acquisition of a company's own shares, the Law on Commercial Companies also restricts acquisition of stakes by the company itself in the case of a limited liability company.[400]

The company may not subscribe its own stakes, but can acquire stakes from its members (including acquisition of parent company's stakes) in full or partially.[401] Naturally, a company cannot acquire all stakes in the company, and must remain with at least one member.

Acquisition of own stakes can be made upon general meetings' decision by two-thirds majority of votes of all members of the company, if no other majority is prescribed, even though it cannot be lower than an absolute majority of all members who have a right to vote on this issue. There are several situations when a company can acquire its own stakes, including acquisition without consideration, in the case of exclusion of a member from the company, by purchase of stakes in full or partially from members, or in the case of compulsory purchase of a stake – if provided in the articles of incorporation in the case of inheritance. Finally, acquisition of own stakes can be a result of statutory change.

A condition for the acquisition of own stakes is that a full consideration was made, except in several situations (in the case of exclusion of a member, compulsory purchase or statutory change), and that payment can be made out of reserves which can be used for this purpose. If company acquires own stakes against restrictions prescribed, acquisition may be pronounced null and void.

Stakes acquired by the company itself are *suspended in certain rights* during their holding, including the right to vote (including quorum composition), as well as the right to profit distribution and cannot be pledged. Upon a general meeting decision, stakes acquired by the company can be *distributed to the members proportionally*. They can be *distributed upon payment or other contribution to members or third parties*, when existing members have a preferential right of subscription in proportion to their share in the capital subscribed. Finally, stakes must be *cancelled*, if not distributed, after three years, when company must apply provisions with regard to capital reduction. A general meeting decision on distribution of company's own stakes must be made by an absolute majority of all members, except when otherwise provided for in the articles of incorporation, or when distribution is not proportional, when an unanimous decision is required, if otherwise is not prescribed in the articles of incorporation.

249.1 Recent amendments of the Law on Commercial Companies in 2019 introduced additional provisions on the reserved company's own stake in order to offer right of acquisition of company's stakes.[402] Reserved company's own stake is a

400. Articles 157–159 LCC 2011.

401. Vladimir Marjanski, 'Sticanje sopstvenog udela društva s ograničenom odgovornošću otkupom od člana društva' ('Acquiring of a Company's own Equity Interest through Redemption of a Company Member'), *Zbornik radova Pravnog fakulteta u Novom Sadu (Collected Papers of Faculty of Law in Novi Sad)* 2/2015, 671ff.

402. *See* Arts 159a-159ž LCC 2011.

stake acquired by the company free of charge from the company's members with the purpose to issue a financial instrument – right of acquisition of company's stakes.

Reserved company's own stake cannot be under pledge, nor it can be disposed or distributed in any other way but according to provisions on the right of acquisition of company's stakes. One company can have one or several reserved company's own stakes, including single-member company, but they cannot represent more than 40% of stakes in the company's capital. Decision on reserved company's own stake has to be made by two-thirds majority of votes of all members of the company, if no other majority is prescribed, even though it cannot be lower than absolute majority of all members who have a right to vote on this issue and can be acquired only from those members who voted for decision, and only for stakes fully paid-up or otherwise contributed. Reserved company's own stake must be registered. It grants to the company no voting rights, while distributions of profit are also forbidden.

The most important purpose of the reserved company's own stake is to issue a non-transferable financial instrument – right of acquisition of company's stakes at a certain date upon fixed price. This financial instrument cannot be under pledge and is non-transferable, including that it cannot be inherited. The issue of this financial instrument is made upon general meetings' decision, if not otherwise prescribed in the articles of incorporation, and contains the most important information on the financial instrument, as well the right of acquisition of company's stakes. It is registered in the Central depository, after which can be used to acquire company's stake or must be cancelled.

## V. Stakes in a Limited Liability Company

*255.* Stakes are not securities and cannot be acquired or disposed publicly on financial markets.[403] Stakes confer membership rights and are acquired in proportion to the value of members' contribution in the capital subscribed. Still, proportion of members' stakes, including proportion of their rights upon stakes, may be determined not only in proportion to the capital subscribed but also otherwise, in the articles of incorporation or an unanimous general meeting decision.

The Law on Commercial Companies promotes a strict principle of *one stake – one member*, applicable also to acquiring new stakes or to their partial transfer. Still, several persons can be *co-owners of one stake*, when considered as one member in the company.[404] Therefore, they are jointly and severally liable for all obligations with regard to their stake in the company. While they arrange their mutual relationships on contractual basis, their rights, including the right to vote, stake co-owners exercise through a joint representative, whose identity must be known to the company. Company can deliver all acts and notifications to co-owner to their joint representative. In case when the company is not informed of the appointment of a joint

403. *See* Arts 150–151 LCC 2011.

404. Article 153 LCC 2011. *See* further in: S. Šogorov, 'Suvlasnički udeo u društvu sa ograničenom odgovornošću' ('Co-ownership stake in the limited liability company'), *Pravo i privreda (Law and Economy)* 5-8/2004, 47ff.

representative, stakes are not included in the majority or quorum at the general meeting, while all acts and information to any one of them have effects on all co-owners.

Stakes cannot be acquired with any *financial assistance* of the company or be pledged by the company itself. Stakes can be *withdrawn and cancelled* only when this was provided in the articles of incorporation at the time of stake acquisition, or by the change of articles of incorporation, if approved by a member whose stake is to be withdrawn and cancelled. It is a unilateral act by the company under stipulated conditions.

Decision on stake withdrawal and cancellation must be made by the general meeting, and must include the basis for withdrawal and cancellation and confirmation that conditions for this decision were fulfilled. The decision must also include the amount and date for payment upon stake withdrawal and cancellation, but no longer than two years. Finally, the decision must include all consequences upon capital subscribed upon stake cancellation. In every case of stake withdrawal and cancellation provisions on capital reduction, except for a general meeting, decision must be respected.

## VI. Transfer of Stakes

*256.* General provisions provide for a free transfer of stakes in full or in part, unless otherwise provided in the articles of incorporation.[405] Obviously, this is the case when stakes are transferred between members, because there are several mechanisms introduced to protect existing members in the case of a stake transfer (in full or in part) to third persons.

Irrespective of protection mechanisms, transfer of stakes must be made in written form, including obligatory certification of signatures. Another form may be prescribed by the law. In case of transfer of stakes, transferor shall be jointly and severally liable with the transferee for liabilities towards the company with regard to unpaid or otherwise performed contribution, or additional payment.

Stakes can be divided (partitioned) upon contract where stakes are partially transferred, upon succession, upon agreement on the stakes division between co-owners or in other cases, prescribed by law. Stakes division can be limited in all (except succession) or some cases in the articles of incorporation.

### *A. Transfer of Stakes to Third Persons*

*257.* Closed nature of a limited liability company, as a key difference compared to a joint-stock company, and its similarity to companies of persons, is best visible in the regime of stake transfer to third persons. Serbian Law on Commercial Companies introduces dispositive provisions on the preferential right of purchase, which

405. *See* Art. 160 LCC 2011.

can be excluded or altered, including possibility to introduce the regime of approval made by the company, including an entitlement of the company to nominate a third person who will acquire members' stake.

1. Preferential Right of Purchase

*258.* Preferential right of purchase is with all existing members of a limited liability company, except when this right is excluded in the articles of incorporation or the law. All existing members have a preferential right of purchase in case of stake transfer to third parties. Therefore, not all transfers, but only those consisting of stake *purchase*, grant the right of preferential purchase to existing members.

If a member wants to transfer its stake to a third-party, he must offer it in writing to all existing members to purchase his stake. The offer must include all details with regard to the transfer agreement, as well as information on the exercise of the preferential right of purchase: address for acceptance, time limit and other conditions for the stake transfer.

Provisions on the *procedure for the exercise of the preferential right of purchase* are of dispositive nature, and provide that all members who exercise their right must accept the offer in full, and in writing within thirty days of receiving the offer, or in other prescribed time (but no longer than ninety days). If more than two members accept the purchase offer, they can agree on the transfer proportion, or if that is not the case, in proportion to the stakes of the members accepting the offer.

In case of a *breach of the preferential right of purchase* existing members can bring legal action and require that a court pronounce null and void the stake purchase contract, stipulates the member to transfer its stake to the plaintiff, or make a judgment on the stake purchase instead of the transfer agreement. The time limit for legal action is thirty days since plaintiff found out that purchase was agreed, but no longer than six months since its registration in the Business Register.

If a preferential right of purchase was exercised by several members, and some of them refuse or fail to form the transfer agreement without transferor's fault, he may agree on the transfer with remaining members. If none of them forms the agreement, transferor may agree on the transfer with a third party under conditions which are not favourable compared to the offer made to existing members, if not otherwise prescribed in the articles of incorporation. Instead of a transfer to a third party, transferor might bring a legal suit against one or several members, and ask the court to determine that a transfer was performed and that members must make compensation in proportion to the stakes acquired.

*Transfer to third parties is allowed* if no existing members accept the offer for transfer. Transfer must be made within ninety days of the time provided for the acceptance of the offer and under conditions which are not favourable compared to the offer made to existing members, if not otherwise prescribed in the articles of incorporation.

If stake transfer was made upon auction or similar procedure preferential right of purchase can be exercised only during this procedure, if not otherwise prescribed in the articles of incorporation.

### 2. Approval Made by the Company

*259.* Articles of incorporation may introduce that stake transfer to third persons must be made upon approval of the company. If not otherwise provided in the articles of incorporation, the prescribed procedure stipulates the transferor to submit notification for approval, including identity of the third person and other details on the stake transfer.

Stake transfer approval decision must be made by an absolute majority of all members of the limited liability company, unless another majority is provided for in the articles of incorporation. If the company fails to decide on the stake transfer within thirty days, transferor is free to transfer his stake to a third person under conditions submitted to the company.

The same consequences provided for the breach of a preferential right of purchase apply, involving a legal suit in front of the competent court. Also, if there is a pledge of stakes (in full or in part) and articles of incorporation provide for the approval of the company in the case of stake transfer, the same restrictions must be applied when a pledge is agreed.

### 3. Right of the Company to Nominate a Third Person

*260.* If stake transfer to third persons must be made upon approval of the company, company may instead nominate a third person to acquire the stake under the same conditions. If fifteen days after the notification of the third person that person refuses or fails to form the transfer agreement without transferor's fault, he may agree on the transfer with a third party under the same conditions.

If purchase was agreed with a third person, the company becomes jointly and severally liable with that person to the transferor for the payment of the purchase price.

### 4. Obligatory Stake Purchase by the Company

*261.* If a company disapproves the stake transfer without nominating a third person, company must purchase a transferor's stake after thirty days of its refusal to give consent for a stake transfer. If company refuses to purchase his stake, the transferor is free to sell his stake to a third person of his choice, upon the same purchase conditions.

## *B. Inheritance*

*262.* Stakes can be transferred to successors of the deceased member according to general rules on inheritance. Still, articles of incorporation can include provisions on the right of compulsory purchase by the company or one or several members within six months of member's death, but no later than three months since heirs' registration into the Business Register as members of the limited liability company.

The right of compulsory purchase can be with the company, when exercise of this right is decided by an absolute majority of all members; or one or more members, who exercise the right of compulsory purchase by written declaration to the company.

Articles of incorporation must include a method for the exercise of a compulsory purchase right, including determination of compensation and time limit for its payment. Heirs of the deceased members are entitled to this compensation if the company or members decide to exercise their right. Still, payments to heirs must be made according to general provisions on the restrictions on payments.

## §5. Members, Management and Control

*263.* In contrast to a joint-stock company, the basic rule for a limited liability company is the freedom of contractual regulation of company bodies. This freedom is manifested through permission that designation of bodies and their competence in a limited liability company might be stipulated according to articles of incorporation.[406] Consequently, we may have a company of this type where all bodies exist, as prescribed by law, either in a one-tier or two-tier system, while their competences can be regulated on an autonomous basis.

A limited liability company may be organized as a company with a one-tier management organization, and includes the general meeting and one or more directors. Also, a limited liability company may opt for a two-tier system, which includes general meeting, supervisory board and one or more directors.

## I. Members

*264.* Members of the limited liability company can be one or more natural or legal persons. Company must register information on its members. According to the Law on Commercial Companies, persons become members of the limited liability company upon registration of their status in the Business Register, which is also determinant for the loss of that status. Company is entitled and must have records on its members, including various information, like address, representative(s), etc., only for practical reasons, including information and other communication to its members.

### *A. General Principles*

*265.* Members of a limited liability company enjoy several rights upon their stakes. They include the right to vote, the right to participate in the profits realized by the company, the right to participate in the liquidation remainder, and to have

406. *See* Art. 141 para. 1 under 8 and para. 2; and Art. 198 LCC 2011.

other rights prescribed by law. Members' rights are in proportion of their stakes in the subscribed capital, but can be determined in another proportion in the articles of incorporation.

### *B. Members' Rights*

*266.* Members in a limited liability company have similar rights as shareholders in a joint-stock company. Similarly, members have various pecuniary rights, among which the most important is the right to participate in profits realized by the company (*see* below under section 1). Members also have preferential right of subscription (*see* above under this chapter §4.III.) as well as the right to liquidation or insolvency distribution of the remainder. The most important non-pecuniary membership rights involve information rights (*see* below under section 2), rights related to the general meeting (*see* below under section 3 and in detail in section D), as well as the most important non-pecuniary right – the right to vote (*see* below under section 4).

#### 1. Right to Participate in the Profits Realized

*267.* Members' right to participate in the profits realized by the company is conditional upon general provisions on payment restrictions. Apart from these provisions, all others dealing with dividend and interim dividend payments in a joint-stock company are applicable to the limited liability company.

Usually, profit distribution will be made according and in proportion to the members' stakes, but can be also made in another proportion, if provided in the articles of incorporation.[407]

#### 2. Information Rights

*268.* In terms of the Law on Commercial Companies, every limited liability company has to keep and retain for a prescribed time period certain acts and documents, including articles of incorporation and other internal acts, minutes and decisions of general meetings, board of directors' reports and supervisory boards' reports and minutes; documents setting up branches and agencies, documents confirming property and other related rights, information on directors and supervisory board members, including transactions made by them or persons connected to them, as well as information and address of company members. All documents must be kept on the company registered office premises or at the place accessible and known to all members. Unlike provision for joint-stock companies providing shareholders' access to certain acts and documents only, members of a limited liability company have access to all documents and acts which must be kept, as well as to financial

407. Article 183 LCC 2011.

reports and other documents with regard to business activities of the company, or connected to their exercise of rights. Members are entitled to inspect and copy these acts and documents during business hours, including the right to have a copy of every general meeting decision in writing.

A member who was prevented (or was not allowed) to access acts and documents can petition the court in a non-litigious procedure. His right to access acts and documents and to be informed on the facts relevant to the business operation of the company or in relation to the exercise of his rights can be denied upon directors' decision when there is a reasonable belief that this right could be used against company interest, or for the purpose in no relation to membership status, or when damage can be caused to another affiliated company.

Also, the director of a limited liability company must inform every member of facts relevant to the business operation of the company or in relation to the exercise of their rights. The same information is duty for every member, who must notify director with regard to the same facts and information. It is, therefore not only a right but also an obligation to inform every member of a limited liability company. If the director or member fails to inform others about facts important for the business operation of the company or in relation to the exercise of their rights, he will be liable for any damage caused.

It must be mentioned here that the director of a limited liability company must also inform the general meeting on accounting practice and financial reporting, business activities and its compatibility with law and other acts, issues with regard to auditors and related party transactions, if that is the case. Also, he must inform every member holding a stake equivalent to at least 10% of the capital subscribed (or supervisory board in a two-tier system) on every extraordinary issue which can be relevant to the company and its business.

### 3. Rights Related to the General Meeting

*269.* In principle, every member is entitled to be present and participate in the general meeting. Similarly to the joint-stock company, members enjoy several rights related to the general meeting. Most important rights related to the convocation, agenda and decision proposals will be discussed below under section D. Finally, the right to vote will be discussed next.

### 4. Right to Vote

*270.* Voting is the expression of members' opinion regarding the decision put to vote, and is one of the most important member control mechanisms. *Every member* is entitled to vote in proportion of his stake in the subscribed capital, if not otherwise prescribed in the articles of incorporation.[408] Nevertheless, it is forbidden to prescribe in the articles of incorporation that a member will have no right to vote.

---

408. On the general right to vote *see* Art. 199 LCC 2011.

The right to vote can be exercised either in person, including voting in writing (unless otherwise provided in the articles of incorporation or by rules of procedure); or by a proxy upon written authorization, which must be certified, if that is prescribed in the articles of incorporation.[409] Voting is performed publicly between members.

The right to vote may not be exercised in cases where members' interest conflicts with that of the company. Exclusion is also applicable for quorum determination, and is specifically introduced when deciding on the renunciation or reduction of obligations of a member towards the company, exclusion or withdrawal of a member from the company; filing or dropping of a lawsuit against him, as with regard to appointments of legal representatives in those proceedings; in the case when deciding on related party transactions, as well as in other cases prescribed by law or articles of incorporation.[410]

### *C. Members' Obligations*

#### 1. In General

*271.* As already mentioned, members of a limited liability company may have several obligations. The most important one is a duty to contribute (*see* above under this chapter §4.I.). Members of a limited liability company may also have an obligation for additional payments which will be explained below in detail because of the particular nature of this obligation and importance in this company form. Because of the closed nature of this company form, members have an obligation to inform directors on all issues relevant to the business activities of the company, as well as exercise of their rights (on this obligation and parallel right to information *see* above under section B.2). Finally, members may have other obligations, stipulated under articles of incorporation. Their subject may be different, and usually includes delivery of goods, rendering services to the company, management, etc.

#### 2. Additional Payments

*272.* Members of a limited liability company may have obligations for additional payments upon articles of incorporation or an unanimous decision of the general meeting, if no other majority is prescribed in the articles of incorporation, although that case can affect only members who voted for the additional payments.[411] This obligation is proportional to members' stakes in the company, but can

---

409. Other provisions on proxy voting for joint-stock company, prescribed by the Law on Commercial Companies are also applicable.
410. Article 214 LCC 2011.
411. On the additional payments *see* Arts 178–180 LCC 2011. *See also*: Stevan Šogorov, 'Autonomni pravni osnov za dodatne (dopunske) uplate članova društva sa ograničenom odgovornošću' ('Autonomous legal ground for additional payments by members of the limited liability company'), *Pravni život (Legal life)* 11/2011, 43ff.

be also prescribed in a different proportion. The purpose of additional payments may vary, and most often they are used to cover losses made, but may also be needed to develop new products, find new markets, etc.

Additional payments can only be in cash and are not considered as contributions, and they do not affect the amount of subscribed capital. Nevertheless, Serbian Law on Commercial Companies prescribed the obligation to return additional payments to members by applying provisions on capital reduction.

Additional payments can be returned to members if not necessary to cover loss incurred by the company or for the payment of creditors. Also, the return of additional payments is not possible before full payment or performance of all considerations. In the case when a company becomes insolvent, payment to members upon return of additional payments can be made only after full satisfaction of all other creditors.

Members of a limited liability company must perform their obligation to additional payments according to provisions on payment of the obligation to contribute. In the case of stake transfer, a member who did not perform his obligation of additional payment is jointly and severally liable to the acquirer of the stakes within three years of the transfer being registered in the Business Register.

A member can be released from his obligation to additional payment only if he paid or performed a full contribution and if he authorizes the company to sell his stake on the auction or in another procedure within thirty days of his obligation to additional payment falling due. A member can still be liable if price received did not cover his obligation in full, or can receive what was left after selling his stake and after the additional payment amount was satisfied.

In case when a member does not authorize the company to sell his stake or if the stake cannot be sold within two years, the company may decide on the exclusion of the member from the company. In that case, the member is not allowed to ask the company for any compensation for his stake, and is still liable for his obligation towards the company.

### *D. General Meeting*

*273.* General meeting is comprised of all members. In the case of a single member company, the single member performs powers of the general meeting. If the single member is a legal person, articles of incorporation can designate the body responsible for performing powers of the general meeting, or if that is not prescribed, this power has its legal representative.

As in the case of a joint-stock company, general meetings of a limited liability company are held at the company's registered office or another location (*see* in detail Chapter 1 §5.I.C), except otherwise provided by a general meeting decision or in the articles of incorporation.

In contrast to a joint-stock company, the general meeting can be *held using different communication methods*, including conference calls. In that case, persons participating in communication are held to be present during the general meeting.[412] Finally, every *decision* in a limited liability company *can be signed* by all members entitled to vote on the issue, where a general meeting session is not necessary.

### 1. Powers of the General Meeting

*274.* According to the Law on Commercial Companies, the general meeting has powers provided. They include *legislative power* of the general meeting, including change of the articles of incorporation.[413] General meeting powers also include powers in relation to *capital and securities*, including capital alterations – increase or reduction and issue of securities and acquisition and disposal of own stakes and reserved own stakes; and issues related to *company's property*, such as the acquisition or disposal of substantial property above a certain threshold. General meeting's authority is also to decide on *business results* – it approves financial and auditors' reports and decides on the profit and loss distribution. Power of the general meeting includes *electoral function and control over management and supervision,* including appointment and dismissal of representatives, directors and members of the supervisory boards, approval of their reports and deciding on their remuneration or criteria to determine remuneration; appointment of auditors and their remuneration. The important power of the general meeting is related to various *statutory issues*, including statutory changes and change of legal form, liquidation and petition requesting the opening of insolvency proceedings. Different to a joint-stock company, a limited liability company has many important powers in relation to *additional payments* and their returns, issues with regard to membership status, including *exclusion and withdrawal* issues, approval of stake transfer to third persons and deciding on conflicts of interest. It also *supervises director*(s), decides on legal suits against members, directors and members of the supervisory board, and performs other issues explicitly provided by law or included in the articles of incorporation.

In addition to the above *legally prescribed competence*, the meeting may decide on other matters established by the constitutive document or other decision or acts (*autonomous competence*). Unlike a joint-stock company, delegation of power from the general meeting to other bodies, as well as vice versa, is allowed, according to party autonomy.

412. *See* Art. 212 LCC 2011.
413. For the extensive list of general meeting's powers *see* Art. 200 LCC 2011.

## 2. Different Kinds of Shareholders' Meetings

*275.* Distinguishing between *an ordinary* (annual) and *extraordinary* meeting is explicitly set forth in Serbian law for a limited liability company, same as for a joint-stock company.[414]

*Annual or ordinary general meeting* is held annually, according to provisions for the annual meeting of a joint-stock company. The same is the case with extraordinary meetings of a limited liability company.

## 3. Convocation

*276.* The *power to call a general meeting* is within the competence of the director (in a one-tier system) or supervisory board (in a two-tier system). Nevertheless, it is expressly provided that articles of incorporation can provide that power to convene a general meeting to a member of the company or another person. Also, a general meeting must be convened upon written request of members holding or representing at least 10% of votes, or a lower percentage prescribed in the articles of incorporation.

If the director or supervisory board fails to convene the general meeting within three days in order to hold the meeting within the next fifteen days, members who filed the request can call the meeting directly within the next eight days.

*Notice of (call for) meetings must be communicated* in writing to each member at his address, kept in the company's records, if no other communication is provided in the articles of incorporation or agreed by members in writing. Notice must be communicated no later than eight days before the general meeting is held, unless otherwise provided in the articles of incorporation. Notice must include date of notice communication, time and place of the general meeting, agenda including decision proposals and other documents related to the agenda.

## 4. General Meeting Chairman, Agenda, Rules of Procedure, Minutes and Other Miscellaneous Matters

*277.* General meeting may adopt *rules of procedure* to specify procedural issues of the meeting. The general meeting has a chairman. Issues with regard to his appointment and powers are regulated by general provisions for a joint-stock company.[415]

*Agenda of the meeting* is determined by a decision on the convocation of the general meeting and communicated to members by notice of the call for the general meeting. Still, different to joint-stock companies where a general meeting is bound by the agenda adopted and can decide only upon issues contained in the agenda, a general meeting of a limited liability company can discuss and decide upon issues

414. Article 201 LCC 2011.
415. Article 209 LCC 2011.

contained in the agenda, *or other issues if all members are present at the meeting and none is opposed*, if not otherwise provided in the articles of incorporation.[416]

Also, one or more members holding or representing at least 5% of stakes in the subscribed capital (or other lower percentage prescribed in the articles of incorporation) can put additional items on the agenda and inform the company or other members directly about that in writing, at the latest three days before the general meeting is held (unless another time limit is prescribed in the articles of incorporation).

Finally, a general meeting of a limited liability company can be held without convocation procedure if all members are present, except if otherwise provided in the articles of incorporation.

Every decision taken during a general meeting must be recorded in writing in *general meeting's minutes*. There are detailed provisions on the content and formal requirements of the minutes, which are under the responsibility of the chairman.[417]

### 5. Quorum and Majority

*278.* *Quorum* necessary for the general meeting is set at a simple majority of the total number of votes, except when a higher majority is prescribed in the articles of incorporation. If conditions for quorum are not fulfilled, the meeting can be *adjourned* with the same agenda and within a time limit of ten to thirty days. Quorum for the adjourned general meeting is one-third of the total number of votes, if a higher majority is not prescribed in the articles of incorporation.

General meeting can adopt a decision by *a simple majority of members present*, entitled to vote upon a certain issue, except when a higher majority is required by law or articles of incorporation. Absolute majority of a total number of members' votes is necessary for a change of the articles of incorporation. Also, the Law prescribed *qualified majority of two-thirds of the total number of members' votes* for decisions on capital increase or reduction, statutory and change of legal form, decisions on the liquidation or requesting the opening of insolvency proceedings, profit distribution and covering of losses, as well as acquisition of own stakes and reserved own stakes by the company. The general meeting must decide by unanimous decision upon additional payments (if no other majority is prescribed in the articles of incorporation), and their return. Articles of incorporation may prescribe another qualified majority instead of the two-thirds majority or unanimous decision-making, but not below absolute majority of a total number of members' votes, entitled to vote upon a certain issue.[418]

---

416. On the agenda *see* Art. 204 para. 5 LCC 2011.
417. Article 210 LCC 2011.
418. *See* Art. 211 LCC 2011.

### 6. Action for Avoidance

*279.* Action for avoidance is prescribed in very limited circumstances for a joint-stock company. Those provisions can be also applied for decisions taken in a limited liability company.[419]

## E. *Minority Members' Rights*

*280.* Development of trade practice prompted modern legislations to design a series of institutes of protection of minority by capital in these companies. Generally, it is considered that the position of minority members is less favourable than the one in joint-stock companies.

The Law on Commercial Companies has certain provisions granting the same rights to minority members as minority shareholders have, and usually grant possibility that another regime might be introduced if prescribed in the articles of incorporation. These rights include withdrawal right of the dissenting member when voting against (or abstaining from a vote) upon issues with regard to change of articles of incorporation on their most important rights, statutory changes, change of legal form, and change of the time scope for which the company was established; in the case of approval of a substantial property acquisition or disposal; as well as other cases when his rights are amended, if that is provided for in the articles of incorporation.[420] Also, the Law on Commercial Companies provides a possibility to apply provisions with regard to special and extraordinary auditing control to a limited liability company, as well as the right to liquidate and to apply other minority oppression remedies.[421]

## F. *Changes in the Membership Status*

*281.* Members of a limited liability company may lose their status if deceased or in the case of loss of legal personality if the member is a legal person (*see* above under this chapter §4.VI.B.). Members can also decide to leave the company through their withdrawal right (*see* below under §1), or they can be excluded from the company (*see* below under §2). Members also lose their status in the case of stake transfer in full (*see* above under this chapter §4.VI.A§), or in the case of withdrawal and cancellation of their stakes (*see* above under this chapter §4.V.).

### 1. Withdrawal Right

*282.* Members of a limited liability company *may withdraw from the company without good cause* at any time and without stating their cause, except when they

419. *See* Art. 217 LCC 2011.
420. *See* in detail Arts 474–476 and especially Art. 477 LCC 2011.
421. *See* Arts 236 and 239 LCC 2011.

have any outstanding obligations towards the company under duty to contribute.[422] In this case of a withdrawal, a member is not allowed to ask for compensation for his stake in the company and must fulfil all his obligations towards company. Withdrawal must be registered simultaneously with the registration of the acquisition of the company's own stake (which is acquired automatically).[423]

Nevertheless, a member can *withdraw from the company if there is a justified reason* (good cause), including damage caused by other members or the company, when prevented from exercising his rights or when non-proportional obligations are introduced; or in other cases, and including those prescribed in the articles of incorporation. If there is a good cause, a member may ask for withdrawal, including reasons and amount to be paid as compensation for his stake, as well as the payment due date. General meeting must decide by an absolute majority of all members, or a higher majority prescribed in the articles of incorporation, upon the request and inform the member within sixty days of its receipt. Otherwise, it is considered that the company accepted the withdrawal including all conditions. If accepted, the stake of the withdrawn member becomes a stake owned by the company itself (and without necessity for a general meeting to decide on the acquisition of its own stakes) while company must reduce capital (if there are conditions for reduction and upon all requirements necessary for the reduction of the capital), upon which the member may establish security for the payment of his compensation.

If a request for withdrawal is not accepted, a member can file a legal suit to the court and ask to be withdrawn from the company because of justified reasons and be compensated for his stake. The court may decide on the withdrawal, including compensation amount upon market value of the stake, but at least equivalent to the proportion of his stake in the subscribed capital. The decision must also include payment due date according to financial situation of the company, but no longer than two years, or another period of time prescribed in the articles of incorporation but no longer than five years; as well as security for the payment, if necessary.

Withdrawn member can be compensated only by reserves collected for this purpose, or with other compensation received after disposal of stake owned by the company upon withdrawal. Company must not make any payments to its members until full payment to the member in withdrawal is made. Withdrawn member also has the right for compensation of any damage caused, which he can claim in other proceedings in front of the court. Compensation for damage can be made only upon the amount received by disposal of the stake owned by the company upon withdrawal. Other members are jointly and severally liable in proportion to their stakes for any compensation of damage to the withdrawn member.

---

422. On the withdrawal right *see* Arts 187–194 LCC 2011.

423. *See* in detail on withdrawal rights in the limited liability company: Vladimir Marjanski, 'Istupanje člana iz društva s ograničenom odgovornošću' ('Withdrawal of a Member from a Limited Liability Company'), *Pravo i privreda (Law and Economy)* 4–6/2016, 120ff.

## 2. Exclusion of the Member(s)

*283. General meeting* may decide by the two-thirds majority of remaining members upon exclusion of the member(s) who *failed to perform his duty to contribute* after additional time for payment or performance of his obligation. The same decision can be made in the case of *failure to make additional payments* to the company.[424]

If excluded, member can be deleted from the Business Register, while his stake becomes stake owned by the company itself. Member who was excluded upon failure to perform his duty to contribute or make payment upon additional payments has no right to be compensated for his stake. He (as well as transferor in the case of stake transfer) must fulfil his obligation upon duty to contribute or to make additional payments, if necessary for the payment of creditors' claims. Company may also claim damages in front of the court.

In all other cases general meeting can decide upon filing legal suit in front of the *court in order to decide on the exclusion of the member(s)* from the company. Decision must be taken upon reasons included in the articles of incorporation – when decision must be made if these reasons were fulfilled. Also, court can decide on the exclusion in other cases when there are justified reasons for exclusion, such as the case when member caused damage to the company intentionally or with gross negligence, or failed to perform duties owed to the company according to the law or upon articles of incorporation; or when he acts or fails to act and makes business operation of the company impossible or difficult to a great extent – when court must decide on the existence and justification of the reasons for exclusion.

Court can temporarily suspend voting or other rights of the member upon whose exclusion will be decided if requested by the company, or introduce receivership (temporary management) in order to avoid damage for the company.

Legal suit must be brought during six months since company found out about existence of the reason for exclusion, but no longer than five years since these reasons occurred.

If excluded, members' stake becomes stake owned by the company itself. Member who was excluded must fulfil his obligation upon duty to contribute or to make additional payments, if necessary for the payment of creditors' claims. Company can also claim damages from the member excluded.

Member who was excluded can ask for compensation for his stake from the company in front of the court during 180 days since he was excluded from the company. Compensation can be made upon value of the stake in proportion to the liquidation remainder if company was liquidated. Decision must include also payment due date according to financial situation of the company, but no longer than two years, or other period of time prescribed in the articles of incorporation but no longer than five years. Assets available for compensation are under the same regime as in the case of withdrawal (*see* above under §1).

424. On the exclusion *see* Arts 195–197 LCC 2011. *See also*: S. Šogorov, 'Isključenje člana iz društva s ograničenom odgovornošću' ('Exclusion of the member from the limited liability company'), *Pravo i privreda (Law and Economy)* 5-8/2003, 71ff.

## II. Management and Control of the Limited Liability Company

*284.* The dilemma of how to organize the internal structure of company bodies was resolved by equivalent option left to limited liability company and its articles of incorporation to decide whether to have one-tier or two-tier system of internal organization. The same option exists in the internal structure of the joint-stock company.[425]

When limited liability company is organized to have *one-tier system*, it has general meeting and one or more directors, appointed by the general meeting. The other – *two-tier system* is adopted by the law alternatively with the first one. It has obligatory supervisory board, appointed by the general meeting. Also, in the two-tier system a company must have one or more directors, appointed by the supervisory board.

### *A. Director(s) of the Limited Liability Company*

*285.* Limited liability company has one or more directors, depending on the articles of incorporation or general meetings' decision. If there are no particular provisions on their number, limited liability company has one director. Director of the limited liability company is not a fully independent body, in comparison to the joint-stock company. Although being a separate body, because of the closed nature of the company, he is under significant influence (and interference) of company members into company management. However, director is also a company's body, managing the company business operation with full responsibility, with its powers based on the law, articles of incorporation and other acts.

#### 1. General Conditions

*286.* The director of the limited liability company may be either company member (one of them, several or all of them), or some other person(s). The Law on Commercial Companies has few provisions with regard to directors of the limited liability company. Most of provisions dealing with directors in the joint-stock company are applicable in this form as well. Therefore, only special provisions with regard to directors of the limited liability company will be explained below.

#### 2. Appointment

*287.* General meeting appoints director of the company in the one-tier system. If company adopts two-tier system, his appointment is made by the supervisory board. Same body responsible for the appointment is responsible for the removal of director, which can be made at any time and without good cause.

---

425. Article 198 LCC 2011.

First director can also be appointed in the articles of incorporation. Once appointed all directors must be registered in the Registration Agency. Mandate of limited liability company director is not limited by law, but can be limited in the articles of incorporation or by general meetings' decision.

In the event of vacancy in the position of director, remaining directors who have power to act individually continue to perform their duties and have same representation powers. If directors are authorized to perform their representation powers collectively, they must inform general meeting or supervisory board in order to appoint vacant directors positions. Until then, remaining directors are allowed to act in urgent cases, unless otherwise is prescribed by articles of incorporation or general meetings' decision.

### 3. Power of Management and Representation

*288.* General provision defines competence of director of the limited liability company to include business management of the company, as well as representation power.[426]

First of all, director is the *legal representative* of the company entitled to represent company towards third persons. Although director represents company towards third persons in accordance with the articles of incorporation, general meetings' decisions and supervisory board instructions in case of a two-tier system, according to general provision on representation, any limits on his powers may not be relied on as against third parties, except in the case of joint signature.[427] Company may have more than one director, when they act collectively in representing the company, unless otherwise provided in the articles of incorporation or general meetings' decision.[428] In the case when company loses its director and the new one is not registered within thirty days, each member of the company or other interested party can appeal to court in order to appoint a temporary representative of the company. Until this appointment, third parties can perform their acts towards member of the supervisory board (if there is any) or any member of the company, and the company will be bound by these acts.

Director of the company has *management powers* according to the articles of incorporation or general meetings' decision, as well as supervisory board instructions in case of a two-tier system.[429] If there is more than one director, all of them have management powers collectively, except when otherwise is provided in the articles of incorporation or general meetings' decision. When the articles of incorporation or general meetings' decision introduce individual power of management for directors, he is not entitled to act when any remaining director(s) is opposing his acts, but must act upon instructions given by the general meeting or supervisory board (in case of two-tier system).

---

426. Articles 218, 221–222, 224–225 LCC 2011.
427. *See* Art. 221 in relation to Art. 33 LCC 2011.
428. On representation *see* in detail Arts 221–222 LCC 2011.
429. *See* Art. 224 LCC 2011.

The most important difference to the joint-stock company with regard to management power delegation exists with regards to so-called presumed competence of director, if they fall outside powers of the general meeting (or general meeting and supervisory board in case of a two-tier system).[430]

### 4. Duties of Directors to the Company

*289.* As already mentioned with regard to joint-stock company, the Law of Commercial Companies introduces duties towards a company for certain persons. For the limited liability company, persons owing duties towards the company are set as following: members having significant stake in the company, or controlling members, directors and members of the supervisory board, legal representatives and procurist, as well as liquidator.[431] Other persons may owe duties if it is prescribed in the articles of incorporation. Their duties are identical to those of the persons holding equivalent positions in the joint-stock company. The same is the case with members with significant or controlling stake in the company, owing duties towards company (and not other members directly), which can be compared with shareholders in the joint-stock company. Therefore, for all details with regard to duties *see* in detail Chapter 1, §5.II. and III.C.

### 5. Liability of Directors

*290.* Unlike joint-stock company, which has only one explicit provision for civil responsibility of members of company bodies, including members of the board of directors, as well as executive or supervisory board members, the same provision is only applicable to the members of the supervisory board in the limited liability company.

Therefore, liability of directors is determined upon general provisions on directors' responsibilities, as well as specific provisions on directors' duties (*see* above under section E).

Directors have several *responsibilities*. His general responsibility is to perform his powers according to law, articles of incorporation and general meetings' decisions or instructions of the supervisory board in case of two-tier system. Also, director's responsibility concerns keeping of business records and accuracy of financial reports, as well as general meetings' decisions records, available to every member of the limited liability company. Apart from obligation to notify general assembly or supervisory board in case of a two-tier system, he must also inform members of the limited liability company. Information includes notification of every member of facts relevant for the business operation of the company or in relation to the exercise of their rights, as well as notification of every member holding stake equivalent

430. Article 224 para. 4 and 5 LCC 2011.
431. Articles 61ff LCC 2011.

to at least 10% of the capital subscribed on every extraordinary issue which can be relevant for the company and its business.[432]

Also, there is a special provision on directors' responsibility to the company in case of unlawful payments, but also to members and to creditors (directly) in case of breach of duty of information of the general meeting which decided on the profit distribution (*see* above under this chapter §4.IV.A.).

### *B. Supervisory Board of the Limited Liability Company*

*291.* Limited liability company might have two-tier management system, if provided in the articles of incorporation, when it must have general meeting, obligatory supervisory board and one or more directors.

#### 1. Appointment and Composition

*292.* General conditions for a person to be appointed as a member of supervisory board, including composition of the board, are the same as for the joint-stock company (*see* in detail Chapter 1, §5.III.A.). They specially include full legal capacity and fulfilment of any special provisions provided in the articles of incorporation, apart from general restrictions valid upon the Law of Commercial Companies for all directors (criminal convictions, multiple directorships, etc.). Members of the supervisory board must not be employed by the limited liability company. They decide on meetings upon same provisions as in the case of joint-stock company.

It is the general meeting who has power to appoint members of the supervisory board, including its chairman. Nevertheless, first members of the supervisory board and chairman may be appointed in the articles of incorporation. They must be registered in the Business Register. Members of the supervisory board have same mandate (including removal and resignation conditions) as members of the supervisory board in the joint-stock company, including that it must not be longer than four years, after which they can be reappointed for a new mandate. Remuneration of the members of the supervisory board is the same as in the case of the joint-stock company.

#### 2. Powers of the Supervisory Board

*293.* Competence of the supervisory board includes issues related to the business strategy and planning and internal control and control of legality in the management of the company, including appointment and removal, as well as control of directors and other representatives, and their remuneration. Further issues are related to the accounting policy and risk management. Important competence of the supervisory board is related to the general meeting, including various proposals,

432. *See* Arts 226 and 242 LCC 2011.

including proposal on the auditor appointment, proposals and control of profit distribution and other payments proposals to members. Supervisory board must submit to the general meeting report in writing on the management of the company and control performed, once a year, if not otherwise provided in the articles of incorporation.

Supervisory board is also competent to approve various acts, including acquisition or disposal of the stakes or shares in other companies, as well as immovable property, and also providing of different kind of security for creditors' protection.

Similar to division of powers between company's bodies in joint-stock company, it is explicitly provided that competence of the supervisory board *may not be delegated* to directors of the company. Nevertheless, it is not excluded that this delegation is made to the general meeting, according to close nature of this company form.

3. Liability and Duties Owed to the Company

*294.* Same provisions of directors' liability for the members of the board of directors in one-tier system is applicable to executive directors and members of the supervisory board in two-tier system in the joint-stock company, and are also applicable to the members of the supervisory board in the limited liability company.[433] The same is the case with duties of directors and members of the supervisory board (*see* above under general regime of duties and directors' liabilities under Chapter 1, §5. II.C. and D.).

## III. Internal Audit

*295.* Law on Commercial companies prescribes *possibility* for the limited liability company to apply provisions on the internal audit, prescribed for the joint-stock company (*see* above under Chapter 1, §5.V.). Nevertheless, these provisions are optional.

## IV. External Audit

*296.* External audit for the limited liability company is mostly prescribed by provisions of the Law on Auditing and the Law on Accounting (*see* above under Chapter 1, §5.VI.).

433. *See* Arts 430 and 447 LCC 2011.

## §6. Liquidation, Statutory Changes, Groups of Companies and Taxation

297. The dissolution of a solvent commercial company is regulated by the Law on Commercial Companies for all forms of commercial companies. Therefore, all provisions are applicable to all company forms, and are different only in issues naturally distinct to these company forms. Such as, for example, the issue of general meeting's decision, for which majority required is two-thirds of the total number of votes of all members in limited liability company.[434] Also, that is the case for method of distribution of the liquidation remainder, which is made to members in proportion to their stakes.[435] For other issues *see* Chapter 1, §6.

Same as the liquidation, all statutory changes and change of legal form are regulated by the Law on Commercial Companies for all forms of commercial companies. Therefore, all provisions are applicable to all company forms, and are different only in issues naturally distinct to these company forms. For these issues *see* Chapter 1, §7.

The same is the case for provisions on affiliated companies, especially groups of companies. Although provisions on contractual groups deal with joint-stock company, it is explicitly provided that they are applicable to all other company forms.[436] For these issues *see* Chapter 1, §8.

Finally, on taxation of the limited liability company *see* provisions of the Corporate Profit Tax Law, briefly explained in Chapter 1, §9.

434. Article 525 para. 1 under 2 LCC 2011.
435. Article 541 para. 2 under 1 LCC 2011.
436. Unlike provisions dealing with the majority required for decision on the control and management contract in joint-stock company, as well as partnerships and limited partnerships, there is no explicit provision with regard to majority necessary for this decision to be made in limited liability company.

# Part II. Partnerships

## Chapter 1. (General) Partnership

*298.* Partnership (*ortačko društvo* – abbreviation o.d. or od) is a commercial company and is legally independent person. It has its own assets and liabilities with which it can be responsible for the debts incurred during business operations. Still, partnership has at least two partners who are jointly and severally liable for company's debts. Their responsibility is of imperative nature, and partners cannot agree otherwise to be effective towards third parties.

### §1. In General

*299.* The former Law on Enterprises, following one of the most important characteristics of this form of company used quite an inappropriate term, naming it as a *company with unlimited joint and several liability of members*. The 1937 Trade Law had the term *public trading company*, which is more appropriate than the definition used in comparative law, i.e.: *societe en nom collectif, societa in nome collectivo, partnership, offene Handelsgeselschaft, societa collectiva.* The Law on Commercial Companies uses the term *partnership*, which is an entirely adequate choice.

The former Law on Enterprises defined the unlimited joint and several liability company of members as a company where all members are liable jointly and severally by all their property.[437] Such definition based on only one of its characteristics, otherwise controversial in the Law itself, is accepted in French law (probably serving as a model for our Law at that time). On the contrary the Swiss, German and former Yugoslav law, contained more acceptable definitions of such type of company, including its other characteristics as well: doing business under a joint name, establishment by contract, legal person's capacity, number and kind of partners, engaging in commercial (trading) activity, and unlimited liability to creditors of the partners for company commitments. All these defining elements are specified in the Law on Commercial Companies.[438]

The Law on Commercial Companies expressly specifies that two is the minimum number of partners for this company, which is also derived from the contractual

437. Article 115, para. 1 Law on Enterprises 1988.
438. Article 93 LCC 2011. *See also*: Ivica Jankovec, *Privredno pravo (Commercial law),* Belgrade, 1999, 66ff; M. Velimirović, *Privredno pravo (Commercial law),* Serbian Sarajevo, 2001, 62ff.

character of its establishment.[439] Consequently, should for any reason such a company be reduced to a single partner, it may not survive in such form. However, although there is no legal maximum regarding the number of partners, due to its contractual nature, establishment and its *intuitu personae* character, it is possible to conclude that these are companies with a relatively small number of partners (although throughout the world there are partnerships with several hundred partners, especially in the freelance professions). Partners, according to Serbian law, may be natural and legal persons, both domestic and foreign, while in some countries these may only be persons having the capacity of a trader (engaged in commercial activity). Therefore, in principle, all persons should be able to become partners in such type of company as well, for the purpose of effectuating various types of interests.

In addition, in some countries there are other restrictions as well. Thus, a natural person may simultaneously be a member (in a public trading company and limited partnership as a general partner) with unlimited liability, only in one commercial company. Also, such a company (partnership and/or limited partnership) may not be a member with unlimited liability in another such company (which does not rule out the membership in a company the nature of which is limited liability). The same motives stood behind the prohibition in the French law for spouses to be members in the same public trading company, although this is no longer the case. Such restrictions are justified in times of privatization, but should be omitted in the future since this should be decided by businesses themselves and by taking into account their own interests (in some cases they may put into effect some of their interests in one partnership, and some in another, and the like).

Regulation of internal relations between partners ('companions'), and between partners and the partnership is a matter of contract (principle of freedom of negotiation, unless otherwise specified by law). Since third-party interest is not at issue here, the Law on Commercial Companies does not intervene with many imperative norms. Similar solutions are present in comparative law as well. Norms of that law, although optional, are an important framework for regulation of partners' mutual relations and their relation with the partnership. These norms are inspired by the principle of making the balance between partners' interests, but having in mind the nature of that company. The freedom of negotiation principle is applied in the following matters: (i) contributions, (ii) disposal of partnership stakes, (iii) decision-making by partners, (iv) management and representation, (v) expenses refund, and (vi) profit and loss matters. Consequently, except for internal relations, the freedom of negotiation principle applies to representation as well, taken as a relationship between the partnership (and partners) and third parties (including partners themselves if involved in business relations with the partnership as a separate legal entity).

---

439. V. Jovanović, *Preduzeća i društva prema Zakonu o preduzećima (Enterprises and companies according to the Law on Enterprises)*, Belgrade, 1990, 52.

## §2. Legal Personality

*300.* According to Serbian Law on Commercial Companies, a partnership has legal personality, acquired from the moment of registration into the Business Register and upon articles of incorporation (with other necessary documents enclosed). Such recognition of legal status (under the French model) eliminates the need of regulating a series of matters otherwise present in many systems of law with a different solution. Therefore, every partnership has full legal personality and may be the holder of rights and duties; it may own property and exercise other property law rights, take part in judicial proceedings, go bankrupt, etc.

Separate legal personality of a partnership include that it has all *essential elements of legal person*, including seat, name, objects clause, commercial character of activities, as well as identification number (*see* above in Part 1, Chapter 1, §3), its own property and is a subject to legal acts and proceedings. Namely, because of legal personality, a partnership possesses property by which it meets its commitments, while company partners are 'owners of the company'. Company property is separate from that of the individual company partners, although the liability of company to creditors is completed by partners' liability.

In legal relations with third parties, the company is the holder of rights and duties. *The separate nature of company property as distinguished from private property of its partners also* entails some legal consequences. First, private creditors of a partner may not be settled out of company property. Second, the company is liable for its commitments by its property (in addition to joint and several liability of partners by their private property). Third, there are no direct legal relations between company creditors and partners (regardless of the fact that partners are liable for company commitments by the operation of law). Fourth, partnership is a taxpayer (profit tax, property tax). Fifth, a partnership may go bankrupt.

Legal personality protects company interests and those of its creditors. It also provides the identity of the company and of its property, even in case of one of the partners withdrawing or others joining the company. In the case of withdrawal partner is only entitled to the amount equivalent to the value of what he would be entitled to receive if company was liquidated. Since partners are not entitled to dispose with their contributions, once contributed to the company (it becomes the property of the company), individual creditors of a partner may not affect the enforcement against contributions, but are only entitled to demand compensation from the company in the amount equivalent to what partner could receive if company was liquidated. In that case partner loses his membership in the company.[440]

A partnership gains legal personality upon *registration* in the Business Register. It has obligatory *articles of incorporation*, which must include a *minimum of required elements:* identification of partners (name, address or seat, identification number) and their contributions according to which it is determined partner's part in the partnership, identification of the partnership (including name and seat), objects clause and other *optional elements* according to individual needs of the partners and partnership.[441] The written form of the articles, including certification of

440. *See* in detail Art. 124 LCC 2011.
441. Article 94 LCC 2011.

signatures by a notary is a prerequisite in Serbian law (*ad solemnitatem* form), which is also the case with other countries recognizing legal personality to this form. As mentioned before for joint-stock company and limited liability company, electronic form is also possible, with same effects for all articles of incorporation, irrespective of the form of the company. The articles of incorporation might be changed by agreement of all partners, unless otherwise specified. That document is particularly important for relations between the partnership and third parties (which is why it is to be filed in the register).

In the case when the company was registered, nullity of the articles of incorporation pronounced by court shall entail the winding-up of the company. Nullity shall not affect the validity of any commitments entered into by or with the company to third parties acting in good faith. Partners in the partnership and limited partnership remain jointly and severely responsible to third parties.[442]

In addition, the company may have additional contract *between the company partners*, signed by all partners, that is not to be enclosed in the register, by which the partners regulate their mutual relations, so that the former document is free from unnecessary text, while on the other hand enables the partners to more closely specify the company management and their relations to the company itself. In case of discord between the constitutive document and the partners' contract, precedence is given to provisions of the former.

## §3. Unlimited Liability

*301.* Serbian law accepts the joint and several liability of partners for company's commitments. Other agreements where partners' liability is limited, either in the articles of incorporation or other act cannot have effect towards third parties.[443] Still, otherwise could be stipulated by contract with individual creditors (departing from the rule could be permitted 'in concreto', but not 'in abstracto').

In this company form partners are liable to all company creditors, including a company partner in the capacity of a company creditor (but not including his/her claims on the ground of membership rights). A partner in such company with the capacity of creditor (i.e., for goods delivered or services rendered, or the claim for participating in the share of a company profit, etc.) may realize the claim from the company in its entirety (just as any other creditor). If this should fail, he may collect the debt-claim from the remaining partners, but after deducting the sum that, according to redress rules between the partners, is specified in the event of settlement of any company commitment falling on such partner.[444]

The liability of partners, regardless of the system, is a *general one*, i.e., it relates to all company commitments (contracts and torts) and to all creditors. This liability

442. *See* Arts 13 and 14 LCC 2011.
443. Article 93 LCC 2011.
444. In reference to the same *see*: Z. Arsić, 'Pravni položaj članova društva sa neograničenom solidarnom odgovornošću' ('Position of the partner in the company with unlimited joint and several responsibility'), *Privrednopravni priručnik (Manual for Commercial law)* 3/1990, 18ff.

is of accessory nature since it depends on the company liability. Therefore, termination of and changes in company obligations have same effect to obligations of partners; partner has his individual, but also objections the company is entitled to; partner can object if company has claims towards creditors which may be set off, etc.[445] Exceptionally, partners' liability has no accessory character in bankruptcy and reorganization.

Partners have liability according to their status in the company, decided upon registration. Thus, a member who has left the company (regardless of reason) is jointly and severally liable with other partners, for all company obligations made while his partner status in the company. However, *a new company partner is liable* just like all other partners, including obligations made before registration of his status, and otherwise cannot be agreed to have effect on third persons.[446] Such legal situation may be qualified, in terms of its legal nature, as a contract of joining a debt.[447]

A partner settling the company obligations acquires creditor's claims against the company, together with all secondary fulfilment rights and warranties (subrogation).[448] Failing to redress from the company, the partner becomes entitled to redress from other company partners in accordance with the terms of the articles of incorporation. Should there be no other provisions, it is presumed that *the redress is effectuated proportionally* not including proportion of that partner. The redress claim may be challenged by all objections which a company partner could have successfully used at the time of fulfilling obligation, with the proviso that the payment has been effected without the company's knowledge.

Finally, *the company creditors* requesting payment from the company partners are not privileged, under the general rules, in relation to *private creditors of company partners*; instead, they compete for collection with these creditors according to the general law of contract rules. However, partners' individual commitments do not bind the partnership at all, save the case of termination of membership status (liquidation stake), in which case the amount in proportion to the value of his stake in the company may serve to settle a partner's creditor (*see* above).

## §4. Contributions and Division of Profits

*302.* Besides partners' unlimited joint and several liability for partnership commitments by their personal property, the Law of Commercial Companies, accepts legal personality of that company, including separate assets. The partnership assets are formed upon members' contributions that may be in cash or in kind. Unlike other company forms, partners may contribute contributions in kind consisting of

445. *See* Arts 115, 116 LCC 2011.
446. *See* Art. 116 LCC 2011.
447. Article 451 Law on obligations.
448. Article 1003 Law on obligations.

work and performance of services.[449] This should be distinguished from employment contract (this, for instance, may be a 'credit' an individual enjoys as a well-known expert or similar service).[450] For third parties it is important that all partners in the partnership are liable without limits for its commitments jointly and severally.

Unless otherwise stipulated in the articles of incorporation, the partners are obliged to contribute equal contributions (*the principle of equality of contributions and equality of partners*). Partners have stakes in the partnership in proportion to their contributions, unless otherwise prescribed in the articles of incorporation.

Partners must contribute what was agreed upon articles of incorporation, although contribution can be reduced if other partners agree. The variability principle is permitted here due to the unlimited liability of partners. Partner is not due to make any additional contribution, if articles of incorporation does not provide otherwise. Articles of incorporation should also include all details with regard to the consequences in case a partner fails to make a contribution; such as the agreed deadline extension, exclusion of the partner, increased payment by others, etc. A delay in the payment of a monetary contribution may be sanctioned by charging interest, or include damage in the case of contributions in kind, as well as grant of other rights to creditors. All general provisions on the possibility to exclude partner in the case of non-performance or payment of the contribution are also applicable, as well as other provisions with regard to contributions and duty to contribute (*see* above under Part I, Chapter I, §2.V. and VI; as well as Part I, Chapter 2, §5.I.F.2.).

According to the Law on Commercial Companies, a partnership is under a *duty to reimburse all expenses* incurred in carrying out company operations to partners and which, in the given circumstances, have been indispensable (a general rule of reimbursing all necessary and useful expenses).[451]

Company profits as determined by the annual financial report (profit and loss statement), as well as company loss are distributed equally to company partners, unless otherwise stipulated in the articles of incorporation. *As a rule, it is stipulated that both profit and loss should be distributed proportionally to the amount invested in the company.* This also applies to company losses (that are deducted from each partner's stake).[452] Exceptionally, partners were formerly permitted to take part only in the distribution of profit, where their contribution included only individual labour and rendering of services (always – if so stipulated by contract), but it was not possible to agree to participate only in bearing company losses.[453] The leonine clause was also not permitted, i.e., that partners with pecuniary contributions participate only in the distribution of profit. Presently, it is increasingly believed that it is unacceptable even for partners who contribute in labour or services to participate only in the distribution of profit.

449. Article 96 LCC 2011.
450. *See* M. Vasiljević, *Preduzeća – pravni aspekti (Enterprises – legal aspects)*, Belgrade, 1990, 49ff.
451. Article 106 LCC 2011.
452. *See*. S. Šogorov, 'Pravo na isplatu dobiti člana ortačkog društva' ('Partners' right to profit distribution'), *Pravni život (Legal life)* 11/2000, 27ff.
453. For more details *see* Vrbanić, *Trgovački zakon (Commercial Code)*, Zagreb, 1893, 82.

§5. Decision-Making, Management and Representation

## I. Decision-Making

*303.* Due to its nature, a partnership has no company bodies, since appropriate functions are, as a rule, exercised by all partners (as contracting parties on the ground of constitutive document and as persons managing the company and acting on its behalf, unless otherwise specified by the above instrument). Consequently, some functions of a company of capital are here exercised by all or only by some of the partners, depending on the articles of incorporation.

Functions of the general meeting, in contrast to the functions of management (but not in terms of the company of capital bodies), are in substance ownership functions and, as a rule, are exercised by all partners of such company. Therefore, according to the basic rule, *decisions in a partnership are made unanimously*, by all partners entitled to vote in the specific matter, on the ground of their equality (partners authorized to participate in decision-making, all partners). It is possible to deviate from the equality principle by introducing an adequate provision in the articles of incorporation. If articles of incorporation provide for majority voting in certain or all issues, all partners have one vote each, if not otherwise provided in the articles of incorporation.

According to the Law on Commercial Companies, such tasks where unanimous decision-making is necessary are not those of the regular management, i.e., regular partnership business operation. This also applies to all matters relating to amending the articles of incorporation, for which consent is required by all partners, unless otherwise specified in it, and also include admission of a new partner, disposal of stakes to third party, liquidation, etc. Taking part in decision-making is a right and, under certain conditions, also a duty for partners. In principle, *the right to take part in decision-making* pertains to *all partners*, as the one derived from the partnership relationship. However, depending on the matter to be decided, it is possible to stipulate otherwise. That right may be defended against the company and other partners in court as well, just as partners exercising that duty may sue the one failing to do it, in order to compel him/her to act accordingly.

The answer to the question: is a partner obligated to vote or not depends on whether the matter to be decided on is in the company interest – when voting would be obligatory and could lead to damage claim, if damage was made to the company. In other cases, when decision-making is not in the interest of the company (such as, the case of the amendments to the articles of incorporation), voting would not be obligatory.

Since this is a typical company of persons, the exclusion and restriction of the right to take part in decision-making are not particularly present, which is not the case in companies of capital. However, the restrictions are possible in certain issues, including: (i) elimination of the conflict of interests (impossibility to decide in one's own matter), (ii) granting the right to vote to a third person – procurator (particularly useful in two-member partnerships in order to prevent decision-making to be blocked). In contrast to that, it is not allowed to transfer the right to vote to a third person – who is not a partner, since that right is non-transferable and individual, as well as related to the partnership relationship, so that such transfer remains impossible even by consent of the remaining partners. This, however, does not mean that the right to vote may not be exercised through a proxy (or a joint representative, i.e., where one partner acts on behalf of another one), unless this is ruled out in the articles of incorporation.

The law does not require the decisions to be in writing or other forms. There are no provisions on the nullity or act of avoidance, which is governed by the general rules of civil law.

## II. Management

*304.* Management includes the performance of legal transactions encompassed by the *regular activity of the company,* including those registered as principal activities of the company.[454]

According to the Law on Commercial Companies, a partnership may be managed by *persons authorized accordingly in the following ways:* (i) all partners of the company – which is the assumption applicable unless otherwise specified in the articles of incorporation – a partner may not validly renounce in advance in this articles or other act, his right to management; (ii) it is possible to specify in the articles of incorporation (or contract between partners) that management is entrusted to one partner or to several of them; (iii) that it may be entrusted to a special body; (iv) or to a special person who is not a company member, i.e., to a procurator.

If more than one partner is authorized to management, it is presumed to be individual, since *every partner is empowered to act independently*, unless otherwise specified in the articles of incorporation or contract between the company partners. In that case remaining partners who disagree on the management have right to veto. If articles of incorporation provide for *joint management*, consent by all partners is necessary for each transaction, unless joint decision-making would cause damage because of the absence of a partner. Also, each partner must follow instructions of other partners having management power, or in the case if thought to be inappropriate, he must inform other partners having management power to make joint decision, except where there is a danger of delay.

In this typical company of persons, *restriction of the right to management*, although legally possible, is not a regular matter. However, they do happen, and their justification is mainly reduced to the need for more efficient management (in large partnerships, the management is limited to a chosen number of partners who may act collectively or the management is entrusted to a special person – proxy or procurator).

Management power may be *withdrawn* in front of the competent court upon legal suit brought either by the company or other partners in the case of a serious violation of duty or management incapacity. Management authority may also be *cancelled,* after notice, on the ground of specific 'justified' reasons. Cancellation of management contrary to law or internal acts gives rise to compensation of damage

---

454. *See* provisions on partnership management in Arts 101–105 LCC 2011.

caused to the company. This should apply, *mutatis mutandis*, to an unauthorized cancellation of power to a person managing the company affairs, although the law fails to mention it expressly.

Management authorization may be *transferred* to another person – third party or another partner upon consent by all partners. In the case of authorized transfer to third persons, the transferor is liable not only for the choice of person the management power has been transferred to but also as if he has conducted the management himself.

## III. Representation

*305.* As a rule, functions of management and representation coincide in a partnership, i.e., are exercised by all partners. Still, representation may be exercised by – as in the case of management, not only by all partners, which is the assumption, unless prescribed otherwise – some of them, a single partner, special body or special person (procurator).[455]

In case when there are several partners authorized for representation, every one of them may act in the name and on behalf of the company autonomously (*autonomous representation*), unless collective representation is stipulated in the articles of incorporation (*collective representation as an exception*). If representation is collective, representatives may authorize one or several to represent company in specific acts or transactions. Also, third parties' acts made to any partner authorized to represent company collectively have effect to the company itself. Articles of incorporation can limit representation power by the collective representation with procurist, when third parties' acts made to any partner or procurist have effect to the company.

In contrast to management, where the law itself distinguishes between regular and extraordinary transactions, in the case of representation, unless otherwise stipulated by articles of incorporation, the representatives, as a rule, are vested with *unlimited powers in transactions within the company activity framework*. In the partnership as well, representatives may grant all kinds of power of attorney (in contrast to the representative determined in the articles of incorporation, who is recorded in the register, attorneys and other representatives, except for the procurator, are not recorded in the register). The representation function may be withdrawn and cancelled under the conditions otherwise valid for the company management (*see* above under II). In the case of collective representation in a two-partner company, where the right of representation is withdrawn or cancelled, the remaining partner authorized for collective representation could not continue representation affairs (unless there is a risk of delay) until the designation of another partner. Withdrawing the representation powers does not always involve simultaneous withdrawal of management power, but it is certain that this happens rather rarely in practice. The termination of representation power regarding third parties is effective from the day that this fact is recorded in the register and is made public.

455. For representation *see* Arts 111–114 LCC 2011.

## §6. Transferability of Partnership Interests and Changes in the Partners' Status

*306.* The status of a partner in a partnership is changed in several situations, including transfer of his interest, death of a partner, when partner – legal person – loses his legal personality upon liquidation or insolvency proceedings, by withdrawal or exclusion of a partner or in other cases provided in the articles of incorporation.[456]

### I. Transfer of Partnership Interests

*307.* Although partnership is closed company, a change in membership may occur, not so easily though given the nature of the company. The transfer of interests *between partners* is generally unlimited, unless otherwise stipulated in the articles of incorporation.[457] Since this involves a change of contracting parties, and a decrease in the number of partners also individually liable for company commitments (increasing thus their respective burdens), such transfer should also be subject to consent by all partners. In any case, the contract should include the mechanism of granting such consent, the assumption of consent, distribution among the partners, etc.

The Law on Commercial Companies regulates also the *transfer of an interest to a third party*. By such transfer, membership rights in partnership are also transferred, which is of an *intuitu personae* nature, so that there is a need to protect the interests of the existing partners. This is put into effect through the consent of the transfer to a third party by all remaining partners, unless otherwise provided in the articles of incorporation.[458] The stake transfer regime is also applicable to contribution of the stake to other company, as well as pledge to third persons. If company refuses to give consent, partner can withdraw from the partnership. The term 'third persons' (third parties) according to Serbian Law on Commercial Companies does not include (all) heirs, bearing in mind special regime of the termination of the membership status in the case of deceased partner (*see* below under II). Transfer of partners' interest includes that transferor and transferee are jointly and severally liable to the company for all transferor liabilities towards company, except otherwise agreed with other partners. This liability is limited to three years after transfer registration into the Business Register.

Transfer of partners' interest must be made *in writing*, including certification of signatures. Transfer is effective upon *registration* into the Business Register.

456. Article 117 LCC 2011.
457. Article 98 LCC 2011.
458. Article 99 LCC 2011.

## II. Death of a Partner

*308.* It is the general provisions of the Law on Commercial Companies to provide that partners' interest is not inheritable, unless otherwise provided in the articles of incorporation.[459] In case of death, partners' stake shall be divided proportionally between other partners in the partnership. Nevertheless, it can be provided in the articles of incorporation that heirs continue to be partners, when they have different rights, including their entitlement to ask for the change of legal form or withdrawal rights. If article of incorporation provides that the company continues to carry out business with the deceased partner's heirs, the heirs may within thirty days from the day of finality of probate proceedings demand from the company to step into the place of the deceased partner. Partner's heirs who do not step into the place of the deceased general partner are entitled to payment of compensation for the share in proportion to their share in inheritance, in accordance with the provisions regarding withdrawal of partner.

## III. Exclusion of a Partner

*309.* All provisions with regard to the exclusion of the member of the limited liability company are applicable for the partners in partnership (*see* above under Part I, Chapter 2, §5.I.F.2.).[460]

## IV. Withdrawal of a Partner

*310.* Partner can withdraw from the partnership by giving written notice to the remaining partners at least six months before the end of the business year, if otherwise is not provided in the articles of incorporation.[461] His membership status ceases by the end of that business year. If partner withdraws from the company, his stake must be divided proportionally to other partners, if not otherwise provided in the articles of incorporation. Partnership must compensate partner for six months since his withdrawal, except other time limit prescribed in the articles of incorporation. His compensation must be calculated in amount of the value of his stake in the case of liquidation, but disregarding pending obligations and incomplete transactions. If company's assets are not enough to cover partnerships' liabilities, partner must compensate the amount equivalent to his stake for six months, if not otherwise prescribed in the articles of incorporation.

459. Article 119 LCC 2011. *See* critically in detail: Nebojša Jovanović, 'Ko nasle uje udeo u ortačkom društvu?' ('Who is the heir of partners' stake'), in: Vuk Radović (ed.), *Uskla ivanje poslovnog prava Srbije sa pravom Evropske unije (2012) (Harmonisation of Serbian business law with EU law (2012)),* Pravni fakultet Univerziteta u Beogradu, Beograd, 2012, 23ff.
460. Article 120 LCC 2011.
461. Article 121 LCC 2011.

Partner stays liable for all liabilities made during his membership status, but no longer than five years since his withdrawal, if articles of incorporation do not provide for other longer period of time. Withdrawn partner has right to participate in the profit and loss from incomplete transactions, unless otherwise provided in the articles of incorporation.

## §7. LIQUIDATION

*311.* A partnership may terminate its activities on the grounds determined for all forms of commercial companies, including decision of the partners, made unanimously in the case of voluntary liquidation. In that case, all provisions on liquidation in general are applicable, with the only exception of the joint and several liability of partners for the creditors' claims after dissolution.[462] Also, a partnership may be terminated and deleted from Business Register upon compulsory liquidation, insolvency or statutory change.

Still, there are special dissolution grounds connected to the partnership and its *intuitu personae* character, and include cases when partner ceases to be in his partner position upon death of physical person or insolvency of the partner – legal person, if not otherwise provided in the articles of incorporation, in the case of withdrawal or expulsion or other cases provided in the articles of incorporation.[463]

Also, the Law on Commercial Companies provides for possibility of a partner to file legal suit in front of the court in order to liquidate partnership on the ground of justified reasons.[464] Justified reasons are defined as a situation when partners cannot do business because of their disputes or other reasons which prevent partnership to continue its business operation pursuant to law and its articles of incorporation. If successful, this is one of the reasons to initiate voluntary (or compulsory) liquidation of the company (*see* above under Part 1, Chapter 1, §6.II.).

## §8. TAXATION

*312.* Some national laws where partnership does not have separate legal personality and is not treated as legal person in taxation matters, and therefore pays no profit tax or the property tax, the taxpayers remain the partners on the ground of partner's revenue, while the value of their participation in the company is added to partners' property. Unlike that, Serbian law recognizes legal personality for partnership. It has many important consequences, including those related to tax law, where it is treated according to general provisions of the Corporate Profit Tax Law (*see* above under Part 1, Chapter 1, §9).

---

462. Article 545 para. 1 LCC 2011.
463. Article 117 LCC 2011.
464. *See* Art. 118 LCC 2011.

# Chapter 2. Limited Partnership

*313.* Limited partnership originated in the Middle Ages from a contract called *commenda* that was used particularly in sea-born trade. The contract involved the act of handing over some goods or amount of money by a person to a merchant or a ship-owner, with the risk limited to the value of his participation in such undertaking and with the right to the share of profit out of that. That was the model of constituting numerous companies, especially because the position of the 'consignor' (dormant or sleeping partner) was more favourable than that of open (public) business partnership. Such special status (secrecy of position and limited risk) was particularly appropriate for the nobility, officers and clergymen who at that time could not be engaged in trading, while still participating with their resources in trading transactions. This was also a way to avoid the canon law prohibition on money lending with interest on principal. According to French theory that prohibition was motivated by forcing rich people to engage in trade and trading operations rather than be only passive money lenders. Such form of company, in spite of its relative unattractiveness due to the nature of liability (which applies to partnerships), is recognized by all legislations, including Serbian. Favourable nature of this company type is the fact that a limited partner is interested in the dividend from the capital invested, but not in management, while on the other hand, the general partner is interested in limited partner's contribution and for his/her own management of the company.

Limited partnership (*komanditno društvo* – abbreviation k.d. or kd) is a commercial company and is a legally independent person. It has its own assets and liabilities with which it can be responsible for the debts incurred during business operations. Still, limited partnership has at least two partners. At least one of them (partner) has joint and several liability for company's debts, and is, therefore, in the same position as partner in general partnership. Limited partnership has at least one member (partner with limited liability) whose responsibility is limited to the amount of unpaid but subscribed contribution.[465]

All provisions with regard to partnerships are applicable to limited partnership, if otherwise is not provided for. Also, all provisions with regard to partners in the (general) partnership are applicable to partners with unlimited liability in limited partnership.[466]

## §1. Legal Personality

*314.* Serbian Law on Commercial Companies accepts the French law concept according to which – just as other companies, the limited partnership is a legal entity. Such status is acquired by filing and registration in the Business Register.

The assets of the limited partnership are, because of the separate legal personality, separate from partners' personal property (founders and partners joining the company subsequently), and even of those liable for company commitments with

465. *See* Art. 125 LCC 2011.
466. *See* Art. 126 LCC 2011.

their own property. By establishing the company, partners become its owners, but whatever has been contributed to the company property becomes the property of the company.

Application form for filing in the register (as in the case of partnership) has to be submitted by persons indicated in the articles of incorporation as company representatives (unless otherwise specified, this involves general partners). The articles of incorporation shall include information about all partners and limited partners (specifying their status of a general or limited partner) and about their contributions.

The articles of incorporation of a limited partnership may be changed by consent of all company members, unless specified otherwise, for example, by consent of all general partners and by a majority of limited partners in terms of their number or in terms of capital, or in terms of both number and capital cumulatively. Still, if such change increases the obligations of company members, or should new obligations be imposed on the partners, those changes may be effected in this part only by consent of all limited partnership's partners affected by the changes.

In addition to the constitutive document, a limited partnership may also have a special internal document – *a contract between company's partners*, which is not submitted to the register, and by which partners regulate the details of their relations, as well as the relation with the company. This is a way of rationally reducing the content of the constitutive instrument. In case of discrepancy between these two instruments, the articles of incorporation shall prevail.

## §2. Unlimited Liability of General Partner and Limited Liability of the Limited Partner

*315.* According to Serbian Law on Commercial Companies, general partners and limited partners may be natural and legal, domestic or foreign persons. It is true that this type of company is primarily created as *intuitu personae,* although personal characteristics of limited partners are not essential (since they participate with specified capital and through this are not engaged in management). However, personal characteristics of limited partners are not entirely irrelevant in the company. It seems that, while appreciating the positions of both categories of partners, this type should be treated as an *intuitu personae* company, although this characteristic is somewhat attenuated as compared to partnership (due to the limited partner's position).

Third-party liability of the company does not rule out the general partners' liability. According to the Law on Commercial Companies, they are liable without limitation, and jointly and severally (by all their property). While partners in the limited partnership have joint and several liability with regard to all company's liabilities, partners with limited liability are not liable for company's liabilities if they paid or performed agreed registered contribution to the company in full.[467]

The limited partner is liable also to company creditors jointly and severally with the general partners, the relevant limit being the amount of contribution stipulated

467. Article 134 LCC 2011.

in the contract that was not paid in (or otherwise contributed). Possible agreement between limited partner and the remaining partners in order for him to be exempted from liability (totally or partially) has no legal effect regarding the creditors.

The Law on Commercial Companies specifies the exceptions from the prescribed regime of limited partner's liability, in which case such partner is liable just as the general one. Exception includes the case where the name of limited partner is indicated in the company business name upon his consent. In that case, he shall be liable as a general partner.[468] Also, provisions of lifting the corporate veil are also applicable to limited partner (*see* above under General Introduction §3).

Finally, liability of a limited partner subsequently joining the company (*new partner liability)* includes his liability only up to the amount of contribution and from the moment of becoming the member of such company. The same rationale applies also to the case of change of partner's status. Should a general partner become limited partner, his unlimited liability for the company commitments remains only for the commitments originating until the registration and making public the status change, while for the new ones his position is that of limited partner. Where a limited partner becomes a general one, the liability in the above-mentioned case is the one characteristic of every other general partner.

### §3. Contributions and Division of Profits

*316.* All provisions with regard to contributions in partnership are applicable to limited partnership as well. Here again the possibility may be accepted of general partner's contributions in kind to be in labour and services to the company.

Profit and loss distribution in the limited partnership is determined in proportion to their stakes, except otherwise is provided in the articles of incorporation.[469] Nevertheless, payments to the limited partner must be made in proportion to his stake, except otherwise provided in the articles of incorporation, in the time prescribed by these articles or general partners' decision if no time is prescribed. If general partners decide on the payment of profits made, it must be within ninety days since financial accounts were adopted.

### §4. Decision-Making, Management and Representation

*317.* As in the case of partnership, the limited partnership, in essence, *has no particular bodies* of the companies of capital type, regardless of the mode of regulation of conducting the affairs (as well as of representation). Although liability-wise limited partners have a position equal to that of members of limited liability company, their position is still somewhat different; limited partner does not manage the company since this is a duty of general partners.[470]

468. Article 135 LCC 2011.
469. Article 130 LCC 2011.
470. *See* Art. 131 LCC 2011.

As a rule, affairs in the competence of the general meeting are performed by both general and limited partners, requiring their unanimous decision, if not otherwise prescribed in the law or articles of incorporation.

In contrast to general partners, the limited partners are under no duty to manage the company or conduct company affairs. The management and representation powers may be performed by all general partners, by few of them, or by a single general partner, or, as the case may be, by a special body (that includes general partners and external professionals) or external specialized person (manager, procurator), but never a limited partner, except when acting as procurator by the unanimous decision of all general partners.

Nevertheless, management of the limited partnership, granted to general partners (or other persons according to party autonomy), is limited only to the regular management, i.e., regular partnership business operation. Limited partner is, therefore, entitled to oppose to extraordinary transactions by general partners. In those transactions, limited partners have right to veto. Status of a general partner representation of the limited partnership is identical to that of a partnership member.

Unlike general partners' right to information on all business activities, limited partners have the right to supervise management of the company through their right to ask for copies of annual financial accounts, and inspection of business records and documents. Limited partner is entitled to petition to court if not allowed to perform his right of supervision.

## §5. Transferability of Partnership Interests

*318.* A stake (allotment, portion) in the limited partnership, as in all other types of company, includes an aggregate of rights belonging to a partner on the ground of contribution made to the company (managing and property rights). Due to dualism of partners' categories in this company, it is necessary to distinguish between the stake in the company capital (both categories of partners) and the stake in membership rights (again both categories). As a rule, a stake in the capital of one category of partners coincides with stakes in membership rights, but this is not always the case. By all means, the latter stakes of both categories differ considerably due to different nature of partners. The amounts of contribution serving as a ground of acquiring the stake in the company depend on the contract, so that they do not have to be equal, both in terms of categories and within a category of partners.

Unless otherwise specified in the articles of incorporation, the internal transfer is generally free. However, in such internal transfer, several situations can be covered by the provisions of the articles of incorporation: (i) whether transfers are affected within the same category of partners or within different categories; (ii) is the transfer total or partial. Disposal within the same category of partners should be subject to the minimum of formalities, since their position in the company does not change (although the number of general partners who are liable without limit becomes reduced). The same regime should apply to the transfer of limited partners' stakes (entire or partial) to the general partners (because the liability property basis is not reduced regarding third parties). This should also apply to the transfer of a part of the general partner's stake to the limited partner (since the former remains to be liable without limit). The strictest regime should be prescribed for the transfer of general partner's total stake (including both the property and the management rights) to a limited partner, since in such a way the existing general partner is exempted from further liability for the company commitments, while the limited partner acquires the status of the general one. Whether a limited partner becomes a general partner where a part of the stake is transferred to the limited partner by the former one depends on whether, together with property rights, the rights to management have been transferred too, because the transfer of property rights does not make this change of status indispensable.

All provisions of the Law on Commercial Companies with regard to transfer of partners' interest in the partnership are equivalently applicable in limited partnership. Therefore, general partners' interest may be transferred to third parties only by the consent of both categories of partners – unless stipulated otherwise. Only explicit provision with regard to transfer of the limited partner interest provides for free transfer (or its part) to other limited partner or third parties.[471]

## §6. Liquidation

*319.* Since limited partnership and partnership fall in the companies of person's category, the reviewed rules regarding the termination of the former type of company regarding the matter of general partner's status change are subject to them as well. The characteristic of this type of company is a different category of partners, i.e., limited partners, so that the issue arises as to the effect of their status change to the limited partnership status.

According to provisions of the Law on Commercial Companies, limited partnership is not dissolved upon death or dissolution of the limited partner, but can be succeeded by the heirs or legal successor of the limited partner.

Should all general partners leave the company, while new ones do not join within legally prescribed deadline of three months, the limited partnership must change its form and become a limited liability company or a joint-stock company. In the event of death of the single unlimited partner, his heirs can inherit a part in the partnership and continue to be unlimited partners, or require the payment of their part. Should all limited partners leave the company, while the new ones do not join within the prescribed deadline, the company must change its legal form. All these changes have to be filed in the register pursuant to law.[472] All other provisions with regard to liquidation of the general partnership are applicable (*see* above under Chapter 1, §7).

471. Article 129 para. 3 LCC 2011.
472. *See* Art. 137 LCC 2011.

## §7. Taxation

*320.* Serbian law recognizes legal personality for limited partnership as well. Therefore, same as in the case of general partnership, provisions of the Corporate Profit Tax Law are also applicable (*see* above under Part 1, Chapter 1, §9).

# Selected Bibliography


Arsić Zoran, Marjanski Vladimir, *Pravo privrednih društava* (*Commercial Companies' Law*), Pravni fakultet Univerziteta u Novom Sadu, Novi Sad, 2013.

Arsić Zoran, 'Povećanje osnovnog kapitala akcionarskog društva iz neto imovine' ('Capital Increase out of Company's Net Asset'), *Zbornik radova Pravnog fakulteta u Novom Sadu* (*Collected Papers of the Faculty of Law in Novi Sad*) 4/2018.

Arsić Zoran, 'Smanjenje osnovnog kapitala akcionarskog društva i zaštita poverilaca' ('Reduction of Share Capital and Protection of Creditors'), *Zbornik radova Pravnog fakulteta u Novom Sadu* (*Collected Papers of the Faculty of Law in Novi Sad*) 3/2017.

Arsić Zoran, 'Zastupanje akcionara od strane banaka koje vode zbirne ili kastodi račune' ('Representation of shareholders by banks that maintain collective or custody accounts'), *Pravo i privreda* (*Law and Economy*) 4–6/2014.

Begović Boris, Bukvić Rajko, Živković Boško, Mijatović Boško, Hiber Dragor, *Unapre enje korporativnog upravljanja* (*Fostering Corporate Governance*), Centar za liberalno demokratske studije, Beograd, 2003.

Cvetićanin Nataša, 'Prav(n)i značaj i mesto dobrovoljne likvidacije u sistemu prestanka privrednih društava' ('Legal Significance and Position of Voluntary Liquidation within Companies' Cessation System'), *Pravo i privreda* (*Law and Economy*) 10–12/2014.

Dabić Ljubiša, 'Postupak prinudne likvidacije privrednih društava u Republici Srbiji' ('Procedure for the Compulsory Liquidation of Companies in the Republic of Serbia'), *Pravo i privreda* (*Law and Economy*) 4–6/2019.

Jevremović Petrović Tatjana, 'Arbitrabilnost sporova u vezi sa pobijanjem odluke skupštine privrednog društva' ('Arbitrability of Corporate Disputes Regarding General Meeting's Decisions'), *Pravo i privreda* (*Law and Economy*) 4–6/2018.

Jevremović Petrović Tatjana, 'Državna pripadnost, *Lex Societatis* i sedište privrednog društva' ('Nationality, Lex Societatis and the Company Seat'), *Pravni život* (*Legal Life*) 11/2010.

Jevremović Petrović Tatjana, 'Elektronska registracija osnivanja privrednih društava u Republici Srbiji' (On-line Registration of Companies in the Republic of Serbia), *Pravo i privreda* (*Law and Economy*) 3/2021.

Jevremović Petrović Tatjana, *Prekogranična spajanja društava u pravu EU* (*Cross-Border Mergers in the EU Law*), Faculty of Law University of Belgrade, Belgrade, 2010.

Jevremović Petrović Tatjana, *Grupe privrednih društava* (*Groups of Companies*), Pravni fakultet Univerziteta u Beogradu, Beograd, 2014.

Jevremović Petrović Tatjana, 'Right of Establishment: Serbian Company Law', in: SEE, EU Cluster of Excellence in European and International Law (Ed.), *South East Europe and the European Union – Legal Aspects*, Verlag Alma Mater, Saarbrücken 2015.

Jevremović Petrović Tatjana, 'Ugovor o statusnoj promeni: trenutak zaključenja, kontrola i drugi povezani problemi' ('Terms on Statutory Change: Moment of Conclusion, Control and other Related Issues'), in: Vuk Radović (ed.), *Uskla ivanje poslovnog prava Srbije sa pravom Evropske unije (2015)* (*Harmonisation of Serbian Business Law with EU Law (2015)*), Pravni fakultet Univerziteta u Beogradu, Beograd, 2015.

Jevremović Petrović Tatjana, 'Ništavost statusne promene nakon registracije' ('Nullity of Merger after Registration'), *Anali Pravnog fakulteta u Beogradu* (*Annals of the Faculty of Law in Belgrade – Belgrade Law Review*) 2/2016.

Jevremović Petrović Tatjana, 'Nullity of companies' registration in Serbian law under the influence of European legal systems', in: Bojan Milosavljević, Tatjana Jevremović Petrović, Miloš Živković (eds.), *Law and Transition: Collection of Papers*, University of Belgrade Faculty of Law, Belgrade, 2017.

Jevremović Petrović Tatjana, 'Pobijanje odluke skupštine o statusnoj promeni' ('Avoidance of General Meeting's Decision on the Statutory Merger'), *Uskla ivanje poslovnog prava Srbije sa pravom Evropske unije* (*Harmonisation of Serbian Business Law with EU Law (2017)*), Pravni fakultet Univerziteta u Beogradu, Beograd, 2017.

Jevremović Petrović Tatjana, 'Ništavost osnivačkog akta u srpskom pravu' (Nullity of the Articles of Incorporation in Serbian Company Law), *Pravo i privreda* (*Law and Economy*) 4–6/2017.

Jevremović Petrović Tatjana, *Modeli osnivačkih akata* (*Model Articles of Incorporation*), Pravni fakultet Univerziteta u Beogradu, Beograd, 2019.

Jovanović Nebojša, *Berzansko pravo* (*The Capital Markets Law*), Pravni fakultet Univerziteta u Beogradu, Beograd 2009.

Jovanović Nebojša, *Udžbenik berzanskog prava* (*Textbook on Capital Markets Law*), Pravni fakultet Univerziteta u Beogradu, Beograd 2010.

Jovanović Nebojša, Radović Vuk, Radović Mirjana, *Kompanijsko pravo: pravo privrednih subjekata* (*Company Law: Law of Commercial Subjects*), Pravni fakultet Univerziteta u Beogradu, Beograd, 2021.

Jovanović Vladimir, *Privredno pravo: privredne organizacije* (*Commercial Law*), Zavod za izdavanje udžbenika Narodne Republike Srbije, Beograd, 1961.

Krulj Vrleta, *Pravni režim i oblici koncentracija u privredi* (*Legal regime and forms of commercial concentrations*), Savremena administracija, Beograd, 1978.

Lepetić Jelena, *Kompanijskopravni režim sukoba interesa: Dužnost lojalnosti* (*Conflict of Interest in Company Law: Duty of Loyalty*), Pravni fakultet Univerziteta u Beogradu, Beograd, 2015.

Lepetić Jelena, 'Jedinstvo članskih prava i ugovori o glasanju akcionara' ('Unity of Membership and Shareholder's Voting Agreements'), *Pravo i privreda* (*Law and Economy*) 4–6/2019.

Lepetić Jelena, 'Jedna akcija – jedan glas: da li je vreme za promene' ('One Share – One Vote: Time for Change?'), *Zbornik radova Pravnog fakulteta u Novom Sadu* (*Collected Papers of Faculty of Law in Novi Sad*) 3/2018.

Marjanski Vladimir, 'Istupanje člana iz društva s ograničenom odgovornošću' ('Withdrawal of a Member from a Limited Liability Company'), *Pravo i privreda* (*Law and Economy*) 4–6/2016.

Marjanski Vladimir, 'Odluka o povećanju osnovnog kapitala društva s ograničenom odgovornošću novim ulozima' ('The Resolution on Capital Increase through New Contributions in Limited Liability Company'), *Zbornik radova Pravnog fakulteta u Novom Sadu* (*Collected Papers of Faculty of Law in Novi Sad*) 3/2017.

Marjanski Vladimir, 'Podobnost nenovčanog uloga kao predmeta obaveze unošenja uloga u društvo s ograničenom odgovornošću' ('Eligibility of a Contributions in Kind as a Subject of an Obligation to Invest in a Limited Liability Company'), *Zbornik radova Pravnog fakulteta u Novom Sadu* (*Collected Papers of the Faculty of Law in Novi Sad*) 3/2019.

Marjanski Vladimir, 'Raspodela dobiti članovima društva s ograničenom odgovornošću i razlike u odnosu na druge isplate korporativno-pravnog karaktera' (Allocation of Profit to Members of Limited Liability Company and Differences in Relation to Other Corporate Legal Payments"), *Zbornik radova Pravnog fakulteta u Novom Sadu* (*Collected Papers of Faculty of Law in Novi Sad*) 1/2020.

Marjanski Vladimir, 'Sticanje sopstvenog udela društva s ograničenom odgovornošću otkupom od člana društva' ('Acquiring of a Company's own Equity Interest through Redemption of a Company Member'), *Zbornik radova Pravnog fakulteta u Novom Sadu* (*Collected Papers of Faculty of Law in Novi Sad*) 2/2015.

Marjanski Vladimir, 'Vrste, cilj (svrha) i načini smanjenja kapitala društva s ograničenom odgovornošću' ('The Type, the Purpose (Goal) and the Ways of Capital Reduction of the Limited Liability Company'), *Zbornik radova Pravnog fakulteta u Novom Sadu* (*Collected Papers of Faculty of Law in Novi Sad*) 3/2018.

Marković Mirjana, 'Pozitivan publicitet registra privrednih subjekata' ('Positive effects of registration of commercial companies'), *Pravo i privreda (Law and Economy)* 5-8/2008.

Mihajlović Borko, 'Diskvalifikacija člana uprave privrednog društva: nova sankcija za povredu dužnosti prijavljivanja poslova i radnji sa ličnim interesom u srpskom pravu' ('Disqualification of the Company's Member of Management: New Sanction for the Breach of Duty to report Businesses and Acts in Which Exists Personal Interest in Serbian Law'), *Glasnik prava* (*Herald of Law*), 2/2019.

Mihajlović Borko, 'Promene u pravnom regulisanju dužnosti prijavljivanja poslova i radnji u kojima postoji lični interes' ('Changes in Legal Regulation of the Duty to Report Businesses and Acts in which Exists Personal Interest'), *Glasnik prava* (*Herald of Law*) 2/2018.

Radović Mirjana, *Čuvanje i administriranje (depozit) hartija od vrednosti* (*Holding and Administration (Deposit) of Securities*), Pravni fakultet Univerziteta u Beogradu, Beograd, 2014.

**Selected Bibliography**

Radović Mirjana, 'Pravo poverioca da zahteva dobijanje odgovarajuće zaštite u slučaju statusne promene privrednog društva – dužnika' ('Creditor's Right to Obtain Adequate Safeguards in Case of a Merger or a Division of his Debtor'), *Pravo i privreda* (*Law and Economy*) 4–6/2016.

Radović Mirjana, 'Odgovornost društva sticaoca za obaveze društva prenosioca kod statusnih promena podele i izdvajanja' ('Liability of the Acquiring Company for Liabilities of the Transferor Company in Case of Division and Separation'), *Uskla ivanje poslovnog prava Srbije sa pravom Evropske unije* (*Harmonisation of Serbian Business Law with EU Law (2017)*), Pravni fakultet Univerziteta u Beogradu, Beograd, 2017.

Radović Vuk, *Mere odbrane akcionarskog društva od preuzimanja kontrole* (*Defensive Measures in the Joint-Stock Company during Takeover Bid*) Pravni fakultet Univerziteta u Beogradu, Beograd, 2008.

Radović Vuk, *Naknada članovima uprave akcionarskog društva* (*Remuneration of Directors of Joint-Stock Company*) Pravni fakultet Univerziteta u Beogradu, Beograd, 2011.

Radović Vuk (ed.), *Uskla ivanje poslovnog prava Srbije sa pravom Evropske unije (2011)* (*Harmonisation of Serbian Business Law with EU Law (2011)*), Pravni fakultet Univerziteta u Beogradu, Beograd, 2011. The same for years: 2012, 2013, 2014, 2015, 2016, 2017, 2018, 2019, 2020, 2021.

Radović Vuk, 'Uslovi za ostvarivanje prava nesaglasnih akcionara' ('Conditions for Exercising Shareholder's Right to Appraisal'), *Pravo i privreda* (*Law and Economy*) 4–6/2017.

Radović Vuk, 'Prava članova u slučaju statusnih promena sa posebnim osvrtom na neke neusaglašenosti srpskog prava sa pravom EU' ('Rights of Companies Members in Mergers and Divisions with a Particular Emphasis on Certain Discrepancies Between Serbian and EU Law'), in: Vuk Radović (ed.), *Uskla ivanje poslovnog prava Srbije sa pravom Evropske unije* (*2018*) (*Harmonisation of Serbian business law with EU law* (*2018*)), Pravni fakultet Univerziteta u Beogradu, Beograd, 2018.

Radović Vuk, 'Nevoljni prestanak privrednog društva' ('Involuntary Dissolution for Deadlock and Oppression'), *Revija Kopaoničke škole prirodnog prava* (*Review of the Kopaonik School of Natural Law*) 1/2020.

Radović Vuk, 'Cilj privrednog društva sa osvrtom na aktuelnu pandemiju' ('Corporate Purpose with a Look on COVID-19 Pandemic'), *Revija Kopaoničke škole prirodnog prava* (*Review of the Kopaonik School of Natural Law*) 2/2021.

Vasiljević Mirko, *Company Law (Law of Commercial Companies of Serbia and the EU)*, Pravni fakultet Univerziteta u Beogradu, Beograd, 2006 (in English).

Vasiljević Mirko, Radović Vuk (eds), *Korporativno upravljanje* (*Corporate Governance*), Pravni fakultet Univerziteta u Beogradu, Beograd, 2008.

Vasiljević Mirko, Radović Vuk (eds), *Korporativno upravljanje: drugi deo – Zbornik radova* (*Corporate Governance: Second Part – Collection of Papers*), Pravni fakultet Univerziteta u Beogradu, Beograd, 2009.

Vasiljević Mirko, *Kompanijsko pravo – Pravo privrednih društava* (*Company Law – Commercial Companies Law*), Pravni fakultet Univerziteta u Beogradu, Beograd, 2013.

Vasiljević Mirko, *Korporativno upravljanje: izabrane teme (Corporate Governance: Selected Themes)*, Udruženje pravnika u privredi, Beograd, 2013.

Vasiljević Mirko, Vuk Radović, 'Teorijske osnove prava nesaglasnih akcionara' ('Theoretical Foundations of Shareholders' Right to Appraisal'), *Anali Pravnog fakulteta u Beogradu* (*Annals of the Faculty of Law in Belgrade – Belgrade Law Review*) 3/2017.

Vasiljević Mirko, 'Privredna društva i privredno sudstvo' ('Commercial Companies and Commercial Courts'), *Pravo i privreda* (*Law and Economy*) 3/2020.

Vasiljević Mirko, *Probijanje pravne ličnosti u kompanijskom pravu* (*član kompanije vs. poverilac kompanije*) (*Piercing the corporate veil in company law* (*company member vs. company creditor*)), Intermex, Beograd, 2020.

Vasiljević Mirko, Jevremović Petrović Tatjana, Lepetić Jelena, *Kompanijsko pravo: pravo privrednih društava* (*Company Law: Law of Commercial Companies*), Službeni glasnik, Beograd, 2020.

Vujisić Dragan, 'Poslovno ime privrednog društva' ('Company's Trade Name'), in: Slavko Đor ević (ed.), *Uskla ivanje pravnog sistema Srbije sa standardima EU* (*Harmonization of the legal system of Serbia with EU standards*), Pravni fakultet Univerziteta u Kragujevcu, Kragujevac, 2017.

Vujisić Dragan, 'Probijanje pravne ličnosti' ('Piercing the Corporate Veil'), in: Miodrag Mićović (ed.), *Uskla ivanje pravnog sistema Srbije sa standardima Evropske unije* (*Harmonization of the legal system of Serbia with the standards of the European Union*), Pravni fakultet Univerziteta u Kragujevcu, Kragujevac, 2019.

# Selected Bibliography

# Index

*The numbers here refer to paragraph numbers.*

www.ingramcontent.com/pod-product-compliance
Ingram Content Group UK Ltd.
Pitfield, Milton Keynes, MK11 3LW, UK
UKHW020139290926
15471UKWH00003B/584

9 789403 506869